Guided by Meaning in Primary Literacy

Guided by Meaning in Primary Literacy

Libraries, Reading, Writing, and Learning

Joyce Armstrong Carroll, Kelley Barger,
Karla James, and Kristy Hill

LIBRARIES
UNLIMITED™

An Imprint of ABC-CLIO, LLC

Santa Barbara, California • Denver, Colorado

Library of Congress Cataloging-in-Publication Control Number: 2016036397

ISBN: 978-1-4408-4398-3
EISBN: 978-1-4408-4399-0

21 20 19 18 17   1 2 3 4 5

This book is also available as an eBook.

Libraries Unlimited
An Imprint of ABC-CLIO, LLC

ABC-CLIO, LLC
130 Cremona Drive, P.O. Box 1911
Santa Barbara, California 93116-1911
www.abc-clio.com

This book is printed on acid-free paper ∞
Manufactured in the United States of America

A child's behavior is always guided by meaning.

—Lev Vygotsky

To all the eager young learners who populate our schools.

JAC

To the students, faculty, and staff of Beneke Elementary for being a vibrant, creative, and inspiring place to teach and learn. Thank-you Cindi, Debbie, and Sarah for years of collaboration in and out of our kindergarten classrooms.

KB

To Leyton, Ethan, and Tristan for being my best writing students, and for all of the kids at ERES who enjoy writing in the library!

KH

To my family, Prentice, P. J., and Christian, who inspire me to live life with meaning. To the students and staff at E. C. Mason, who share my passion for writing.

KJ

Contents

PART II: WHY WRITE IN THE LIBRARY?
Kristy Hill

PART III: GUIDED BY MEANING THROUGH EARLY LITERACY
Kelley Barger

PART IV: GUIDED BY MEANING IN TEACHING LESSONS
Karla James

Foreword

First Day of School

Here, take my child.
He has a fistful of crayons,
Is ready to begin
To enter the halls that smell of chalk dust and lemon oil.
He wants to colour a picture.
Help him to see that the colour he chooses,
The pictures he makes, are beautiful . . .
Before you ask him to paint the Sistine Chapel.

Here, take my child.
She knows one and one makes two.
I want her to learn to add,
Without being subtracted from.
I want her to multiply her abilities,
But not if it divides her against herself.

Here, take my child.
He has a book he wants to read.
Let him read it first,
Tell you why he likes it,
Before you ask him to read a book
You think he should read . . .
To be up to "the level."

Here, take my child.
She has written a poem:
"dandy lions are golden buttons in the grass"
Smell those dandelions, see the image,
Before you tell her dandelions are weeds or
Dandelions is not spelled correctly.

Here, take my child
but . . . TAKE CARE.

Sheree Fitch

A few years ago, I was invited to be the visiting author for a beautiful new elementary school in South Carolina. As I drove up, I noticed the marquee that proudly announced that this school had been named a Blue Ribbon Campus, meaning that the test scores for this group of children had consistently been on the higher end of the spectrum.

I could tell, before I even got to the front door, that this was a school that had been carefully tended. The grounds were clean and orderly, the playground was large and sunny, and there was a grove of friendly trees lining the back fence. It was obviously a well-cared-for neighborhood school, one to which from all appearances any parents would love to send their children. I was happy to be there.

Walking through the doors was no different, at least at first. The halls were painted with lively primary colors, and they were shiny clean. In the office, I was greeted by the school librarian and escorted to the cafeteria where I would talk to the kids—one grade level at a time—about my life as a writer, something I've been doing for so many years now, I can't count them. As I set up my laptop and adjusted the projector, the children began to file in and sit in rows on the floor. They were orderly, clearly used to coming to the cafeteria for presentations. As they plopped down, one by one, the librarian gently prodded them, "Crisscross-applesauce."

Oh how I love *crisscross-applesauce*. For me, it's a signal that stories are about to happen. It's code for *snuggle up, my homies, and listen*. Whenever I hear it, my heartbeat picks up, and I am suddenly the luckiest person in the world to be with these children, in this beautiful school, in the midst of Story, with a capital S. The lights in the room went down, and we were off.

Like I always do, I started my presentations by reminding everyone that we—we humans, that is—are the only ones in the animal kingdom, so far as we know, who tell stories. We know that other animals communicate, that they give signals and mark trees and sing and whatnot. But so far as we know, they do not gather at the base of the elm trees and discuss the state of the world or what their mothers fed them for dinner the night before. Armadillos aren't in the habit of regaling other armadillos about the anthills they have conquered, and flamingos don't remind their chicks about how they flew 2,000 miles to visit their flamingo relatives. At least as far as we can tell.

So we are the *story animals*, the ones who share our lives through stories. And this, I remind them, is what makes our stories so darned important. Stories are what separate us from the other animals. They're what make us most human . . . and they have the added benefit of making us most *humane* as well. Our holiest books are compendia of stories that have been with us for thousands of years.

In fact, stories, I told my young audience, are so sacred and so powerful that we actually go to war over whose stories are best. A tragic misuse of story, for sure, because they also have the power of bringing us together, something they've done for centuries. The caves of Lacaux, which Dr. Carroll describes so eloquently in these pages, are one example of that ancient, most basic human act, telling stories.

In that darkened school cafeteria in South Carolina, the stately trees just outside the door, I talked to those 200 children, all crisscross-applesauced, and invited them to come along with me as I shared some of my stories, and I encouraged them to think about their own stories as we went along. It was all good.

However, somewhere in the middle of my second or third presentation, I realized that these well-mannered, orderly students only peripherally seemed to engage with me. They were polite, no question. They laughed at the right moments. They asked plenty of questions. But despite so much "rightness," there was something reserved about these small story animals. Too reserved.

I began to feel "itchy," as if there were something I had missed. What was I doing wrong? It just seemed that something was *off*. But I couldn't seem to put my finger on it, especially considering the situation: a lovely, well-situated Blue Ribbon Campus, in a solid middle-class neighborhood, where everything seemed to be in place.

At the end of the day, I thanked the librarian, packed up my laptop, and made my way to the front door. Normally, after a day like this, I leave feeling exhausted, but in a happy way. That day, I just felt exhausted. Nothing had gone wrong, but that itch wouldn't go away.

And then, somewhere between the cafeteria and the door, walking down the hallway with its merry primary tones, so cheerful and bright, I figured it all out. I saw what was missing. There was not a single piece of student work on display. No art. No writing. No bits and pieces of student-generated stories. Nothing but clean, empty color.

And in the absence of Story, the story became clear. This school had lost its best Story—the jubilation of creativity that occurs on lined notebook pages and manila paper, caught in the swirls of soft pencil leads and markers and tempera paints, and then displayed for the world to see.

Anyone who has visited those beautiful caves in France knows that at the heart of those drawings is the story that the artist was working to tell. The overwhelming emotion is one of connection. When we gather around a campfire, or sit next to each other on the bus, or curl up with a good book, we are making connections. Through those ancient drawings, we're connecting at an elementally human level to our forebears. Even after all these centuries, the story still matters.

Walking down the halls of a school that displays the work of its students has the same effect. We don't have to understand the creatively spelled words of our youngest students to get the message: *my story matters*.

Life is short, isn't it? And because it is, every bit of our children's lives count. When they leave school, whether that's in their late teens, their early twenties, their fifties, or whenever, *no one* is going to care what their test scores were. I've never, in my entire life, had anyone ask me about my SAT or GRE scores. Not a single person. Who needs or wants to be bored out of their minds? Unless we've had a particularly harrowing experience with a test or an unusually wonderful experience with one, the whole thing is irrelevant *to life*.

Only when something about taking a test is unusual does it matter. Why? Because then it becomes a *story*.

The children at the Blue Ribbon school in South Carolina were good test takers. They had proof. But the joy of crisscross-applesauce was missing. So, I am worried. Worried that in our quest to improve test scores, we're missing out on what is fundamentally human—Story—and our ability to both listen/read and tell/write it. We don't make connections with each other while engaged in testing. We do make connections, even across time, through stories.

The very fact that you have picked up this book by Dr. Joyce Carroll, Kristy Hill, Karla James, and Dr. Kelley Barger is testament to your own belief that our stories matter, and just as important, our children's stories matter. Knowing that this book is in your hands right now makes me worry a little less. I want to encourage you to curl up with it and let it soak in.

Because what these four authors bring to these pages is their collective wealth of experiences in the classroom and library. Together, they provide you with the hands-on tools, grounded in solid research, to create the spaces necessary for the care and feeding of young story animals. My gosh, it's a treasure trove. This book gives me hope not only that you can find the "golden buttons in the green grass," of Sheree Fitch's poem, but that you and your students will leave your own marks on the world. It's what we're built for. It's what helps us make sense of our surroundings, and yes, gives us meaning in the world. Nothing is more important than that.

Kathi Appelt

Introduction

Joyce Armstrong Carroll

Moment by moment throughout our lifetime, our brains hum with the work of making meaning: weaving together many thousands of threads of information into all manner of thoughts, feels, memories, and ideas.

—Daniel Tamment

I enrolled Joyce Elizabeth, my namesake, in a wonderfully progressive teaching school (as opposed to babysitting day care) when she was one year old. In this loving, knowledgeable environment, she flourished for three years, learning, almost as play, her colors, shapes, numbers, the alphabet, songs, nursery rhymes, and social skills.

When she entered the class for four-year-olds, everything changed. This teacher was one of those "Letter of the Week" teachers. As Harste and Woodward describe in their essay, "Fostering Needed Change in Early Literacy Programs":

> During this period, it was not uncommon to find the language curriculum in preschool and kindergarten organized around "Letter A Day," "Letter B Day," and so on. Often these programs were formal, asking children to *study* rather than *use* language. This instructional trend was primarily the result of misconceptions about how young children learn. (1989, 147)

So Joyce Elizabeth labored over her letters, worrying them into correctness, hesitating to make a mark lest it be wrong. She never wrote what she wanted to write; rather, she practiced her first name over and over. Toward the end of the year she brought home four pages filled with just her last name. Another time she did (I don't know what other verb to use) a "book" (I use the term loosely). A pitiful thing, 5½ by 8½ inches, comprised of already stapled worksheets of already written text; it was titled "Spring." Page 1: "I see green grass." Page 2: "I see tulips." Page 3: "I see buds." Well, you get the idea. Joyce's disengagement showed in the sloppy way she colored the pages. The only writing she was allowed to do was her name on the proper line on the cover.

But—and there is always a "but" in a good story, and this story is both good *and* true—one day her sister was assigned a school project, so Mami bought her one of those tri-foldable display boards. Joyce begged for one, too.

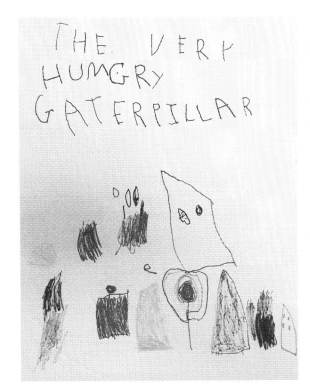

At home, while the sister worked on her project, Joyce Elizabeth worked on hers.

She carefully copied the title from her favorite book, *The Very Hungry Caterpillar*, in the center panel. Under the title she created a series of ideographs depicting each of the items the hungry caterpillar ate. Related to the book and to her, each ideograph held meaning.

She filled the left panel with writing: letter strings, approximations, some named scribbles, and her name.

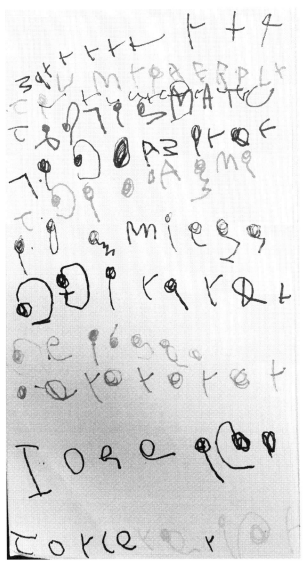

Donald Graves often advised when he spoke, "Pay attention to children; they will tell you what they know and what they need to know." Joyce Elizabeth told me loudly and clearly that a phony book duplicated, stapled, and already written held no meaning for her. It was nothing more than a disguised coloring book, what we used to call "busy work," and that's how she treated it. Yet when given big white panels of her own choosing, she was *guided by meaning—her meaning*. She basically wrote a completely literate response to literature and when asked— even now almost a year later—she can read what she had written. That's true literacy.

I think the above anecdote is telling: when children—like adults—find meaning in a task, they undertake it with zeal and relish. In the doing of it they find satisfaction and want to repeat the act in order to feel that satisfaction again and again.

What Kelley, Karla, Kristy, and I present in this book are ways to introduce true literacy and ways to keep it moving forward. Our title, *Guided by Meaning*—a phrase borrowed from Lev Vygotsky—both liberates and equips us foundationally. We believe that instruction must be as meaningful to those who teach as to those we teach. Brain research has supported meaningful instruction for decades and continues to support it by offering experiment after experiment proving that the brain neither attends nor retains what it perceives as meaningless (Ebbinghaus 1913; Bartlett 1932; Alkon 1992; Given 2002; Caine, Caine, McCintic, and Klimek 2005; Dowshen 2013).

In short, learning is meaning that sticks. That's the core of this book.

Part I

True Literacy

Joyce Armstrong Carroll

1

Play and Literacy for the Young Learner

Experiments and day-to-day observation clearly show that it is impossible for very young children to separate the field of meaning from the visual field because there is such intimate fusion between meaning and what is seen.

—Lev Vygotsky

Aside from interactions with family and the immediate environment of the home, little children develop literacy through play, books, and the act of writing. It's basic neuroscience.

When we are born, our brains contain about 100 billion neurons. That number looks like this:

100,000,000,000

Some researches contend it's more like 200 billion:

200,000,000,000

Those staggering numbers of cells are the building blocks of our knowing. Those neurons do amazing things—not the least of which is growing dendrites that make all kinds of connections. Those connections ultimately define what we know and how we know it. They are what make us unique.

Barbara Clark, who wrote *Growing Up Gifted* (now in its eighth edition) and who keynoted at the Abydos Conference in 1997, said it this way, "All children have the potential to be phenomenal."

So what makes some children appear more phenomenal than others?

There is an axiom among "brainers" (people who study the brain): "neurons that fire together wire together." That means the more connections neurons make, the more connections they *can* make. When children engage in play, books, and the act of writing, they activate—or set afire—certain neurons. When they repeatedly play or reengage with books, or make connections between books and writing, they rekindle those neurons. The more this happens, the more often neurons sprout dendrites, which enable further connections to be made and more easily. In short, this connectivity builds better brains. It follows then that the more children are occupied in play and with books and writing, the more phenomenal they become.

So it makes sense to involve children in play that promotes patterning and in books and through writing that strengthen knowing. Whether we realize it or not, patterning promotes adult learning as well. Our brains recognize and store information. We learn when we make connections by fitting something new into an already stored pattern. For example, in science children learn early on the difference between a predator and prey. But when the class went on a field trip to a state park, the ranger increased the distinction by explaining, "You can tell the difference between a predator and a prey by the eyes." The children were riveted. They knew the words *predator/prey* and they certainly knew the concept of eyes. Then the ranger recited a little rhyme, a pattern: "Eyes in front, they like to hunt. Eyes on the side, they like to hide." I could almost see the children's brains swallowing the new information, fitting it into what they already knew. When she showed them skeletons, she pointed again and again to the hollows that were once eyes, and the children never faltered in the correctness of their responses. So simple, yet so brilliant, a natural way to increase learning through patterning with no worksheets, no programs, no computers.

Play in the Growth of Literacy

Watch a child when she is drawing or painting. You will see a worried look on her face—a look of intense concentration. Is she working or playing?

—Corita Kent

Play as Guided by Meaning

Corita Kent is not the only one to connect work and play. Vivian Gussin Paley's *A Child's Work: The Importance of Fantasy Play* both reminds and cautions us.

There is no activity for which young children are better prepared than fantasy play. Nothing is more dependable and risk-free, and the dangers are only pretend. What are we in danger of doing is delegitimatizing mankind's oldest and best-used learning tool. (2004, 8)

If I searched the world over I could not find a better thesis for this section than Vygotsky's words, "The influence of play on a child's development is enormous" (1978, 96). Many of us associate play, especially the play of children, with fun—random running around, screaming, and nonsense—not with learning, yet we sometimes fail to understand that play is guided by meaning. In the world of young children, the acts of discovering, exploring, and learning dwell within their games.

Vygotsky tells us that as adults we know things abstractly, but children come to their knowing in concrete ways. What makes teaching children so challenging is what I call the process of "bringing the wonders down"; that is, taking what we know abstractly and reconstructing it in concrete ways so the child can grasp it. Vygotsky says the process of taking an abstract concept and concretizing it is as difficult for adults as taking something concrete and abstracting it is for children. Now we call this process scaffolding, but it is based on the age-old concept of heuristics.

By scaffolding the learning, the child first comes concretely to whatever is being taught, but eventually works through that into a more sophisticated knowing. Phrased another way, children begin in the real, the actual, but through play they are able to move their thinking from that tangible reality into the intangible world of ideas, concepts, and abstractions.

That scaffolding process describes Vygotsky's zone of proximal development (ZPD):

_____ here is where we want the child to be

here is the ZONE OF PROXIMAL DEVELOPMENT

_____ here is where the child is

Through good teaching, we metaphorically reach down to where the child is, take the child's mind by the hand, and cognitively move that child up, up, up to where we want that child to be. This can happen in many ways—one sure way is through play. As Mischel says, "Ultimately, all biological processes are influenced by context, including the social-psychological environment"(2014, 87). We call this strategy *making meaning*.

Play from the Concrete to the Abstract

Games bring the wonders down, because play helps move the thinking from concrete to the abstract.

Recently I overheard one bossy little miss on her way to play in the "house center" in kindergarten. "I'll be the mommy," she said with authority, pointing to herself. "You be the daddy," she said as she nodded her head in the direction of a little guy in the class. "And you be the other daddy," she said confidently, poking her finger into the chest of a third little boy.

And so they assumed these roles, doing exactly what Vygotsky described:

> In play a child is always above his average age, above his daily behavior; in play it is as though he were a head taller than himself. While imitating their elders in culturally patterned activities, children generate opportunities for intellectual development. Initially their games are recollections and reenacts of real situations; but through the dynamics of their imagination and the recognition of implicit rules governing the activities they have reproduced in their games, children achieve an elementary mastery of abstract thought. (1978, 129)

While these three tykes were imitating their elders, they were using their imaginations and following rules for their activity.

As if to prove that point, Little Miss Bossy overstepped her role, to which "Daddy Number One" protested, "Mommy wouldn't do that!" The play momentarily stopped but then continued with "Mommy" carefully staying inside the rules.

What happened here is that Little Miss Bossy violated the reenactment, so Daddy Number One reminded her of the more abstract rules, which she immediately understood and embraced.

Play as Self-Control

There is something in play that is imaginative (as if the act of imagination *becomes* the action of play), motivated (as if the motivation *becomes* personified during play), and (strange as it may seem to those of us who watch play with adult-centric eyes) there are rules.

The rules of children's games demand mastering self-control. In Walter Mischel's *The Marshmallow Test*, he describes how the preschoolers in Stanford University's Bing Nursery School reacted to a simple challenge: get one marshmallow immediately or wait until the return of the researcher for a bigger reward. Interestingly, "the more seconds they waited at age four or five, the higher their SAT scores and the better their rated social and cognitive functioning during adolescence. At age 27–32, those who had waited longer during the Marshmallow Test in preschool had a lower body mass index and a better sense of self-worth, pursued their goals more effectively, and coped more adaptively with frustration and stress. At midlife, those who could consistently wait ('high delay'), versus those who couldn't ('low delay'), were characterized by distinctively different brain scans in areas linked to addictions and obesity" (2014, 5). So being able to delay gratification when one is young clearly increases future development.

Think of play this way: play advances a child's development in two ways. First, it provides motive for action. Second, it helps the child deal with what Vygotsky calls "unrealizable tendencies" (1978,93). That play calls motive into action is important because without it a child would never advance from one developmental phase to the next. Hence, there is a basic need to teach through scaffolding as that strategy actually moves the changes along a specific cognitive path.

These "unrealizable tendencies" can cause temper outbursts, crying, all manner of machinations demanding immediacy by the very young child. During preschool, though, the child begins to realize that all demands cannot or will not be met, so the child creates the world of play, in which these "unrealizable tendencies" can be met.

Play as Higher-Level Thinking

What happens in that magnificent malleable brain is the prefrontal cortex—the area behind the forehead—moves from simply receiving sensory information to being able to manipulate and regulate new information. That, in turn, allows what we call "higher-level thinking." Play thus enables cognitive activities such as problem solving, planning, predicting, and self-control.

How brilliant the child's mind!

As Joyce Elizabeth reached three, I broke my ankle, which confined me to a wheelchair for a time. Joyce Elizabeth would sit on my lap, and we would play with big pieces of white paper and colored markers. We would talk write. It was great fun! One day a marker she loved fell to the floor. She looked at me as if to say, "Get it for me, Nina."

"Joyce Elizabeth," I said, "Nina can't get your marker. What are we going to do? We can't play with it anymore." She looked at me, then she looked at the marker, then she looked at me again while I tried to maintain an "I-can't-help-you look." All of a sudden, she slid off my lap and retrieved the marker, holding it up triumphantly. She had solved the problem. Those dendrites in that frontal cortex were firing lickety-split. That early venture set the scene for the "you can do it" philosophy, which in turn has fostered an independent-thinking child.

The Power of Play

When I was a kid over seven decades ago, Mom would say, "Go out and play!" Half mandate, half invitation, I obeyed. We didn't have video games or TV then, so we invented games—involved games with rules and boundaries and awards.

Years later, while in college, I read a long-since lost (by me) article by S. I. Hayakawa in which he said (if my memory serves me correctly) that kids today go through the motions of play, say in Little League, but not through the important decision-making process. As I read his brilliant words, I thought of how we kids played baseball. The process was consistent:

- Jackie and Bo were the team captains—always.
- Someone threw the bat to one or the other of the captains, who caught it close to the bottom with one hand. Then together, alternating fist over fist, the two boys worked their way toward the top of the bat. If Jackie's fist was the last one on top, he got first pick; if Bo's fist won, he got first pick. No one ever questioned the wisdom of chance. (If either Jackie or Bo dropped the bat, the other got first pick.)
- The rest of us were chosen according to our baseball acumen. Bobby was chosen first, Larry next, then Janet, and then Nancy, until the choices eventually trickled down to me. None of us minded that—because we knew we had different skills. Anything creative—I was picked first. Athletics? Not so much. We were already adjusting, accepting, accommodating, realizing, and being guided by meaning.
- Sometimes Bo and Jackie got into a scuffle. We hated that because it always ended the game. But in time they, and we, learned that negotiation worked better than fighting, as it allowed the game to continue. The point is that the kids made the decisions.

As I think back, I realize all the lessons embedded in that command, "Go out and play"!—everything from imaginative choice to problem solving, from setting goals to determining rules, from guided meaning to making meaning.

Essentially (before this turns into a memoir) we were developing naturally in a way that, as Vygotsky puts it, "permeates the attitude toward reality" (1978, 104). As an adult, I depend upon that.

To Recap

Play is the magic dust of cognitive development: 1. it moves the mind from sensory input (the concrete) to higher-level thinking (the abstract); 2. it moves from imagination to action; 3. it fosters the development of those all-important dendrites; 4. it helps children deal productively with things they cannot have; 5. it builds confidence and self-control.

DR. JACs Six Play Pointers

1. *Make learning seem like play.* Have fun teaching it. In the now classic piece of writing by first-grader Heather Mitchell (Carroll and Wilson 2008, xxi–xxii), it is clear Heather considers her learning play. As she wrote on the first page of a four-page story, "The Meanest Sub":

> Once upon a time there was a nice teacher. Her name was Mrs. Chamberlin. She had a big class because everyone liked her very much. The reason everyone liked her was because she let her class play a lot. And she let them play for a long time too. But one day the teacher was sick. We had the meanest substitute. She made us do 50 worksheets.

That being said, there is no doubt that Heather's "play" led to wonderful pieces of writing, whereas the work assigned by the sub did not. That yielded 50 worksheets.

2. *Collect loose parts.* To help stimulate meaningful play, I recommend the use of what Simon Nicholson calls "loose parts." (See *Loose Parts: Inspiring Play in Young Children* by Lisa Daly and Miriam Beloglovsky, 2015.) These wonderfully captivating, open-ended, mobile objects, and materials allow children to turn them into whatever they want—the cap of a marker becomes a baton when stuck on the index finger, an acorn turns into a miniature doll, grass and leaves morph into the makings of a super soup.

A former colleague, who owns and operates progressive early children centers, has long been a proponent of loose parts. Four-year-olds in her school learn the concept of small, medium, and large by sorting and classifying pinecones; three-year olds practice the early rudiments of design by placing rocks and stones along cracks in the playground and then deciding what the pattern looks like. My colleague once told me, "I had a parent ask why I don't use those expensive concept kits. I explained it's because children love natural things so much more." They love turning an egg carton, for example, into a train, or by turning a corrugated cardboard coffee drink holder inside out, they have a musical instrument they can strum. Children quickly get bored with something with a predetermined function. They want to create their own worlds. How many times can a child slide down the plastic slide? But give children a box and some rocks and they will invent buildings, cities, and games all day long.

Daly and Beloglovky offer ways to use loose parts for color, texture, sound, art, design, symbolic play, movement, transporting, connecting and disconnecting, constructing, investigating, and correlating. So, collecting loose parts for play pays dividends.

3. *Treat play as important.* If play holds a prominent place in the curriculum, children recognize that. So honor play and treat it seriously.

When Joyce Elizabeth and I play "Cosmetic Counter," Joyce plays the saleslady, while I assume the role of customer. I am always awed at how Joyce watches my choices and calculates my bill, "That will be twenty dollars," she always says as she takes the play money and carefully puts it into the "cash register." This is serious business she seems to say—no matter how often we play.

4. *Create lots of situations for role-playing.* Remember what Vygotsky says about play permitting a child to be "taller than himself." When children role-play, they are guided by meaning in a way that helps them make sense of the world and their place in it. Nancy Carlsson-Paige illustrated this best when she shared the following anecdote with Temple University graduates in May 2015:

> It was a winter day, after my teaching and the boys' day at school. The three of us were together in the living room of our rented apartment. An accidental fire started from the fireplace—accidental in the sense that I wasn't trying to burn down the house, but tired after work, I'd made a sloppy fire. I do wonder as I look back now how overwhelmed I might have been as a young, single working mom. So the flames were leaping out of the fireplace, lapping the wooden mantle. I began trying to suffocate them with a heavy blanket. My older son Kyle was trying to help. But my younger son Matt, who was then five years old, ran out of the room.

I started having success suppressing the flames but then I was wondering: Where is Matt? And then after some moments, he ran into the room. He was dressed in his red corduroy bathrobe, his fire fighter's hat, his black galoshes, and a sea diver's mask. He had a little piece of rubber tubing in his hand. It wasn't connected to anything, but he was spraying it in the direction of the fireplace.

The outfit Matt had on was the one he wore for his rescue hero play. He had it on now because wearing it was what he could do to put out the fire.

A young child in a rescue hero outfit IS a hero in that moment—and he can fully believe that by wearing firefighter clothes and with his rubber tube, he can put out a fire.

5. *Establish ground rules and an "out place."* Even during self-sponsored play, children make rules, so they expect rules from us. Rules give children both security and freedom. What Corita Kent, artist and educator, once said about assignments applies to ground rules. Paraphrased: with ground rules, children are free not to have to do everything.

As for an "out place," every child does not always feel like playing every time or playing every game, so giving children an "out place" not only helps them decide when and what to play, but also honors their unique abilities and preferences.

6. *Model often and praise honestly.* Kids need to know and see adult expectations, and they need to experience validation. A "well done" or "I loved that" goes far to support a well-accomplished skill or a risk-taking effort, as kids know when they have done something well or when they are trying hard. But don't be adult-centric. Look at play through the eyes of the children—not through adult eyes.

I watch in admiration as Miss Hazel teaches swimming and Miss Carla instructs ballet. They never "tell" the kids what to do; rather, Hazel is in the water moving her arms and then their arms with proper strokes. Carla is off to the side performing the steps while the children watch and imitate. Both model— they show; they don't tell. And when all is said and done, hugs and high fives are the rewards. The kids understand and love it.

2

Books and the Growth of Literacy

Reading Guided by Meaning

If you have ever watched young children—even toddlers—choose a book, you will see how meaning guides their choice.

One day while waiting in the school library for teachers to arrive for my staff development session, a kindergarten child wandered in and proceeded to examine the books. He gingerly removed a few, looked at them, turned a few pages, returned each one in turn, and moved on. I watched, fascinated.

In time he made his way from the fictional world of wordless books and picture books to the nonfiction section. There he got busy. He looked like a little man on a mission. But nothing seemed to suit him. His frustration was palpable as he sighed and scratched his head and sighed some more. Then all of a sudden he apparently saw what he wanted. Excitedly he pulled out a red-covered book, quite a hefty book compared to the other books he had tasted. He smiled and took it over to the librarian.

To my dismay, and although well-intentioned, she said, "Oh, no! You can't check out his book. You can't read it yet!"

Crestfallen, the little guy just stood there; I quite expected tears, but just then the principal walked in. I quietly and quickly told her what had happened. She wasted not a minute but walked over to the librarian, retrieved the red fire truck book from her, gave it to the little boy, whose name was Leroy, and said, "Miss X, I think he can check this book out—his daddy is a fireman."

Leroy brightened as if she had given him the sun, and he fairly skipped out of the library, holding the book tightly.

When he was out of earshot, the principal told both of us that Leroy's daddy was something of a hero. Apparently several years ago he had saved a child from an apartment fire. She inferred Leroy had heard that story many times.

As the teachers piled in for the staff development session, I thought, *choosing a book is always determined by meaning—even at five years old*.

Then, almost as a gift, I read an interview with Pulitzer Prize–winning author Anthony Doerr in the *New York Times Book Review*. He said in part, "I was incredibly blessed, because neither my mother nor the local librarians ever said: 'This is outside your age range, Tony. You can't handle this.' They trusted us to make our own paths through books, and that's very, very empowering" (2015, 8).

Granted, Doerr was almost a teenager at the time—not an emergent reader—but the same dictum holds true for our youngest readers. Children need to be empowered to make their own paths through books. Choice empowers.

The Evidence

I know of no serious educator who does not extol the power of reading to and with youngsters. Authors, too, praise the power of reading. On July 10, 2015, Meghan Cox Gurdon wrote in the *Wall Street Journal*:, "For 45 minutes or an hour adults can give children—and themselves—an irreplaceable gift, a cultural grounding, a zest for language, a stake in the rich history of storytelling." While lamenting the fact that "childhood itself is fast disappearing into the bewitching embrace of technology," she wrote convincingly about the power of reading aloud. Quoting one of our favorite authors, Kate DiCamello (who keynoted at our annual conference in 2002), "'We let down our guard when someone we love is reading us a story. We exist together in a little patch of warmth and light'," Gurdon made a compelling case for snuggling up with a book and a child as a way to begin a literacy journey.

But when pediatricians begin to see the power, when medical doctors quote the brain research behind reading, educators receive the added boost to deflect any naysayers.

In 1989 the American Academy of Pediatrics, citing the mounds of research that support reading as a powerful means of stimulating brain development, began "Reach Out and Read" (ROR). Making literacy a standard part of pediatric care, they built a relationship between parents and health-care providers through books—millions of books. The results were so stunning that in 2007, ROR was awarded the UNESCO Confucius Prize for Literacy. (http://www.prnewswire.com /news-releases/20-million-kids-books-distributed).

In truth, it is meaning that guides reading; that's what makes reading make sense, makes it fun, makes it exciting, makes it worthwhile. Frank Smith says it this way:

> Nonvisual information is critically important in reading because meaning is not directly represented in the surface structure of language, in the sounds of speech, or in the visible marks of writing. Readers must bring meaning—deep structure—to what they read, employing their prior knowledge of the topic and of the language of the text. (2006, 85)

If that deep structure, that comprehension, that meaning, is not present, the reader— regardless of age—becomes frustrated or bored, because the brain is not making sense out of the symbols. I once asked a group of struggling readers this question, "What is reading?" Their answer? "Reading is saying the words." No wonder they were struggling.

Think about a struggling reader dealing with this sentence, provided by Frank Smith (2006, 81):

She runs through the sand and waves.

Even struggling readers could probably say all the words in that sentence correctly (excepting, perhaps, a stumbling over the word *through*) so the reader "gets" the surface structure. But if that reader is not guided by meaning, does not get the deep structure (Smith's synonym for *meaning*), does not crystallize the ambiguity with another clarifying sentence, there is danger of a misread. Smith says "Meaning lies beyond mere words" (2006, 81); I like to say, "Reading is the brain making meaning."

The reading brain will ask of the sentence above: Is she running through the sand and waves, or is she running through the sand and then waves to someone?

So it follows that the little guy who chose a fire truck book beyond his "reading level" could indeed read it. Not only was he guided by reading in his choice, but also by meaning as he read it. Because of his daddy, he had lots of experiences with fire trucks and could tease out the meaning from the pictures and words by using his magnificent brain, just as we had to bring our prior knowledge to the sand and waves sentence. Our brains do the reading because meaning must connect to experience. If children have no context for "beach and sand and waves," the girl could be running through a sand box or in a grassless backyard in their minds. That is why reading must be guided by meaning.

Further Evidence

Maryanne Wolf opens her remarkable book *Proust and the Squid: The Story and Science of the Reading Brain* with this corker of a hook, "We were never born to read" (2007, 3). So if we weren't born to it, why did it happen? It happened because our brains constantly tried to make sense of our world; that trying to make sense hastened the growth of neurons and their dendrites, which in turn continued to try to make sense of the world. Ever changing in an upward spiral, our brains continue to fit into an increasingly complex environment:

> There are few more powerful mirrors of the human brain's astonishing ability to rearrange itself to learn a new intellectual function than the act of reading. Underlying the brain's ability to learn reading lies its protean capacity to make new connections among structures and circuits originally devoted to other more basic brain processes, such as vision and spoken language. . . .We are, it would seem from the start, genetically poised for breakthroughs. (Wolf 2007, 4–5)

Nicholas Carr tells us in *The Shallows*, a book that explores the cognitive complex challenges of the Internet, "My mind isn't going—so far as I can tell—but it's changing" (2010, 5).

Wolf quotes cognitive scientist David Swinney, who "discovered that the brain doesn't find just one simple meaning for a word; instead it stimulates a veritable trove of knowledge about that word and the many words related to it" (2007, 9). Obviously the more experiences we have, the more meaning we bring to each word and their interrelationship to other words and pictures, if there are pictures on the page—there goes those neurons again! Wolf takes Dr. Seuss's *Oh, the Places You'll Go!* as one of her examples. She flatly states, "Children who have never left the narrow boundaries of their neighborhood, either figuratively or literally, may understand this book in entirely different ways from other children" (2007, 9).

But they make sense out of it. They make its meaning. That is why when working with young children, their responses to a book strike us as sometimes funny, sometimes outlandish, and sometimes so off the wall, we are tempted to ask, "Where did that come from?" But instead we say, "Tell me how you came to think that."

I am reminded of a time when I observed in Kelley's class, which was always an amazing experience.

In an effort to help kinders understand a corpus of work by an author, Kelley followed up her reading of Margaret Wise Brown's *The Important Book* by asking, "Do you know any other books by Margaret Wise Brown?" One child offered *The Runaway Bunny*, while another confidently said *Good-Night Moon*. But a third child, waving her hand frantically, blurted out, "The lady who drives the school bus is named Margaret."

Clearly the little girl wasn't making a connection with the book, but she was making a connection; she was making meaning.

And of course I have an example from Joyce Elizabeth when she just turned three. We were reading *Maisy's Rainbow Dream* by Lucy Cousins (2003), talking about the colors, when Joyce Elizabeth said, "I dreamed I was purple all over!" That's a text-to-self connection if I ever heard one.

One of the world's most recognized researchers on the cognitive neuroscience of language, Stanislas Dehaene (and this précis does not do his book justice) tells us something we must bear in mind when we separate phonics from a context. "The brain network that analyzes word meaning is quite distinct from that which converts letters into sounds" (2009, 109). Dehaene explains how teaching reading should focus on "the grasp of the alphabetic principle whereby each letter or grapheme represents a phoneme" (228), but then he presents this caveat. "Of course, learning the mechanics of reading is not an end in itself—in the long run, it only makes sense if it leads to learning. Children must know that reading is not simply mumbling a few syllables—it requires understanding what is written" (229).

What Dehaene refers to as "mumbling a few syllables" reminds me of the phrase "barking at print," which I first heard from Beth Egmon, an Abydos trainer and a specialist in early childhood literacy. While doing research I discovered the phrase actually dates back to 1915–1916. P. B. Ballard, in "Norms of Performance in Reading," seems to have coined the phrase when discussing a test he constructed of isolated words. He admits, "much scorn has been leveled at this type of reading . . . contemptuously called 'barking at print'" (1915/1916, 154). We find this phrase handy, as it best describes the children who, when reading, say the words but have no earthly idea what they mean. Therefore, all the words are "barked" equally. No variation in tone or inflection signifies comprehension—a sure sign of a struggling reader. Also, they often "bark" *any* word if they don't recognize the word. For example, they may say *wool* for *wolf* or *stick* for *sick* even if it makes no sense in the context. Naturally this impedes any progress in understanding the text.

Finally, weighing in on the side of making meaning, I offer Louise Rosenblatt's succinctly precise analysis, which is called "transactional theory." Eschewing the two prevailing notions that (1) the reader finds meaning in the text and (2) the reader finds meaning solely in his or her mind, Rosenblatt contends, " The finding of meaning involves both the author's text and what the reader brings to it" (1978, 14). To do anything less, it seems to me, is not to *read* but to *say*. It is Dehaene's "mumbling" without *connection to thought*.

Books as Foundational

The Power of the Focal Book

We at Abydos Literacy have been using what we call "focal books" for several decades, designing reading/writing connections for all disciplines, for different themes, and most especially for different skills. Focal books set the tone, set the genre, set the grammar, set the characterization, set the way authors begin, develop, and end narratives and informational texts. They may be used to introduce skills or culminate a lesson on a specific skill. They are an absolute necessity for showing, and thereby teaching, the parts of a book, or even how to turn the pages of a book. I find them indispensable for priming students. They are the mentor texts, to use the term of the day, because they provide the model for just about anything a teacher wants to teach during that lesson. If well chosen, focal books are nothing less than a perfect way into, through, or concluding a lesson. So in a real sense, they are the foundation of the lesson.

An Example of a Focal Book

Let's look at one focal book to get the idea: I recently received *Kindergarten Luck* by Louise Borden (2015). Loving her since I successfully used her book *The Day Eddie Met the Author*, I stopped what I was doing to read it.

Before even beginning the reading, I noticed its hardcover had a dust jacket. Hello? There is an immediate lesson on the difference between a dust jacket and a cover. And a knowledgeable teacher will be able to share just why we have dust jackets on books—a bit of history.

Upon opening the book—what do I see? Dark clouds and gigantic raindrops cover the end pages. The copyright page shows a forlorn looking little guy holding back the curtain inside the house only to see a gloomy scene outside.

The title page depicts some Legos® close to a teddy bear, who looks as forlorn as the little boy. *Ah ha!* I think—*the end pages foreshadow the story. This is one of those books that begins before it begins.*

But the beginning of the story changes everything. Even though it's a gloomy morning, Theodore (isn't that a wonderful name for a character?), on his way down the stairs for breakfast, finds a shiny penny with Abraham Lincoln face up. *Just on page one,* I think, *I could show how there is a connection* (coherence) *from the end pages to the first page. I could teach (or review) how proper names take capital letters, how there is a comma between the words "bright" and "shiny" and another after "Lincoln."*

Then I notice the words *"What luck!"* Those two words are like finding a lesson on exclamation marks. Page two has dialogue (in color for young readers) that contains the grammatical structure called "direct address." I quickly flip to the back end pages and am delighted to see a pink sky with white fluffy clouds. Kindergarten luck had changed the day.

I shall stop there. My point here is to illustrate the richness of focal books. Of course not *every* book will do, but neither will *any* book do, so teachers and parents must be well read, with one eye on the potential of the book and the other on the objective for reading the book. The third eye—that "inner" eye that provides perception beyond the obvious—is the one that knows just the right book has been found and knows what to do with it.

Extensions of the Focal Book: Themes to Discuss and Possible Writing Prompts

In addition to that sampling from the book's first several pages, two major messages emerge: (1) noticing how much luck there is in the world; and (2) sharing that luck. These themes furnish the opportunity to talk about positive perceptions, meaningful actions, and connections to the students' lives.

Leaping from this book are the possible writing prompts of a lucky day or finding, discovering, or uncovering something. And when students read what they have written, they will hold everyone's attention because their writing will be real, it will be authentic, and it will be guided by meaning.

To Recap

A focal book focuses the literacy. It both precipitates and prods, it is both mentor and guide, and it enables and inspires. It is not just a book to read aloud, but also a book to show the way. It is not just a reader, but also a shepherd into writing. A focal book is the powerhouse that guides students into meaningful further reading, authentic writing, and deeper thinking.

Focal books must be chosen with care and wisdom; they are foundational and provide the support for the many lessons yet to come.

DR. JACs Six Book Pointers

1. *Spend lots of time talking about the book's cover and its pictures.* When Martin Waddell, author of many wonderful children's books, spoke at an Abydos Literacy conference, he explained that little children "see more in the pictures than we do." Essentially, they "read" the pictures. By giving them time and encouragement to do that with each book, we are validating what they do well, and we are setting the scene for a good reading experience. This was further reinforced when reading scholar and author Cris Tovani, speaking at yet another Abydos conference, shared research she had done on how teachers in different disciplines read. She astonished us all by reminding us that our colleagues outside of English often primarily rely on the graphs, charts, photos, diagrams, maps, and other visual symbols to convey meaning—the text is then checked secondarily for the meaning, whereas English Language Arts Reading (ELAR) teachers depend primarily on the written text and only secondarily check the visuals. So supporting the "reading" of pictures with little ones helps them guide their own meaning.

2. *Point out any unusual features.* Little kids grow to love books when they see features in them that appeal to their senses: pop-ups, sounds, moving parts, sparkles, spangles, flaps, places that invite touching such as shiny paper, sandpaper, corrugated paper, different shapes. The brain loves color, and no brain loves it more than the child's does. However, some fine, fine wordless books contain little color, so that provides an opportunity to discuss why that would be so. The wordless book *The Wave* is simply hues of blue and charcoal that enhance its meaning, which makes it an interesting contrast to the wordless book *The Apple Bird* where color enhances its meaning.

Two of Joyce Elizabeth's favorite books before she could read were Hervé Tullet's *Press Here* and *Mix It Up!* The former invites the child to press and rub on dots, only to turn the page to find the results of such whimsy. The latter invites the child to tap on the dots to find the magic. Joyce Elizabeth never tired of turning the page to find her handprint! Guided by this meaning, she learned that books hold surprises, meaning, fun, magical things, information, and invitations to the imagination.

3. *Encourage the child to hold the book, turn its pages.* In this way the book becomes part of the child's experience. The child takes on the ownership of the book. "This is my book," the child will say.

This also allows for micro-minilessons on how to hold a book, how to turn its pages, and how to treat a book. This in turn helps the child realize that books are precious and should be respected.

4. *Read the book with great authentic expression.* There's no need for histrionics, but there is a great need for voice modifications and intensifications of tone. Reading a book to a child also calls for changes in facial expression. This helps the child process the thoughts and feelings of the characters; it also helps children paint images in their minds and understand changes in emotions, which helps them later when they must visualize and hear what they are reading silently. Bark when the dog barks, growl when he growls, pant when he pants. Then invite the child to do the same. This additional level of meaning brings the book to life.

5. *Most of all—enjoy the book you are reading.* Nothing turns a child off to reading more quickly than an uninterested adult. *Brown Bear* must be read with the same enthusiasm on its fiftieth reading as on its first reading. Laugh at the funny parts, look sad at the sad parts, guffaw, tease out a tear, smile, frown, and settle in to enjoy the book. Emotion is contagious.

6. *Be sure to read the book to yourself first.* I am astonished at the number of parents and teachers I see reading a book "cold" before reading it to a child. This is a bad idea, because children's books are often so sophisticated, you need to read them beforehand to be sure you "get" it.

3

Writing Guided by Meaning

Children develop language through interaction, not action. They learn to talk by talking to someone who responds. They must therefore learn to write by writing to someone who responds. It's not a new theory, but it's one I keep forgetting even though it's so clear and simple. Please keep it somewhere safe.

—Mem Fox

The Delight to Write

Young children delight in the act of writing. They write on foggy windows, in cereal, in sand, and (much to the dismay of parents) on walls in their homes. *Harold and the Purple Crayon* by Crockett Johnson shows us that delight as Harold uses his big purple crayon to make everything from his imagination real. Writing does that. Actually, writing does *just* that. It takes ephemeral thought, fleeting as it is, and plants it firmly on the paper. And when children read their thoughts, they delight in the process. They consider it magical. Many adults when re-reading something they have written a while back will often exclaim, "Did *I* write that?" as if the words magically appeared over time or rearranged themselves while time passed.

But imagine, if you will, what it must have been like when writing was first conceived! The notion that marks could extend memory, be read by others, and give someone power by conveying meaning was considered spooky stuff. Robert Silverberg put that imagining in his novel *Gilgamesh the King,* a fictional account of the Sumerian god-king who lived over 5,000 years ago. This excerpt describes Gilgamesh recalling when he learned to read and write:

> What attracted me to writing was my notion that it was magical. To be able to work magic, that magic or any other, was tremendously attractive. It seems miraculous that words could be captured like hawks in flight and imprisoned in a piece of red clay, and set loose again by anyone who knew the art of it. . . . I learned my writing-signs well, and know them still, and can never be deceived by some treacherous underling who means to play me false. (1984, 31)

Now, it is true that this novel is a fabrication, but in these words Silverberg nailed the essence of the early wonder of writing and its power.

Wolf, in discussing how the discovery of writing and then the reading of that writing caused our brains to adapt, tells us that writing was actually discovered several times, enabling us to read everything from "tiny tokens to 'dragon bones' in the period that stretches from the eighth millennium to the first millennium BCE" (2007, 27). But write we did, we do, we will.

Why Children Write

Aside from the fascination of making the pencil or crayon an extension of their index fingers, aside from feeling the power of putting a mark where there wasn't one, children write for the same reasons adults write: they want to capture something meaningful because they have much to express. They want to construct their reality like Harold did with his purple crayon, and they want to show their relationship in the world.

In this book we consider all marks made by children as writing. As Vygotsky says, "Gestures, it has been correctly said, are writing in air, and written signs frequently are simply gestures that have been fixed" (1978, 107). So even if something in our samples looks like drawing, we consider it writing—that is, the effort to make meaning. (For a detailed examination of developmental writing, see Carroll and Wilson 2008, chapter 11, "Early Literacy.") (See also Karla's section IV, Chapter 22, pp. 215–224.) Let's look at a few examples from our youngest writers that verify their writing is guided by meaning.

Student Sample 1 (Two Years Old)

Little William, age two years and eleven months, has written what holds meaning for him. Researchers tell us that the first shape an infant recognizes is the circle. They theorize that this is so because infants look into their caregivers' eyes, seeing circles within circles. They also see the head and face shapes as circles. So it is not surprising that William has written circles when writing about his mother. Most of his writing is in red, with touches of green like hair on top of the large circle. A line of green extends from the circle that might be a "mouth"; the mouth itself is purple. Brainers tell us that the brain loves color and that colors hold meanings for children.

Figure 3.1. Williams's writing.

Student Sample 2
(Four Years Old)

Here we see a leap from circles that hold meaning to a few controlled scribbles, some approximations, and a few letters. This writing by four-year-old Cary expresses a meaningful message to his relative. When nudged, "Tell me about your writing," Cary read: "Cary [he stated his name first and we can see he wrote it first]. Thank-you for the hat." Looking closely at the writing, we can see C A R, maybe a T, and the word YOU. And then we move into what appears to be approximations and random scribbles. Still, as if receiving a hat isn't meaningful enough, Cary extends that meaning by thanking his relative for it. This is not idle scribbling.

Figure 3.2. Cary's writing.

Student Sample 3
(Four Years Old)

This page of approximations almost obscures the fact that Elizabeth is practicing the letters in her name on lined paper. We also see a distinct circle, bright red in the original, and wedge-shaped characters that resemble the Sumerian cuneiform. Many researchers of early writing contend that the writing of children subsumes in a short period of time the eons of writing development undertaken by humankind. Interestingly, most of her cuneiforms were written in brown crayon. Elizabeth wrote the upside-down L in the top left corner of the paper and the letters BET in the color green. In Elizabeth's world, her name holds meaning for her, so her writing is guided by that meaning, and she wants to get it just right.

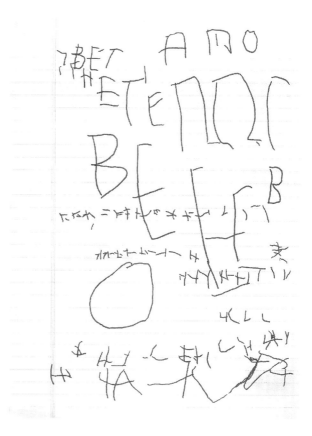

Figure 3.3. Elizabeth's writing.

Student Sample 4 (Four Years Old)

Of course we must include an example from Joyce Elizabeth. When she was barely four (four years and two months), she was attending school. One day she brought me a sheet of rough ecru construction paper to be hung at "Joyce's place" on the kitchen wall. Clearly there was writing at the top, but the remainder of the paper was filled with colored dots.

I invited, "Read me what you have written, Joyce Elizabeth." She immediately read what she had written at the top as, "This is my bracelet." I responded. "How lovely and look at all these colors—purples, oranges, green, and black, and even some pink. But tell me, Joyce Elizabeth, about this part here?" I pointed to the purple dots that started at the left side of the paper but trailed to the bottom right side and off the page.

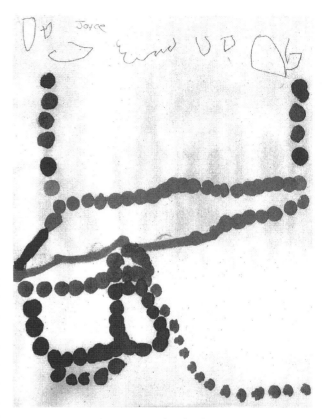

Figure 3.4. Joyce Elizabeth's writing.

"Oh," she said without missing a beat, "my bracelet is broken."

It turns out the broken bracelet was one of her favorites. Breaking it disappointed her, but she mended it with meaning when she wrote.

Student Samples 5 and 6 (Kindergarten)

Kindergarten is the perfect place to see most of the arenas of writing at one time. While most children are beyond **random scribbles** and even **controlled scribbles**, many still make deliberate marks that resemble random scribbling and talk write as they do. We call these **named scribbles**.

But most kindergarten children have been exposed to writing long enough to make marks that look like letters, often in letter strings. These approximations, as they are called in the field, provide a prelude to pre-phonemic spelling. In addition, many kinders do **symbolic drawing**, which divides itself into **pictographs** where children use pictures, signs, and symbols to capture what they know, not what they necessarily see, and **ideographs** where children use written or graphic symbols to represent an idea or depict some relationship.

One favorite pictograph comes from two-year-old Jenny. She "wrote" a smiley face with five lines radiating around it. Everyone thought it was the sun, but fortunately we asked Jenny to tell us about her writing. She did. The writing was her mommy, who bore little resemblance to the pretty lady upon whose lap she sat. Jenny explained, "She smiles a lot and gives me hugs." Pointing to the five lines, she said, "Those are her arms." Jenny didn't write about the mommy she saw; she wrote about the mommy she knows—the warm, loving, happy woman who hugs her often. In doing so, Jenny produced a perfect pictograph.

We see an excellent example of an archetypal ideograph in Amanda's writing. The teacher told us that Amanda wrote this piece of writing a week after her grandmother's death. Her grandfather's name is Tom, which is sprawled across the top. Amanda explained to her teacher that the cross between the name *Tom* and the actual ideograph means Jesus is taking her grandmother to heaven. There seems to be a church steeple to the right of the page, surrounded by what looks like scribbles.

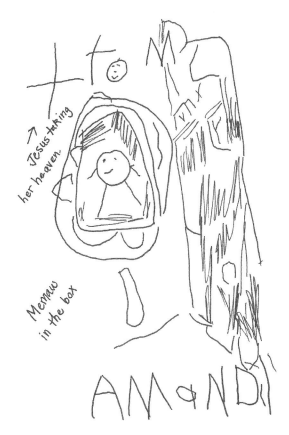

Figure 3.5. Amanda's writing.

But the most powerful part of this writing is centered. Amanda declared to the teacher, "Memaw in the box." Evidence enough that this writing was guided by meaning. Amanda wrote this entire page in blacks and browns.

But Amanda wrote still another page that may even be more telling about her relationship with her grandmother.

The teacher told us that the big heart was in bright red with the arms of Amanda's grandmother reaching out to "Amanda," which is written on both sides of the heart. The tiny heart, also in red, is Amanda's. Notice the cross at the top. Clearly Amanda's message is fraught with meaning, showing relationships and great love but also anxiety or even stress at this loss. She told the teacher, "I love my Memaw."

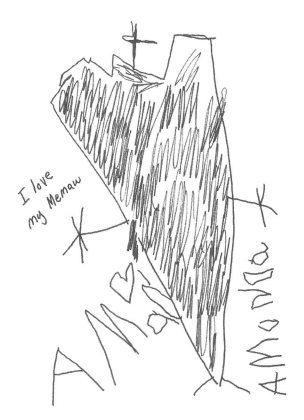

Figure 3.6. Amanda's writing.

Student Sample 7 (Kindergarten)

This sample dates back in my files to 1994. Lest you think this writing is about "fart money," the teacher transcribed the writing on the back to prove that even little children can write an analysis. She put the child's age (5) but not the child's name. Still, "anonymous" proves that some children, even in kindergarten, already flirt with the arena of **transitional writing**, even primitive transitional writing (where children move from rudimentary writing to standard writing). Here is the teacher's transcription: "My favorite movie is to watch My Girl 2. In My Girl 2 the girl kissed the boy."

Can anyone doubt the meaning this movie held for this young writer?

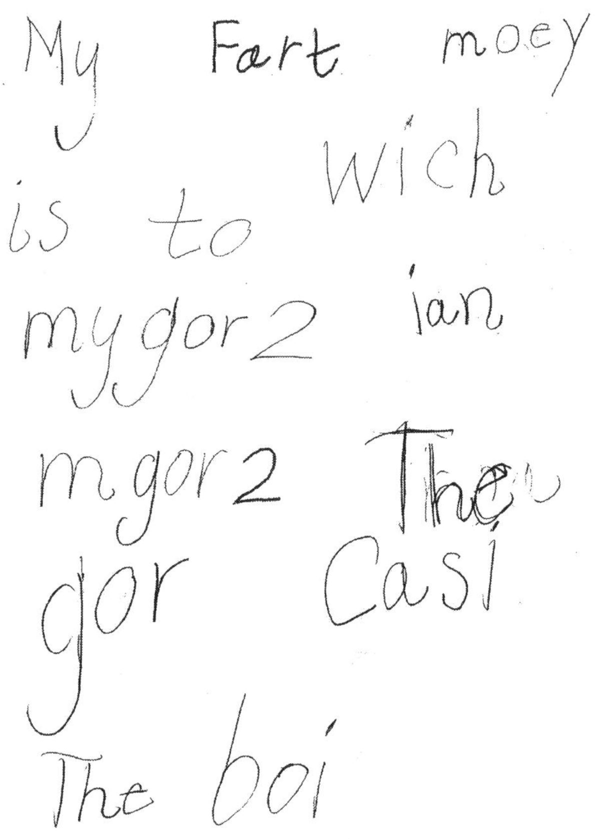

My Fart moey
is to wich
mygor 2 ian
mgor 2 The
gor Casi
The boi

Figure 3.7. Writing by anonymous.

Student Sample 8: First Grade

We see more evidence of transitional writing in first grade. One of my favorite pieces literally floored me when I first read it because it is so sophisticated. Writing in the genre of a play, Diana, not yet quite seven, creates a dialogue between Alisha and Robert. She even supplies the first letter of each of their names down the left side of the page in the manner of a script so the reader can keep things straight.

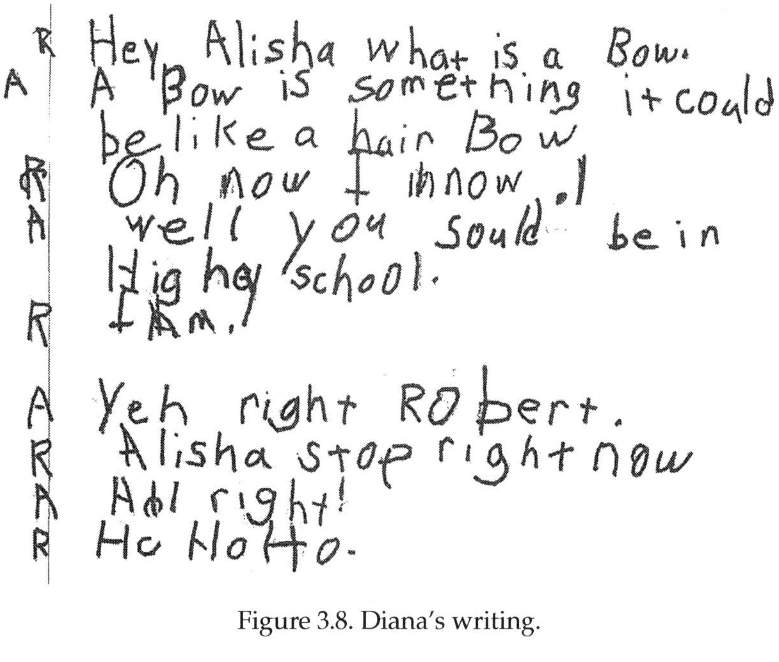

R Hey Alisha what is a Bow.
A A Bow is something it could be like a hair Bow
R Oh now I know.
A well you sould be in High school.
R I Am.
A Yeh right RObert.
R Alisha stop right now
A All right!
R Ha HoHo.

Figure 3.8. Diana's writing.

What makes this piece of writing all the more meaningful is that Diana, in the first grade, assumes a different persona in her writing. Young children do this easily in play, but it is a higher cognitive step to do it in writing.

Three other interesting things emerge here:

1. The reader wonders about the original question. Was Diana playing with the word *bow*, as in a knot with loops, or was she thinking of the weapon that shoots arrows (shades of Disney's Merida), or does she or someone in her experience play a musical instrument that uses a bow? Or is she trying to ascertain what Robert knows? In any case, wordplay of this kind at this level indicates a child who has many experiences with language and knows language holds meaning, maybe many meanings.
2. How did Diana pronounce the word *bow*? What experience does Diana have with high school? Does she have siblings or relatives who attend? She obviously realizes that high school students know more information than do first graders. Perhaps Diana chose to create a riddle—that ancient play on words—or is studying homophones, but her risk taking in writing by playing one child off the other child shows a bright mind.
3. This writing takes on a tone that is most unusual for this level, an almost mocking tone, "Yeh, right Robert." And then Diana has Robert "get it" because he responds "Alisha, stop right now!" Capturing tone is difficult even for students in the upper grades, but Diana has an ear for it. But Robert gets the last laugh with his "Ho, ho, ho!"

Student Sample 9: Second Grade

I chose this sample not because it is closer to standard writing than some others I have, but because it shows the recursiveness of these arenas. Amelia wrote a perfectly cogent, coherent piece of discourse but reverted to an ideograph—to the symbolic drawing arena—to be sure her readers got the idea of the "flower bed" with the flowers at different stages in their growth and blooming.

Astonishingly, she has both the *it's* spelled correctly with the apostrophe in the right place. She spelled the correct *too* the first time but missed it the second time. But she is seven! High school students goof on those demons. So who will ding her for *maid*?

As for meaning? Well, with a sense of panache for a good ending, she concludes with her most meaningful sentence, "We made it."

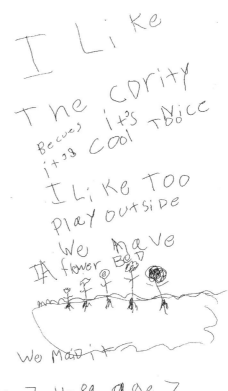

Figure 3.9. Amelia's writing.

Student Sample 10: Summer of Second Grade

Driving home the other afternoon, I noticed some kids and an adult mulling around the esplanade that separates the road leading into our subdivision from the road leading out. As I drew closer I saw what was happening—a lemonade stand was in the making. Three kids were setting up a table and some chairs, an umbrella, and a banner. I inferred they were siblings as they all resembled each other—an older brother, a middle sister, and a younger sister. The adult was clearly Dad.

I couldn't resist. I lowered my window and called, "Gee, I really feel like a lemonade today; it's so hot."

The youngest ran over to the car with a plastic glass half full. After the transaction, this young entrepreneur asked, "Would you like the recipe?"

"Of course!" So she whipped out a notebook-sized page covered with colorful print and handed it to me. "Thanks and good luck," I said and drove off.

At home I studied my windfall. Once again we see the power of writing coupled with the power of color. The title: "Ingredients, " although misspelled, is written in big brown letters. Underneath we find the list in red. She deliberated over the word *sugar* because at first it was spelled *s u g u r*. The second red *u* was then corrected in orange marker to make an *a*.

The dotted lines alternate in brown and gray. Interesting bit of coherence because the second title "How to make" is written in gray. Brown and gray; makes sense to me. She uses the two colors to draw the two parts of the recipe together as both are important.

This little girl understands revision. She crossed out in bold yellow whatever she had written after the first sentence. She crossed out *But* in the second sentence. (Might some well-intentioned but ill-informed adult have told her that you never start a sentence with *But*?)

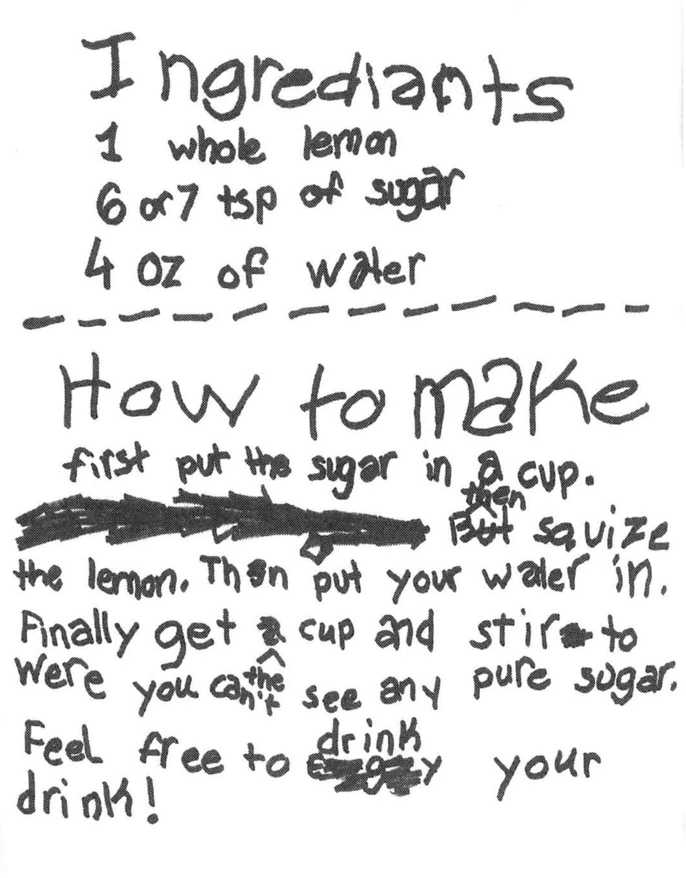

Figure 3.10. The writing of a budding entrepreneur.

Notice, too, that she has been taught the caret. She uses two of them.

My favorite part is the cross out in the last sentence. I think she was attempting to write the word *enjoy* but got flummoxed by that annoying *g,* so she abandoned *enjoy* and opted for *drink,* which happens to make sense in that context.

Was our tiny tycoon interested in making meaning? You bet. She wanted to be part of not only the sales but also the advertising. Not only does she have a firm grasp of the recipe genre, but she also knows what catches her eye—color, line, and white space— and applied that to her recipe. Most important, though, is her desire to share. She wants her customers to have her recipe. I once had a college student who said profoundly of writing, "This solitary work we cannot do alone." Janet Emig and other scholars tell us that "writing and reading are social acts" (Bruffee 1983, 149; Emig 1991).

To Recap

Children write because they have something important to share. They write to leave their mark. This human urgency was captured perfectly in an interview between David A. Sohn, then director of curriculum research with the National Film Study Project at Fordham University, and Saul Bass, graphic and industrial designer and Oscar award winner:

> Humankind creates to leave its mark on its time, as a denial of mortality, to say, "Look at me; I was here." Each of us also creates out of a need to identify ourselves, to ourselves. To say, "I am unique. I am here. I am." (Sohn 1970, 58)

Children create—they write for the same reason.

DR. JACs Five Writing Pointers

1. Have lots of materials available. Literally stock their rooms or play area or the den or the kitchen or wherever children feel comfortable working with large sheets of colored and white paper. Butcher paper is best. Large Post-its® are the easiest. Least favored by children is the rough (but cheaper) construction paper. Fill jars or cans with all types of writing implements: markers, crayons, pencils, highlighters, pens that write sparkly and those that write in multiple colors, and anything else that would encourage a child to try writing with them. Add tape and glue sticks and safe scissors; magazines; newspapers; and tons and tons of miscellaneous "stuff" such as colored paper clips, sidewalk chalk, glitter, stickers, wool, string, small staplers for those tiny fingers, various sized Post-its® in bright colors, index cards, lined and unlined paper.

The larger the paper, the more children will write. And don't use that dreaded "story paper," which invites children to write something anorexic that will fit the given lines and then end when the lines end.

2. Set aside writing time. Call it writing time and not art or drawing time. When children make meaningful marks, they are writing. Applaud that. If possible, sit with the child and write too. Those mirror neurons are activated when adults and older siblings model. When you are finished, read what you have written and encourage the child to do the same. Sharing is important as it validates the act. Writing is a social act, one that becomes more delightful when shared with another.

3. Read first and then write. Read a book to a child and invite a piece of writing out of that focal book. For example, if the child loves *Brown Bear, Brown Bear*, read it together and then talk about it—all the animals, all the colors. Then it would be organic to say something like, "Gee, I wonder if I could write a page with a different animal and another color. Hmmmm. . . . I am thinking of a chameleon because I could color it all different colors." Or "Hmmmm, this book is about animals and colors, I think I could write a book about animals and the sounds they make." Then write an example and let the child do the same.

4. *Find real reasons to write.* Kids love to feel important, so what could make them feel more important than writing their names on birthday invitations, birthday cards, or birthday thank-you notes? They love helping Mom with the grocery list or Dad with some how-to instructions to remember. When they do these things, they realize the many functions of writing even though they cannot put words to them yet. Although letter writing is becoming a lost art in our society, children still love to write letters. Encourage them to write to Santa Claus, their grandmother or grandfather, a favorite aunt, you!—anyone in their world. And encourage the recipient to write back. As we have seen, children love to write and share recipes. Let them.

5. *Publish the writing.* Make a big deal out of what they write. Hang it on a special "publishing wall," create books so they can "publish" their stories or whatever they write. Send their letters out and invite the recipients to respond. Try to keep the correspondence going. Create a "family journal" or a "class journal." Place it somewhere for easy accessibility. Anyone in the family or class may write anytime to anyone else or to everyone. (This also encourages reading.) At some auspicious point, such as Thanksgiving, some family holiday, or a designated day in school, arrange a READ-AROUND. Everyone sits in a circle and reads aloud some piece of writing he or she has chosen. Everyone applauds each reader.

4

The History of the Alphabet

But of all other stupendous inventions, what sublimity of mind must have been his who conceived how to communicate his most secret thoughts to any other person, though very far distant either in time or place? And with no greater difficulty than the various arrangement of two dozen little signs upon paper? Let this be the seal of all the admirable inventions of man.

—Galileo

From the Beginning

A, B, C, D, E, F, G,

Can you hear the melody of this now classic alphabet song?

H, I, J, KLMNOP,
Q, R, S,
T, U, V,
W, X,
Y and Z
Now I know my ABC's
Won't you sing along with me?

Most of us know some version of this "Alphabet Song," but many of us don't know the history of what has been called one of the greatest inventions of all time. "Of all mankind's inventions, with the possible exception of language itself, nothing has proved more useful or led to more innovations than the alphabet" (Logan 1986, 17–18).

While there are roughly about fifty alphabets in use today, "our own alphabet is the most widely used of any in the world" (Ogg 1948, 5). Considered the gateway to knowledge, these twenty-six letters "are the keys not only to reading and writing but also to a whole philosophy of organizing information" (Logan 1986, 18). So it is not surprising parents sing the alphabet song as a lullaby to their babies, preschoolers sing the alphabet song repeatedly throughout their day, and kinders jump and hop and write the letters in the air as they sing the alphabet song again and again.

But this ingenious invention of humankind did not pop into existence at some magical point in time. Rather, it began with the chipped stones of our earliest ancestors, dating back some 600,000 years. Flash forward to somewhere around 35,000 BC, when those chipped stones had morphed into implements for drawing and carving, for making notches and marks; in short, for memory helpers. Even today we use writing to nudge our memories as we make a grocery list or create a mnemonic for a personal spelling demon.

With these so-called primitive devices, the concept that was to blossom into the alphabet was born.

In the "Glossary of Language Arts Concepts" for *Phonics Friendly Books* (1998, 177), I make the point that letters evolved as forms from thing-pictures to idea-pictures to word-sound pictures to syllable-sound pictures and finally to letter-sound pictures as humans tried for a more efficient way to write thoughts. Yet many of these forms existed side by side for centuries. Interestingly, children evolve into the act of writing in much the same way. It is as if the natural writing development of children mirrors a truncated version of the writing development of humankind.

One of everyone's favorite parts of a workshop I conduct on early literacy shows that development vividly—bear in mind that development did not happen in such a lockstep way—but it serves as an apt example. I use a phonogram, sometimes called a pictograph, an ideogram, sometimes called an ideograph, and a letter from Ogg's *The 26 Letters* (41). Before I begin, I talk about how the Sumerians and then the Egyptians—both of whom preceded the Greeks and Romans—had a system of letters but not exactly an alphabet. First I place a transparency of a pictograph, which is a *thing-picture,* on the overhead. It is a stylized eagle, drawn to look like an eagle and meant to mean *eagle.*

Next I superimpose the ideograph, which is the *idea-picture.* It fits over the pictograph perfectly and shows how the eagle now has a human face, so it is no longer *eagle*; rather, this idea-picture means *soul.*

Finally, I superimpose upon the *thing-picture* and the *idea-picture* the letter *a.*

eagle

Figure 4.1. Pictograph.

soul

Figure 4.2. Ideograph.

That's when I hear the "ahas," gasps, and "I got it!"s The progression is unmistakable.

We see this progression with emergent writers. Often—actually more often than not—children will draw *thing-pictures* and/or *idea pictures*, then add some approximations or even legitimate letters in and around them. These all hold meaning for the child. But equally intriguing, children who have transitioned to standard writing often add *thing-pictures* or *idea pictures* or both to their writing as if they still don't totally trust the words to convey their intended meaning.

letter

Figure 4.3. The letter.

From Caves to Classrooms

My husband and I were fortunate enough to visit the caves along the banks of the Dordogne River in France. There we entered the famous caves of Lascaux. What wonders we beheld! Grand, detailed drawings of bison and reindeer, woolly rhinoceroses, mammoths, hippopotami, cave bears, horses, aurochs, and other paleolithic and mesolithic animals conveyed as static thing-pictures. These exist on the cave walls side by side with more dynamic idea-pictures: charging bulls, a fresco of five deer swimming or running through tall grass with heads up and necks outstretched, galloping horses, a stallion pierced by seven arrows, a cavalcade of mares, ponies, and ibexes.

Galleries of large and small animals run along the base of some areas of the caves with multiple feet and legs as if in a Duchamp painting, while Chagall-like cows seem to indeed jump over the moon. Stories all.

A mythical, dappled unicorn with an almost human face lopes easily alongside a darker horse. One stunning painting depicts a hunter and a bison juxtaposed in mortal combat. Spears and rope appear in the foreground along with what appears to be a bird sitting on a pole or shaft. No doubt several ideas are expressed in this painting: fear, valor, courage, the thrill of the hunt, or the idea of life and death. Again, whole stories. Interestingly, it seems humankind began with picture-stories (pictographs) just the way emergent writers begin their literacy journey.

I have three favorites. The first is an upside down horse. Perhaps driven off a cliff by hunters, the details of its vertiginous fall are captured in surrealistic suspension for perpetuity, which embeds itself in the memory and as such it becomes a favorite.

While studying my second favorite, I wondered at the notion of "primitive people," as its sensitivity is palpable. A stag stands over a pregnant doe, her belly painted over a protruding rock formation, his head bowed over her head as he licks her face.

My favorite favorite (as the kids like to say the word twice for emphasis) is the outline of a human hand, small, suggesting that the author was a woman. Standing before it I could almost hear the writer say, "I am"; I could almost see the author claim ownership; I could almost feel the cave wall's texture as the author "signed" the piece. Even today, children often "sign" their work by outlining one or both hands.

All this description does not include many enigmatic symbols such as dots, lines of various thickness, boxes, geometrical grids, arrows, the monochromatic and polychromatic use of reds and yellows, blacks, and whites which were applied by scraping, spraying (through a reed pipe or a hollow bone), rubbing, blending, and dabbing techniques. All this, coupled with a somewhat consistent superimposition of images, becomes part of the scene that no doubt reinforced the idea and helped convey the story.

Standing there, where our guide emphasized, "This is where civilization was born," I could easily imagine the flickering images made by lamps filled with animal fat and tufts of moss, which caused the images to move on the cave walls like the images in an old silent movie. I could hear the stories being told and retold. I could understand the illusions.

Simultaneously, I could easily see the walls of the caves as our ancestors must have seen them—as huge canvasses upon which to write. The experience was probably not unlike a child regarding a wall at home, or large unlined paper in preschool or kindergarten. These are spaces to be filled. These blank spaces are invitations to capture a thing or an idea. And children fill their spaces as our ancestors filled the walls, with realism and myth, with color and texture, and with their own idiosyncratic symbols. When children move from telling us about their thing-pictures to explaining and showing the complex relationships, sequences, captured chronologies, troubles, characters, and settings, we call it story.

The Wonder of Symbolic Language: The Alphabet

So ubiquitous is the alphabet in today's world, we take it for granted. Yet when we think about it, the alphabet is a wonder. Starting in the Middle East about 1700 BC with the twenty-two letters of the Semitic language, the Phoenicians picked it up and traveled and traded with it. The Greeks used that alphabet as a model but "added letters for vowels" (Crystal 1996, 258). Logan contends, "By introducing vowels explicitly, the Greeks created the most accurate and unambiguous phonetic writing system ever known to man" (1986, 40). The Etruscans, in turn, used the Greek model, and that brings us to the twenty-three-letter Roman alphabet. But Ogg reminds us that "to some extent the Greeks and the Romans were working out their alphabets *at the same time*" (1948, 104).

When I was working on *Phonics Friendly Books*, I actively researched the alphabet and shared this:

From the standard Greek alphabet the Romans took A, B, E, Z, H. I, K, M, N, O, T, X and Y with hardly any change at all. The letter B, for instance, was merely a rounded form of the Greek character. Remodeling and finishing other Greek letters, the Romans produced C (and G), L, S, P, R, D and V. F and Q were taken from two old characters abandoned by the Greeks themselves. And that makes twenty-three.

Meanwhile you may have been wondering why Z comes at the end of the alphabet, for with the Greeks it had been number six. When they allowed Z to return to the alphabet, it had lost its place in the regular order and had to get to the end of the line. We have kept Z there ever since. The three missing letters J, U and W were not used by the Romans at all. U and W developed from V about a thousand years ago, and J developed from the letter I about five hundred years ago. (Carroll 1998, 177)

Kids love this story of how Z lost its place in line—they understand and giggle at the telling. Any children with J in their names are fascinated to learn that they have the youngest letter of the alphabet tucked in there, and forming the J from the letter I strikes them as some ancient task. Teachers understand better how the pointed V morphed into the softer curve of the U and how the two Us came together to become W (double U). When said, the double U sound is softer, too. That helps them explain why W takes the sound of the wind phonetically, not the sound of D—dah!

A Visual History of the Alphabet

The information in this section was painstakingly culled from Ogg's *The 26 Letters*, Crystal's *The Cambridge Encyclopedia of the English Language*, and Dowdell's delightful *Secrets of the ABC's*.

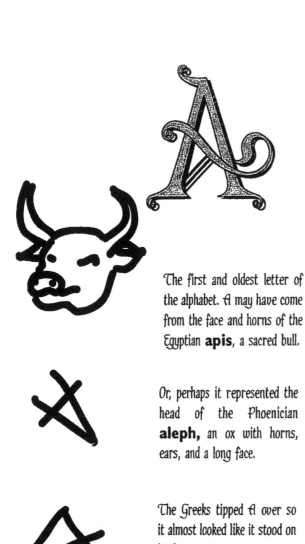

The first and oldest letter of the alphabet. A may have come from the face and horns of the Egyptian **apis**, a sacred bull.

Or, perhaps it represented the head of the Phoenician **aleph,** an ox with horns, ears, and a long face.

The Greeks tipped A over so it almost looked like it stood on its horns.

The Romans wrote it without the ears and stood it solidly on its horns. The **A** has remained that way every since.

B is a blueprint.

Then someone made a hallway.

T h e Phoenicians turned the blueprint on its side and widened the hallway.
The Greeks added another room.

The Romans softened the angles, and the **B** was built.

At first it was drawn like the outline of a camel's head.

Then it was simplified.

C came from the Semitic word for **gimel** which sounds a bit like camel.

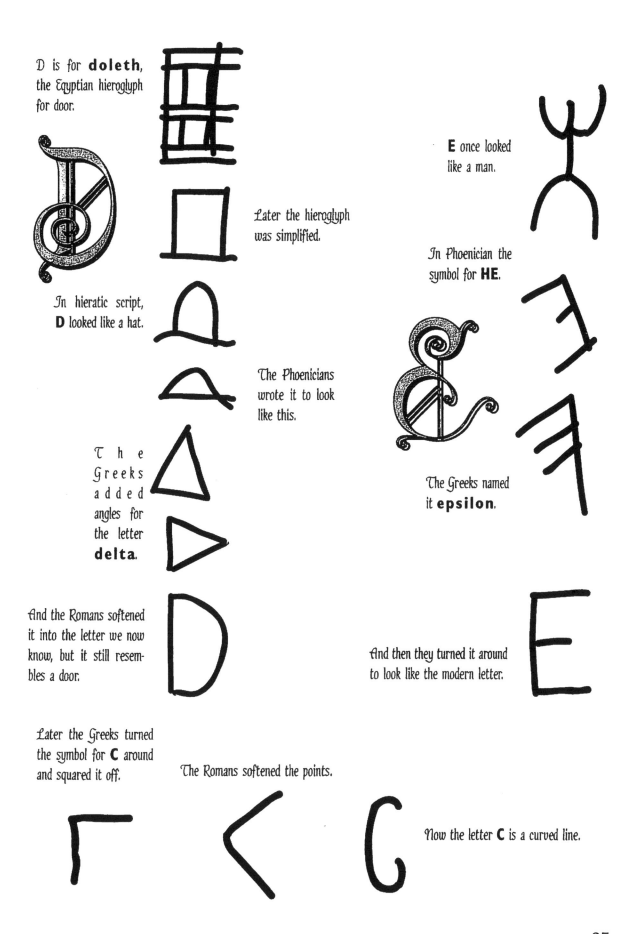

D is for **doleth**, the Egyptian hieroglyph for door.

Later the hieroglyph was simplified.

In hieratic script, **D** looked like a hat.

The Phoenicians wrote it to look like this.

T h e G r e e k s a d d e d angles for the letter **delta**.

And the Romans softened it into the letter we now know, but it still resembles a door.

Later the Greeks turned the symbol for **C** around and squared it off.

The Romans softened the points.

E once looked like a man.

In Phoenician the symbol for **HE**.

The Greeks named it **epsilon**.

And then they turned it around to look like the modern letter.

Now the letter **C** is a curved line.

From *Guided by Meaning in Primary Literacy: Libraries, Reading, Writing, and Learning* by Joyce Armstrong Carroll, Kelley Barger, Karla James, and Kristy Hill. Santa Barbara, CA: Libraries Unlimited. Copyright © 2017.

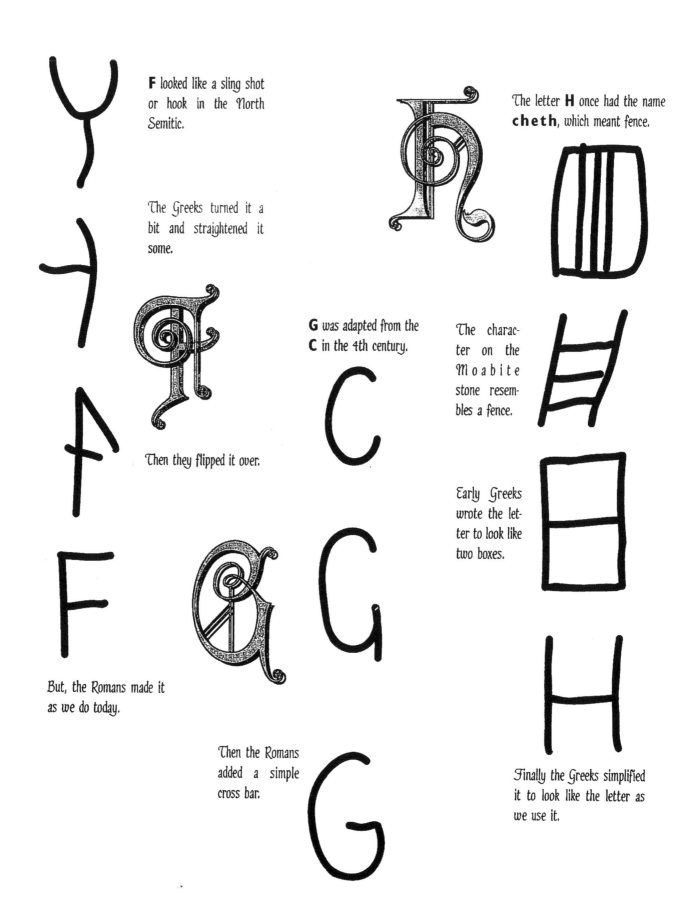

F looked like a sling shot or hook in the North Semitic.

The Greeks turned it a bit and straightened it some.

Then they flipped it over.

But, the Romans made it as we do today.

G was adapted from the **C** in the 4th century.

Then the Romans added a simple cross bar.

The letter **H** once had the name **c h e t h**, which meant fence.

The character on the M o a b i t e stone resembles a fence.

Early Greeks wrote the letter to look like two boxes.

Finally the Greeks simplified it to look like the letter as we use it.

The North Semitic symbol for **I** looked like a long numeral **2** with a line through its middle.

The Greeks made it look like a **Z**

The Phoenician word **k a p h** was first a picture-word that meant palm of the hand.

The **J** is the youngest letter. It is only about 500 years old.

Later they straightened it out to the letter of today.

During the medieval period, a graphic variation of the letter **I** lengthened it and added a left-facing curve at its bottom.

The Greeks slightly modified the symbol for **k a p p a** in form and sound so that it was quite like our **K**.

But when the Greeks began to write from left to right, they flipped it over to make the letter K as we know it.

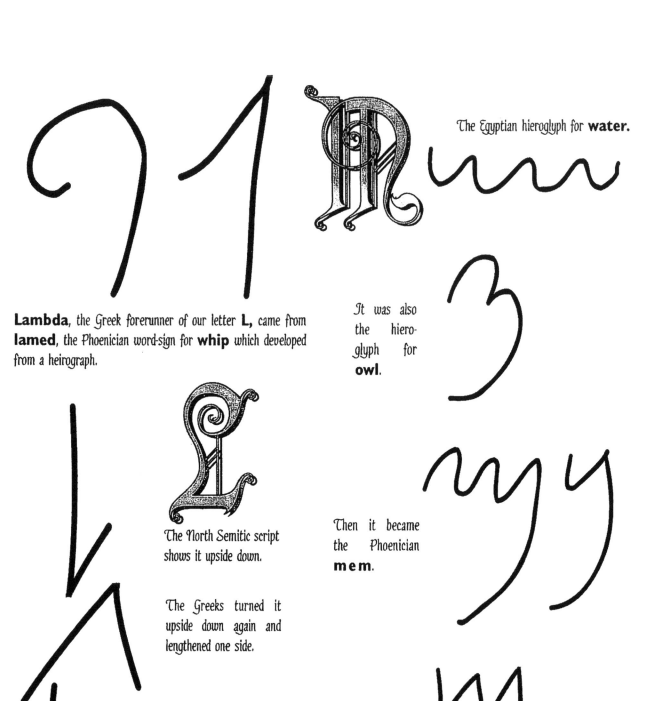

The Egyptian hieroglyph for **water.**

Lambda, the Greek forerunner of our letter **L,** came from **lamed**, the Phoenician word-sign for **whip** which developed from a heirograph.

It was also the hieroglyph for **owl**.

The North Semitic script shows it upside down.

Then it became the Phoenician **m e m**.

The Greeks turned it upside down again and lengthened one side.

The Romans planted it on its side where it has remained ever since.

In Greek **m e m** became **m u**

Eventually, it became our letter **M**.

N came from an early hieroglyph meaning **snake**.

O began as the symbol for an eye.

The Phoenicians used this symbol for **nun**

It was written in an oval by the Phoenicians.

This symbol was adopted by the Greeks as **nu.**

Sometimes it was written with a dot by the Greeks.

Eventually it was flipped into place as the modern **N**.

The letter **O** has changed little throughout its history.

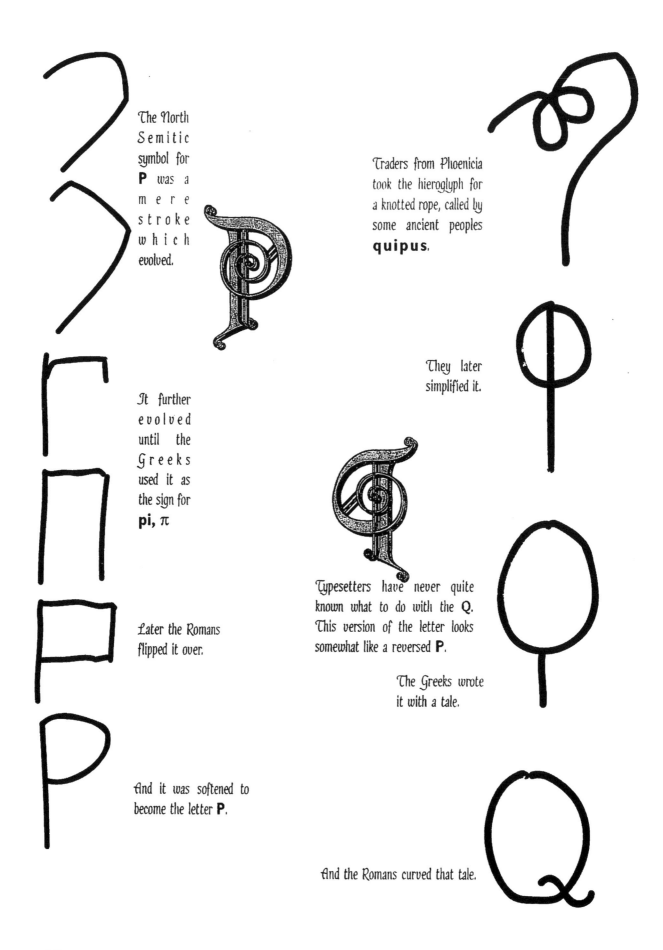

The North Semitic symbol for **P** was a mere stroke which evolved.

It further evolved until the Greeks used it as the sign for **pi, π**

Later the Romans flipped it over.

And it was softened to become the letter **P**.

Traders from Phoenicia took the hieroglyph for a knotted rope, called by some ancient peoples **quipus**.

They later simplified it.

Typesetters have never quite known what to do with the **Q**. This version of the letter looks somewhat like a reversed **P**.

The Greeks wrote it with a tale.

And the Romans curved that tale.

40

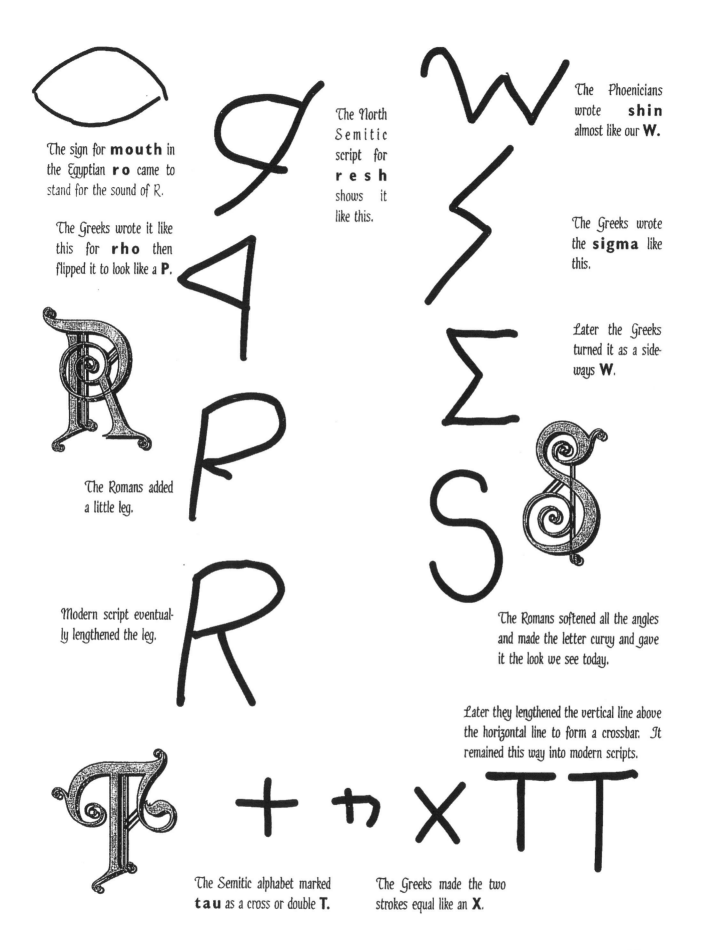

The sign for **mouth** in the Egyptian **r o** came to stand for the sound of R.

The Greeks wrote it like this for **rho** then flipped it to look like a **P**.

The Romans added a little leg.

Modern script eventually lengthened the leg.

The North Semitic script for **r e s h** shows it like this.

The Phoenicians wrote **shin** almost like our **W**.

The Greeks wrote the **sigma** like this.

Later the Greeks turned it as a sideways **W**.

The Romans softened all the angles and made the letter curvy and gave it the look we see today.

Later they lengthened the vertical line above the horizontal line to form a crossbar. It remained this way into modern scripts.

The Semitic alphabet marked **t a u** as a cross or double **T**.

The Greeks made the two strokes equal like an **X**.

U, **V**, and **F** have the same roots moving from the North Semitic...

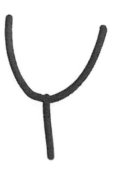

...to the Greek form...

V was called **U** for many years.

...to the Latin pointed letter which was softened to a curve.

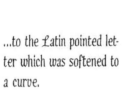

Old manuscripts show the **U** and **V** used interchangeably but later the soft curve **U** was used as the vowel.

The angular, pointed **V** was used as the consonant.

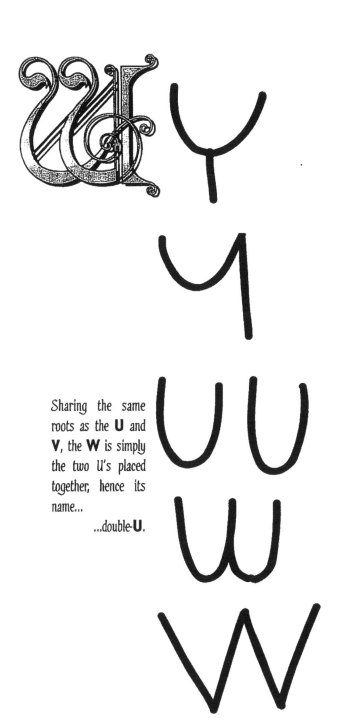

Sharing the same roots as the **U** and **V**, the **W** is simply the two U's placed together, hence its name...

...double-**U**.

An early Semitic sibilant letter led the Greeks to **chi** at first formed this way, but eventually given way to simple two crossed lines.

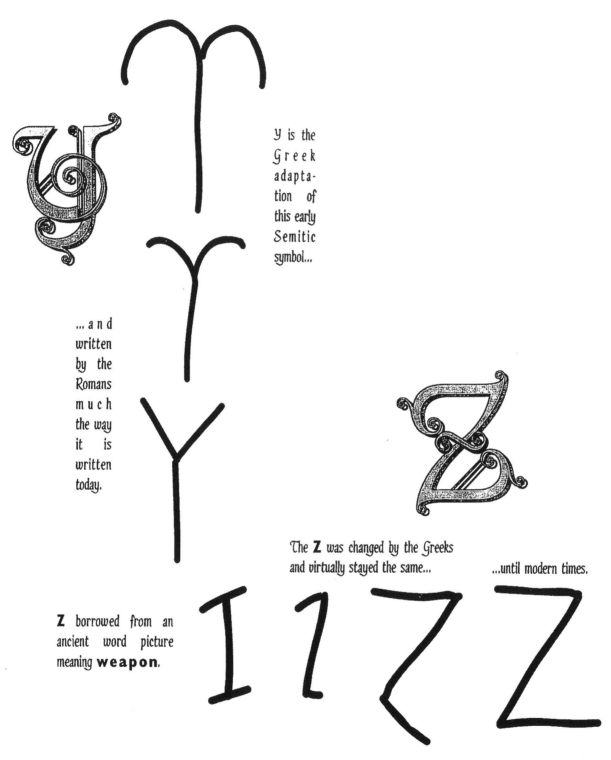

Y is the Greek adaptation of this early Semitic symbol...

...and written by the Romans much the way it is written today.

Z borrowed from an ancient word picture meaning **weapon**.

The **Z** was changed by the Greeks and virtually stayed the same...

...until modern times.

Interesting, the **Z** was the seventh letter of the Greek alphabet, but since Romans only used it when writing Greek, it lost its place. When reintroduced into the alphabet it had to go to the end of the line. Some people call the **Z** **izzard** and some say **z e d**.

To Recap

Before the alphabet, knowledge was mysterious; after the alphabet, knowledge became power. It's that simple. Parents know it, teachers know it, and children come to know it. Without the knowledge of the alphabet, the ability to arrange and rearrange those two dozen plus signs, as Galileo described them in the quote at the beginning of this chapter, not only gives us power, but also contributed to humans' highly developed analytical consciousness. So by signing the alphabet song, playing with the letters, and using them in real ways, we empower students.

DR. JACs Four Alphabet Pointers

1. Learn the "Alphabet Song" and sing it often. When Joyce Elizabeth was just a baby, the alphabet song became both a learning tool and a lullaby. I sang it to her to insinuate the letters into that malleable brain, and often sang as she drifted off to sleep at nap time or bed time. When she entered school, she already had the notion of alphabet and quickly picked up the letters, understanding their names in other contexts. Children learn many things through rhythm and song, so other alpha songs can be introduced. One immensely successful alpha song is "A You're Adorable." This song of the late 1940s, made popular by entertainers such as Perry Como and Jo Stafford, was also used on *Star Trek: The Next Generation* and *Sesame Street*. There are versions on YouTube. For ways to use this song, see "Dr. JAC 59" in *Phonics Friendly Books* (Carroll 1998) and "Family Literacy Activity 59" in *Phonics Friendly Families* (Smith 1999).

2. Begin a collection of alphabet books. Not only do alphabet books reinforce the letters in colorful interesting ways, but many deal with themes such as farmers, Jewish holidays, animals, geography, trees, quilts, and so forth. Several bring in other concepts, such as alliteration, the Afro-American experience, multicultural studies, science, the connections between letters and meaning, and even sensory imagery. All are guided by meaning, and children want them to be read again and again until they can pick them up and read them all by themselves. The alphabet is an amazing tool for organizing and categorizing.

3. Have fun with the alphabet. Invest in those jumbo foam alpha letters, alpha magnetic letters, stencil letters, letters you can punch out or fit in, letters in puzzles and on tiles, letters with pictures, fuzzy letters, and sandpaper letters. Lots of letters can be manipulated, copied, traced, or reinforced with a drawing or picture. Others can be counted, shared, and eventually made into words. Copy letters with Sharpies® on those plastic lids that cover almost everything these days and invite the children to do the same. Children need to play with letters, say them, sing them, get silly with them, and even eat them as in cereal letters. One of the best early childhood classrooms I ever visited had the alphabet displayed around the room BUT this teacher allowed the students to make the uppercase and lowercase letters and draw or find the appropriate picture to accompany the letters—which was less expensive and guided by meaning for the students.

4. Categorize letters into vowels and consonants. Use books such as *The War Between the Vowels and the Consonants* by Priscilla Turner or just about any version of *Old MacDonald Had a Farm* to make the distinction. With Old Mac, instead of singing E-I-E-I-O, sing the vowels A-E-I-O-U. These ideas and others may be found in *Phonics Friendly Books* (Carroll 1998) and *Phonics Friendly Families* (Smith 1999).

5

Literacy in Schools

Where are Bellerophon and Pegasus when you need them? Credited throughout Greek mythology with slaying Cimeraera, the fire-breathing mythical monster with a lion's head, a goat's body, and a serpent's tail, who terrorized Lycia and other lands in Asia Minor, is needed now to slay educators and educational systems who hold to what Janet Emig, in one of her characteristically brilliant essays, labels "magical thinking" (1983, 135). Indeed, she claims, "Most North American school are temples to magical thinking" (1983, 135).

So exactly what do she and others mean by "magical thinking"? Not to oversimplify, this term comes to us principally from Latin American writers such as Gabriel García Márquez and Isabel Allende and from such artists as George Tooker, Paul Cadmus, and Frida Kahlo, who wove the unreal with the real. But as Mexican critic Luis Leal once answered when asked to define magical realism, "If you can explain it, then it's not magical realism." So, too, with magical thinking—so subtle is the blend of what is true with what is preposterous, that one subsumes the other; therefore, and in exactly that way, the world of magical thinking slid into academia.

I think the image of Cimeraera apt as too many of our schools breathe fire and terrorize those who do not believe their magical thinking. And like Cimeraera, it comes as a monster with one kind of head, a different body, and a third type of tail. For example, to attribute learning to constant testing (even when the tests themselves prove little or nothing) deserves in our minds a good douse of fire. The tenet is to terrorize teachers into testing, to convince parents that testing is teaching, and to kowtow to large testing corporations. So we must slay this "monster" that has been hurting and continues to hurt students and teachers.

To believe children cannot write before they know their ABCs *in alpha order* even though we have caves replete with proof—not to mention reams of past and recent research to the contrary—gives rise to the monster of magical thinking. So again, we must slay this "monster" and give children the permission and freedom to write what is in their minds and hearts. After all, we write best what we know.

Bellerophon and Pegasus need to slay the "monster" that rises up with punitive machinations for children in any given class who choose the books they want to read. How preposterous to think that all children have the same interests, that children of a given chronological age are also at the same stage in reading, and that experiences and socioeconomic influences don't influence what children can read and want to read!

Ironically, schools and school districts eschew "magic" of any kind, yet they embrace fantasies. Like Gabriel García Márquez, a leader in literary magical realism, educators blend their fantasies with the real world. Truly, it would be awesome if all children learned at the same exact rate, a rate that matched their chronological years. But that's magical thinking. Truly, it would be amazing if all children learned in the same way. And wouldn't we live in a fairy tale if children all liked the same book, the same author, the same theme, the same genre? Even as I write that, the possibility rings absurd.

I remember once conducting a staff development session in a midsize city in Texas. The room was configured so my back was to its door. At the moment of making a point about diversifying instruction, I reiterated a phrase from reading guru Frank Smith (2006), "There is no one way to teach reading that works for every child every time, so every teacher needs a repertoire of strategies." Hearing the clapping of one person behind me, I wheeled around to see the superintendent standing there. He said, "How refreshing. So many consultants come here extolling their way as *the* way and *the only way* to teach reading." So even consultants engage in magical thinking. What is frightening is that magical thinking, like magic realism, ascribes the fantastic as real, so it all to often misguides instruction.

Take phonics in isolation, for example. All recent brain research and cognitive developmental research points out that it is far more difficult to learn something—anything—in isolation than in a meaningful context. This makes sense, common sense: without a context, there is nothing to hang the new learning on, nothing to connect it to, nothing to associate it with anything else. So teaching phonics in isolation is the most magical of magical thinking. That is, until you add to that the notion of non-sense—nonsense words. (The person who came up with that idea should be crowned the grand wizard of magical thinking.) There are so many words in our language that experts are reluctant to give an estimate of the exact number because so many words hold multiple meanings. For example, take the common word *table.* Would we count that as one word if used as a noun, e.g., Mom set the *table* for dinner; or would we count it as two words since *table* can be an adjective, e.g., The *table* top was cluttered with dishes; or perhaps we should count it as three words given *table* can be a verb, e.g., When you go to the meeting, *table* the motion. And what about compound words with the word *table*, for example, tablelands, tablespoon, tableware. Or what if we added its multiple meanings, which total some thirty-nine words? Certainly a table lamp is different than a table napkin, which is more specific than table linen. You get the idea. With this simple fact, then, why in the world do we want to clutter kids' minds with nonwords, nonsense words just for the sounds? Magical thinking strikes again, and we need to counterstrike.

Not to belabor the allusion, but I wonder what Bellerophon and Pegasus would make of Richard L. Allington's article "What Really Matters When Working with Struggling Readers" (2013).Whom would they slay? Surely not Allington. He makes the case that we know how to teach reading, but schools don't pay attention to the research. If that's not magical thinking, nothing is. Educators go to conferences, read their scholarly journals, write and share papers, conduct research, but then something dastardly happens because the research is ignored. Instead of good solid teaching, districts pour tons of money into "programs," sit children in front of a computer with a disembodied voice, give them inhumane amounts of homework, insist they attend tutorials where they do what they already did in class—ad nauseam. If they didn't get it when it was first taught, consider the magical thinking that they'll get it at four in the afternoon or on Saturdays. Or better yet, consider the way it was first taught or how the child's life might be impacting the learning.

I am in contact as I write this with an educator who is attending a mandated staff development for five days with 1,400 other educators for the sole purpose of improving scores in their schools. The sessions are boring combinations of lecture and Power-Point™ presentations that would deaden the most active intellect. Interestingly, this same group attended this expensive training (plus paying for hotels, travel, and meals) last year. This reminds me of the line in a song, "Same song second verse a little bit louder but a little bit worse." Nothing came of this training last year, and I'd bet one of my degrees nothing will come of it this year. Instead of using that investment of time and money (and magical thinking) and concentrating that energy on strategies that work, that have been proven, that are research based, these educators are reenacting the same song. They—or whoever has mandated their attendance—are deep believers in magical thinking. But I read once that if you do the same thing over and over again expecting to get different results, that's insanity.

Homework, too, has raised its ugly monster head. I don't know about you, but I do know about me (and most everyone else I've talked to). After a full day of consulting (or almost any kind of labor-intensive or brain-intensive work), I am not in any mood to do more work. I want to get into comfortable clothes, kick off my shoes, and do something that relaxes my mind and body. Yet we assign young children and adolescents hours more work at home after a full day at school. As research professor Peter Gray asks, "What have we done to childhood?" This within a chapter where he records the skyrocketing "rates of stress-related mental disorders in young people" and quotes the work of Jean Twenge, a psychology professor who conducted research on the topic: "[A]nxiety and depression have increased continuously, linearly, and dramatically in children, adolescents, and college students over the decades" (2013, 14).

When do we feel anxious? When do we feel depressed? When do we get tinfoil stomachs and sleepless nights? When we feel a lack of control over our lives, over our decisions. Young people are no different. We have taken away book choices, writing topics, projects; we have even taken away free play.

Adults orchestrate everything. Birthday parties happen in places with inflatable slides and mazes where kids have an allotted amount of time to participate before they sit down to a structured "party." Games are now totally supervised by "coaches," teams of parents. Even kids who live across the street from their school MUST ride the school bus to ensure safety. I echo Gray, "What have we done to childhood?" We have infused it with adult-centric, magical thinking:

> And yet, the hue and cry that we hear from pundits and politicians today is for more restrictive schooling, not less. They want more standardized tests, more homework, more supervision, longer school days, longer school years, more sanctions against children taking off a day or two for a family vacation.

This is one realm in which politicians from both the major parties, at every level of government, seem to agree. More schooling and more testing are better than less schooling and less testing. (Gray 2013, 19)

That's pure magical thinking. But it is the order of the day. So I call upon Bellerophon and Pegasus to destroy this monster that has stolen childhood from children, because "we have forgotten that children are designed by nature to learn through self-directed play and exploration, and so, more and more, we deprive them of freedom to learn, subjecting them instead to the tedious and painfully slow learning methods devised by those who run schools" (Gray 2013, 65). We then try to devise ways to keep them from abject boredom, dropping out, loss of motivation to learn, and even violence.

To Recap

There are places, tiny spots among the huge behemoth of schools in the United States, that have slain the "monster" of magical thinking by creating sound, research-based educational venues. The Center for Teaching and Learning in Edgecomb, Maine; Sudbury Valley School in Framingham, Massachusetts; and The Center for Teaching and Learning in the Woodlands, Texas, stand out as exemplars. These are democratic schools where in a real way the children educate themselves. These schools are loving, caring places where kids feel safe, successful, validated, and encouraged. They are proof that schools do not have to be punitive places that kids dread, hate, endure, or where they learn to play the game. As Joyce Elizabeth, who now attends CTL in the Woodlands, said to me just this past week, "I wish I could go to school *every* day!" Remember: Don Graves told us to listen to the children; they tell us in many ways what they need. They know when they are learning, and because of brain research, we know we are happiest when we are in the learning mode.

**DR. JACs Four Pointers
for a Successful School**

1. *Check your school not for its test scores but for its curriculum.* Successful schools encourage higher-level thinking, imagination, and true rigor. And interestingly, they usually do well on tests, but conversely, those that concentrate solely or almost solely on test prep do less well on tests and typically deaden the sense of exploration, the joy of discovery, and the desire to really write (and read) what one wants.

2. *Successful schools are happy places where learning is fun but not trivial.* If you have visited a successful school, you see the mark of success on the faces of the students and teachers. They know they are learning, and they realize they are learning important things. Further, successful schools are built on a philosophy of sharing and helping and working together toward a common goal. They mimic successful places in the world where combative competitiveness takes a back seat to resourceful accord. Exploration is key.

3. *Choice of all kinds characterizes a successful school.* In successful schools, students choose topics for their writing, choose books for their reading. They choose projects, have a say in the classroom governance, and discuss freely without fear of being ridiculed or admonished. They learn to respect the opinions of others, understand valid argument, and learn the basics of civility and courtesy. I always say, "Choice equals voice." By *voice* I not only mean developing each personality and style in writing and presenting, but also developing apt expression, the ability to articulate an opinion, and the ability to assert without offending.

4. *You can tell much about a school by the language you hear.* Words of joy and delight replace words of threat and punishment in successful schools. Students work in a positive, not negative, environment toward realistic goals that hold meaning for them. Teachers spend time priming the students and priming the text so that students understand not only what they are learning, but why they are learning it.

Part I References

Alkon, D. L. 1992. *Memory's Voice: Deciphering the Brain-Mind Code*. New York: HarperCollins.

Allington, Richard L. 2013. "What Really Matters When Working with Struggling Readers." *The Reading Teacher* 66: 520–530.

Ballard, P. B. 1915/1916. "Norms of Performance in Reading." *The Journal of Experimental Pedagogy and Training College Record* 3: 153–161.

Bartlett, F. C. 1932. *Remembering*. Cambridge, UK: Cambridge University Press.

Borden, Louise. 2001. *The Day Eddie Met the Author*. New York: Margaret K. McElderry Books.

Borden, Louise. 2015. *Kindergarten Luck*. San Francisco, CA: Chronicle Books.

Brown, Margaret Wise. 1949. *The Important Book*. New York: Harper & Row.

Bruffee, Kenneth A. 1983. "Reading and Writing as Social Acts." *Journal of Teaching Writing* (May): 149–154.

Caine, Renate Nummela, Geoffrey Caine, Carol McClintic, and Karl Klimek. 2005. *12 Brain/Mind Learning Principles in Action*. Thousand Oaks, CA: Corwin Press.

Carle, Eric. 1987. *The Very Hungry Caterpillar*. New York: Philomel Books.

Carlsson-Paige, Nancy. 2015. "Keynote Address." Temple University Graduation Speaker, School of Education, May.

Carr, Nicholas. 2010. *The Shallows: What the Internet Is Doing to Our Brains*. New York: W. W. Norton.

Carroll, Joyce Armstrong. 1998. *Phonics Friendly Books: Teaching Phonics through Children's Literature*. Spring, TX: Absey & Co..

Carroll, Joyce Armstrong, and Edward Wilson. 2008. *Acts of Teaching: How to Teach Writing*. 2nd ed. Westport, CT: Teacher Ideas Press.

Clark, Barbara. 1979. *Growing Up Gifted: Developing the Potential of Children at Home and at School*. 4th ed. New York: Macmillan.

Cousins, Lucy. 2003. *Maisy's Rainbow Dream*. Cambridge, MA: Candlewick Press.

Crystal, David. 1996. *The Cambridge Encyclopedia of the English Language*. New York: Cambridge University Press.

Daly, Lisa, and Miriam Beloglovsky. 2015. *Loose Parts: Inspiring Play in Young Children*. New York: Redleaf Press.

Dehaene, Stanislas. 2009. *Reading in the Brain: The Science and Evolution of Human Invention*. New York: Viking.

Doerr, Anthony. 2015. "By the Book." *New York Times Book Review*, July 5, 8.

Dowdell, Dorothy. 1965. *Secrets of the ABC's*. Fayetteville, GA: Oddo Publishing.

Dowshen, Steven. 2013. "Memory Matters." http://kidshealth.org/kkid/health_problems/brain /memory. October 20.

Ebbinghaus, Hermann. 1913. *Memory*. Translated by D. H. Ruyer and C. E. Bussenius. New York: Teachers College Press.

Emig, Janet. 1983. *The Web of Meaning: Essays on Writing, Teaching, Learning, and Thinking*. Upper Montclair, NJ: Boynton/Cook Publishers.

Emig, Janet. 1991. "Yes, Writing and Reading Are Social Acts." *Education Week*, March 20. http:// www.edweek.org/ew/articles/1991/03/20/10190999.h10.html?qs=janet+Emig.

Given, Barbara K. 2002. *Teaching to the Brain's Natural Learning Systems*. Alexandria, VA: Association for Supervision and Curriculum Development.

Gray, Peter. 2013. *Free to Learn*. New York: Basic Books.

Gurdon, Meghan Cox. 2015. "The Great Gift of Reading Aloud." *Wall Street Journal*, July 10. www.wsj.com/articles/the-great-gift-of-reading-aloud-1436561248.

Harste, Jerome, and Virginia A. Woodward. 1989. "Fostering Needed Change in Early Literacy Programs." In *Emerging Literacy: Young Children Learn to Read and Write,* edited by Dorothy S. Strickland and Lesley Mandel Morrow, 147–159. Newark, DE: International Reading Association.

Johnson, Crockett. 1955. *Harold and the Purple Crayon.* New York: HarperCollins.

Kent, Corita, and Jan Steward. 2008. *Learning by Heart: Teaching to Free the Creative Spirit.* 2nd ed. New York: Allworth Press.

Lee, Suzy. 2008. *The Wave.* San Francisco, CA: Chronicle Books.

Logan, Robert K. 1986. *The Alphabet Effect: The Impact of the Phonetic Alphabet on the Development of Western Civilization.* New York: William Morrow.

Mischel, Walter. 2014. *The Marshmallow Test: Mastering Self-Control.* New York: Little, Brown.

Ogg, Oscar. 1948. *The 26 Letters.* New York: Thomas Y. Crowell.

Paley, Vivian Gussin. 2004. *A Child's Play: The Importance of Fantasy Play.* Chicago: University of Chicago Press.

"Reach Out and Read." n.d. http://www.reachoutandread.org.

Rosenblatt, Louise M. 1978. *The Reader, the Text, the Poem: The Transactional Theory of the Literary Work.* Carbondale: Southern Illinois University Press.

Seuss, Dr. 1960. *Oh, The Places You'll Go!* New York: Random House.

Silverberg, Robert. 1984. *Gilgamesh the King.* New York: Arbor House.

Smith, Frank. 2006. *Reading Without Nonsense.* 4th ed. New York: Teachers College, Columbia University.

Smith, Kelley R. (Barger). 1999. *Phonics Friendly Families.* Spring, TX: Absey & Co.

Sohn, David A. 1970. *Film: The Creative Eye.* Dayton, OH: Geo. A. Pflaum.

Tullet, Hervé. 2008. *Press Here.* San Francisco, CA: Chronicle Books.

Tullet, Hervé. 2014. *Mix It Up!* San Francisco, CA: Chronicle Books.

Vygotsky, Lev. 1962. *Thought and Language.* Cambridge, MA: MIT Press.

Vygotsky, Lev. 1978. *Mind in Society: The Development of Higher Psychological Processes.* Cambridge, MA: Harvard University Press.

Wildsmith. Brian. 1983. *The Apple Bird.* Oxford: Oxford University Press.

Wolf, Maryanne. 2007. *Proust and the Squid: The Story and Science of the Reading Brain.* New York: HarperCollins.

Part II

Why Write in the Library?

Kristy Hill

6

What Does the Teacher Librarian Have to Offer?

The library is the temple of learning, and learning has liberated more people than all the wars in history.

—Carl T. Rowan

Making the move from the role of a classroom teacher to that of a school librarian wasn't an easy decision for me to make. I had always thought my place was in the classroom, and I couldn't imagine giving up the instructional role I played in the school setting. It wasn't until it occurred to me that I could continue teaching from the library that I was set on making the change. When a library position opened up on my campus, I approached my principal to share my interest in making the move and actually sold myself by telling her I could teach reading and writing to every student on our campus. Not only could I continue my instructional role, but I would now have access to every student in our school. I didn't have to stop being a teacher to be the school librarian. My classroom is now much larger, and I have almost 800 students on my roster. I could not feel more in my element.

The role librarians play in public schools is changing drastically. Gone are the days when librarians were the keepers of the books, sitting behind a circulation desk checking books in and out and maintaining quiet in the library. Today, libraries are becoming a learning commons, a flexible environment in which continuous communication and collaboration are taking place. Students are using libraries as learning centers and not just as places to pick up a new book. Librarians are collaborating with teachers to support curriculum. What better place for writing to take place than in the library, where students are surrounded by the works of beloved authors?

As librarians, we've taken on the vital responsibility of generating enthusiasm for literacy. We have programs in place to encourage reading. We make displays to show off books we think students will enjoy. We have contests that require kids to pick up books they might not otherwise choose on their own. It seems a logical progression to then encourage writing as well. Research proves that writing is a mode of learning and improves student growth across the curriculum. Librarians are in the perfect position to teach not only research writing skills, but narrative and creative writing as well. In the lower grades this will include the use of mentor texts and modeling

Figure 6.1. Cozy reading nooks invite students to get comfortable for quiet reading.

writing for younger students. It will require librarians to use think alouds, sharing their own thoughts while reading to students, to model how readers think like writers and writers think like readers. It will involve games that allow students to use the print-rich nature of the library to increase their sight word vocabulary, their creative thinking skills, and collaboration with peers to grow as writers in a safe, nurturing environment.

Advocating for Writing Instruction in the Library

Librarians need to advocate for this service if they want support from administrators and teachers. Dr. Keith Lance, director of library research services at the Colorado State Library, has conducted an extensive study of libraries in twenty states and in Canada to prove the link between quality library services and instruction and student achievement. His research has shown that "the school library is one of the few factors whose contribution to academic achievement has been documented empirically, and it is a contribution that cannot be explained away by other powerful influences on student performance" (Lance 2002, 22).

Figure 6.2. Whole group area for reading aloud to students and for large group instruction.

Librarians are teachers first. My classroom has evolved—desks replaced by tables, white boards replaced with book shelves and technology—and my class is made up of every student on my campus, but I am still a teacher.

In addition to collaborating with teachers, librarians should try to meet regularly with school administrators to keep them informed of what is happening in the library. Let administrators know that students come first and that the library is just as much a place of learning and instruction as the classroom. Libraries are vital to student success. Librarians are in a position to spark a passion for reading and writing in students, because they aren't bound by the confines of a specific grade-level curriculum. When I first moved to the library I knew that what I wanted most was to impact the learning of every student on my campus. This was a lofty goal, but it is also what got me the job. I told my principal that I could teach writing to every student in our school, and that's exactly what I am doing.

So how can librarians get the word out to teachers, school administrators, parents, and students about what they have to offer? The most effective means of sharing with others what you can do is to offer professional development to teachers. Teach them the strategies you are using with students in the library when you are reading and writing with students. Share mentor texts that can be used for reading and writing minilessons. Display student writing in the library and in the hallways, on library social media sites, Web sites, and blogs. Meet regularly with school administrators to show them firsthand what is happening in the library. The more support you have from school administrators, the bigger your impact will be. That support will give you momentum to continue and might possibly help with budget requests in the future. If administrators know that you are increasing student engagement and achievement, they will be more willing to support library services in the future. In addition, if you don't communicate this with them, teachers won't know what you are able to do to support their instruction and won't understand how you offer an additional layer of learning that supports their efforts in the classroom.

Librarians can also offer staff and district workshops, present information to staff members at staff meetings, lead staff book studies, and work with administrators and paraprofessionals to help support curriculum instruction. Topics that might be helpful for sharing during professional development sessions include the use of library databases, copyright information, how to search the library information retrieval system, how to place books on hold, and making lists of resources to be pulled for classroom use (McGhee and Jansen 2005).

Collaboration between teachers and library media specialists benefits everyone. Administrators benefit when staff members work together to create a collaborative culture in a school building. The library media specialist benefits because teachers and administrators will see the value in the librarian and in library programming. Teachers benefit from the support and knowledge provided by the library media specialist. Most of all, students benefit from an entire school system working together to create meaningful learning experiences for them (Buzzeo 2002). Collaboration supports all stakeholders in a school.

A school library impact study conducted in Pennsylvania found six main areas that administrators focused on when considering excellent library programming. Librarian-led professional development, coteaching between classroom teachers and the librarian, and this collaboration being included in the teacher appraisal system, regular meetings with principals to keep them in the loop, librarians serving on school committees, and flexible scheduling were found to be "essential" to determining the value of library programming and its impact on student learning (Lance and Kachel 2013). Librarians who collaborate, become involved, and play an instructional role in their school create value and purpose for the library, something that is becoming necessary in an economy always looking to cut corners, even in education.

Integrating Technology

Many school libraries, or library media technology centers, are now being referred to as a "learning commons" in more and more schools across the country. Technology instruction is just as important as literacy instruction. What better way to teach students how to use available technology than to allow them to use it for writing? I used to think that to get students to use library databases and software I had to teach the teachers, so they could pass that on to their students. Now I understand that I, myself, can empower students to become researchers and authors by teaching them how to do authentic research in the library. I don't have to wait for the research unit to come up in the curriculum. I can teach students how to use subscription databases to research topics that interest them through library minilessons. Pretty much my entire library curriculum is project-based learning, a hands-on approach to learning that involves relatable issues, and I love giving students the opportunity to find their passions and explore them.

In addition to databases, students can use available technology to publish their writing. They can take a book they enjoyed and create a book trailer video to share with other students using iMovie, or they can create a poster in their Google Drive that portrays the personal and literary connections they made to what they read, along with an evaluation of the story. The very youngest students can find sight words in books they are reading, take pictures of them, and create presentations or quizzes to help other students learn alongside them. I recently discovered an app called YouDoodle that I downloaded onto our library iPads. Students can take pictures and draw or write on top of them. I love reading a book to my students and then asking them to illustrate their thoughts about the book using the app. The students love it, and they are so creative! Technology is an excellent tool that allows students to share their voice and their learning with others. It is constantly evolving, increasing student access to print and meaning.

Joyce Kasman Valenza, an advocate for the changing role of the twenty-first-century librarian, describes the paradigm shift occurring in libraries: "In school libraries we can do a lot for learners. We have a unique opportunity to offer customized, 24/7, just-in-time, relevant and authentic service and instruction—but only if we retool" (2007, 18). Students of any age will benefit from this retooling of the library when it engages them in learning through the use of technology. The aspect that some schools often overlook is the instructional role the librarian plays: not just instructing the use of technology, but the content instruction as well. Students can take the skills they learn in the library back to the classroom as an additional tool to use for classroom learning. I can teach students how to make book trailers in iMovie. The classroom teacher can then ask students to create films documenting what they have learned in class. My instruction can help students learn to analyze literature and then to turn that analysis into a product to be shared with others. They will then have a new skill using filmmaking software to apply to personal and educational projects.

Becoming a Champion of Writing

The library's reputation for promoting literacy is often limited to reading and research. But the library should champion all of the traditional literacies, including reading, writing, speaking, and information literacy, as well as literacies related to technology. We have several platforms available to us to establish this routine in the library. One way we can champion writing instruction in the library is through professional development for teachers. Another is through direct instruction with students. Librarians can also participate in curriculum development by attending planning meetings. Show teachers how you can support their efforts in the library. Write with students and share samples of student writing with teachers. Line the halls with anchor charts that you develop with students to show evidence of text analysis and reading and writing connections. Showcase student writing in the library.

Making Literacy Fun

The beauty of reading and writing instruction in the library is that we have freedom to truly make learning fun by exploring topics that students find interesting. We can take advantage of the many resources we have available in the library to ignite a passion for reading and writing in students. Show your youngest students where they can find books on their favorite topics. Point out the information in library databases. Read aloud from books that interest students. Then talk about them. Let the kids share their stories while you are reading. Admire the beauty and the humor of the illustrations. Keep an interest inventory chart in the whole-group area. Every time students talk about something they are interested in, add their ideas to the chart. This will give you a living document that will help you select texts to share with students, and it might spark an idea for creative writing or student research.

Create learning games, scavenger hunts, and fun activities that get kids moving and excited about reading and writing. Making learning fun will make it memorable, and students will look forward to reading and writing with you during their library time.

Figure 6.3. Areas for collaboration or for student writing.

Creating a Space That Promotes Literacy

The library serves many purposes, and our space should accommodate each of those purposes equally. There should be cozy nooks for private reading time and spaces for student collaboration, as well as areas for whole-group instruction and read alouds. Just as important as the space are the supplies needed for each purpose. Have plenty of sticky notes, chart paper, construction paper, writing supplies, crayons and markers, pencils, and scissors in your writing centers. It's important to create a space that inspires creativity. Once you have the space, make sure you use it! Give students plenty of time for reading on their own, conduct whole-group lessons, then send students to tables to try out new strategies with peers. Gone are the days of the quiet library! Libraries are now spaces in which learning and collaboration take place. It's all about balance, and in the next few chapters I'm going to share my strategies for utilizing my space to maximize student learning while fostering creativity and a love for reading and writing. The library is the literacy hub of the school, and it will be a favorite place among students when you help them achieve success in a fun, engaging way.

Figure 6.4. Writing center with supplies needed for students to write.

7

Librarians Can *Teach* Literacy

Librarians have always been among the most thoughtful and helpful people. They are teachers without a classroom. No libraries, no progress.

—Willard Scott

School libraries are classrooms, and school librarians are teachers. Our student roster includes every child who walks through the doors of the school building, as well as the teachers. Librarians are teachers first. Our curriculum is created using school and district goals, as well as state criteria, but most important, it encompasses topics that are of interest to students. "School librarians' teaching experience inspires literacy by providing a broad, carefully selected collection of resources to support every student at any level and in many interests to encourage reading for pleasure and lifelong learning" (Hand, Grissom, and Briggs 2015, 5). The library is an exciting place to be, now more than ever. One of my favorite things about being a librarian is that I get to teach every grade level and get to know every student on my campus.

My lesson plans look a little different than they did when I taught in the classroom, but they share some likenesses with those of the regular classroom teacher. My library runs on a fixed schedule. Hopefully we will eventually be able to run the library on a flexible schedule, as is considered to be a best practice, but the lessons and ideas in this book can be utilized no matter your schedule. I generally follow the same routine with each lesson. I spend one-quarter of my time with students reading aloud to them, varying the genres in order to expose them to as many different voices and styles of writing as possible. I use the second quarter of my time teaching a minilesson. The third quarter is for student exploration or practice with whatever skill I have taught, and the final quarter is for students to check out books.

Teaching minilessons is the easiest way for the librarian to impact student learning. There's not enough time in our class period with students to delve too deeply into one particular skill and still give them time to practice the skill and check out new books. In addition to the skills outlined in AASL's *Standards for the 21st Century Learner* (2007), I incorporate literacy skills into my lessons for even my youngest learners. These lessons tend to fall into one of four categories: sight word games, genres, grammar integration, and modeling reading and writing. In addition to these four categories I incorporate alphabet skills when the opportunity presents itself. Showing students how to find books in the library is a great way to call attention to alphabetical order. When students struggle with writing letters I can give them an opportunity to practice by finding letters in books and letting them practice writing them.

Sight Word Games

Sight word games are a fun way to engage students in learning through play. Librarians can request sight word lists from classroom teachers or use the Dolch or Fry sight word lists available online (http://www.sightwords.com/). Collaborating with the classroom teacher will ensure that the librarian is teaching words that students are currently learning in class and will make the lesson more meaningful for the students.

- Word Ball: The librarian places words from grade-appropriate sight word lists on sticky notes and sticks them on a wall in the library. Two students at a time take turns using a foam ball to "tag" the words on the wall when the librarian calls them out. Students can work in teams to earn points or play just for fun.
- Sight Word Scavenger Hunt: The librarian places enough picture books on each table so that each student has access to a book. The librarian then calls out sight words or projects them onto a screen in the library, and students try to find the words in their books.
- Sight Word Lists: Students use picture books to find as many sight words (or any words they recognize) as possible and then write the words on a piece of paper. Students can compete in groups to find the most words or track their progress each time the game is played, to show growth.
- Sight Word Records: The librarian gives each student an index card to keep in the book pocket of his or her library book. Students record sight words found in their books on the index cards and turn in the cards when they return the books. The librarian can then create a class record of how many sight words were found in each check out period.
- Sight Word Illustrations: The librarian helps students locate a sentence in a library book that contains a sight word. Each student, with help from the librarian if necessary, writes the sentence on a piece of paper and illustrates the sentence.
- Sight Word Read Aloud: During read aloud time the librarian and students record sight words contained in the story on a piece of chart paper. Students can take the chart paper back to their classroom and read the words for their teacher.
- Sight Word Musical Chairs: The librarian arranges chairs in a circle, then places sticky notes with one sight word written on each inside library books and puts a book on each chair. The librarian plays music, and students walk in a circle inside the circle of chairs. When the music stops, students claim the chair closest to them and try to find the word on the sticky note inside the library book. This game requires a little prep work for the librarian to go through each book and locate a sight word contained in the book, but the

students love it, so it will be worth the extra effort. Students can record sight words found on index cards to take back to their classrooms.

Genres

Exposing students to a variety of genres increases student experience with literature, as well as with writing styles. When the librarian identifies a piece of literature by genre and explains the genre, the students will engage with the style of writing in a way they never have before. I try to read a poem to students each time they come to the library, and usually I try to make some connection to another piece of literature I'm reading aloud, whether it is a picture book or a nonfiction book. Discussing text features as you go along will increase comprehension and will get the students to think like writers while they are listening to stories or nonfiction texts being read to them.

Figure 7.1. Kindergarteners illustrated a stanza from the poem *Hello Harvest Moon* by Ralph Fletcher.

- Poetry Illustrations: Share various poems with students and invite them to illustrate one of them, or even just a stanza from a poem. I love emphasizing a stanza that really speaks to me, even to the youngest students, and then seeing their interpretations through their illustrations. Drawing is a wonderful way for prewriters to experiment with getting meaning down on paper.
- Nonfiction: Read a nonfiction book that is of high interest to students. I try to invite students to make lists of topics they are interested in, then I choose a nonfiction book that I think will appeal to them. As we read through each book, I point out the features of nonfiction books: the boldface words, subheadings, pictures with captions, and the glossary if there is one.
- Picture Books: Picture books are an obvious favorite for read aloud time because they are short by nature. They pack an educational punch when you think aloud while reading. Notice character development, plot progression, and when the story comes to a climax, and invite students to make inferences and draw conclusions as you go. Picture books encourage students to make connections, and often they will raise their hands to share a story or memory

the book invoked for them. I try to allow as many students as possible to share their stories, and I point out that they are making connections.

- Novels: It's difficult for librarians to read entire novels with classes of students due to time constraints, but I do love reading the first chapter of novels, even to my youngest students. Often they will really get into the story and want to check out the book. I don't discourage beginning readers from checking out chapter books. I talk to them about asking older siblings or parents to read those books with them. Once I have read the first chapter, I ask students to make predictions about the rest of the story. Usually I will read the back of the book, the title and dedication pages, and chapter titles if there are any. We flip through the book to look for any illustrations and talk about what might happen next. It's not uncommon that novels I share with students don't make their way back to the shelf for quite a while.

Grammar Integration

Another way librarians and teachers can collaborate is through sharing lesson plans and skills being taught for grammar. The librarian can integrate grammar instruction into read aloud time by focusing on skills being taught in the classroom and looking for ways authors use the skill in published literature. Grammar is a courtesy writers extend to readers. Librarians can highlight grammar skills as they read to students and discuss why authors choose to use grammar the way they do. We want our readers to think like writers and our writers to think like readers. The two are so closely intertwined that one cannot exist without the other.

- Grammar Anchor Charts: Create class anchor charts to record student learning, to display in the library reading area. Students can record their own version of the anchor chart in their library journals, which are discussed in the next chapter, or the librarian can arrange for students to bring their classroom writing journals to the library with them and transfer the anchor chart to them. Sharing classroom journals is a great way to show solidarity between the classroom teacher and the librarian and to highlight the library as an extension of the regular classroom. Perhaps kindergarteners are learning to capitalize the first word of each sentence. Use literature to find examples and discuss how this is one way authors show they are moving their thoughts along by creating new sentences.
- Grammar Illustrations: We talk about illustrators a lot in the library. Have students create an illustration of a grammar skill and write a book page to go with it. Better yet, have the class divide up and assign specific skills to small groups, which can then be compiled into a class grammar book. Students can use examples from literature in their illustrations, further creating a bond among authentic literature, grammar, and the writing process. For example, first graders might be learning about prepositions. When Pete the Cat stepped in a large pile of strawberries, his shoes were stained red. If he had walked

around the pile of strawberries or stepped over the pile of strawberries, the story wouldn't have been as much fun.

- Writing Time: Give students an opportunity to write in the library. The library is full of rich material to inspire creative and expository writing. Encourage writing to the extent that students are able to publish and display their work in the library. Grammar skills can be reinforced throughout this process by allowing students to collaborate on writing projects and by using authentic literature as examples of how meaning is expressed through grammar. Second graders learning the nuances of declarative and interrogative sentences could focus on this skill in their writing time. The librarian would be supporting classroom instruction, which solidifies the foundation of grammar needed for writers to adequately say what they want to say in their writing.

- Play Grammar Games: Take well-written lines from literature and have students rewrite them using different punctuation. Allow them to experiment with how grammar can change the way a sentence is delivered and how it can alter the meaning of the writing itself. Challenge students to find ways that authors defy the typical standards of grammar. The English language is consistent only in its inconsistencies. Students love it when they can find authors' "mistakes," and it makes for great conversations about how grammar is used to convey meaning. For the youngest students this requires a lot of modeling, but some first and second graders could do this on their own and in small groups.

Model Reading and Writing

One of the most effective ways to teach anything is through modeling. I've never seen a child learn how to tie his or her shoes by being told how to do it. The same is true of any learning. Teachers, both in the classroom and in the library, can best share their knowledge by repeatedly modeling the desired skill for students.

Librarians are gateways to information. We teach students how to use databases by modeling the steps for them. We walk them through it, and usually we have to do it again and again before students finally feel the confidence required to do it on their own. We teach students to locate library materials by modeling how to use the information retrieval system and how to search by keyword, title, and author, and then physically walking to the shelves to show them where their requested materials are stored.

Librarians can also model reading and writing. For our youngest students we may have to begin by modeling how to hold a book, which direction to turn the pages, and how the words are presented on the page. We can use our fingers to follow the text and physically demonstrate how the words tell a story when we follow them from the left to the right side of the page. We can point out that spaces between words help authors separate ideas into small chunks that are related to the words that surround them. We model for our students how the illustrations support the text by discussing them as we read along.

Modeling reading comes quite naturally to many librarians. I know some librarians who are amazing storytellers. What may not come as naturally is modeling writing. This may be a scary concept for some librarians. I know that when I was a classroom teacher, the idea of writing in front of my students and for my students was very intimidating to begin with, but confidence came with practice. The more I wrote in front of my students, the easier it was and the more they learned. The idea becomes less daunting when you start with what you know and with your areas of interest. Librarians are information seekers, and we love a challenge. We teach our students how to find information, and this is an excellent starting point for modeling writing. We can show students how we make lists of questions when we are researching a topic. We can model the gathering of information through note taking and paraphrasing texts used. We can then model how we put all of our gained knowledge together for a presentation.

When sharing unique poems I often stop and very quickly begin forming a short poem in the style of the poem I was reading to my students. Sometimes I verbalize it, and sometimes I actually write it down on a whiteboard that I keep near the area where I read to my students. Once when I read the book *Dogku*, the story of a family that takes in a stray dog told in haiku by Andrew Clements, to my students I was inspired to write my own haiku about books. I quickly jotted my poem on a piece of chart paper:

> Oh, that new book smell!
> A spine not broken . . . intact.
> New books are the best.

When I write down my own ideas I'm showing my students how it's done and demystifying the process of creating literature. I'm making the task just a little more approachable for my students. I'm showing them that if I can do it, so can they. I'm also showing them how I get ideas. I mentioned previously that we need to teach our students to read like writers and to write like readers. When we are reading a picture book, poem, or nonfiction text that gives me an idea, I write it down in front of my students to hopefully inspire them to do the same, but I am at the very least planting a seed within them that will help grow them into readers and writers.

8

Library Notebooks

Librarians are the tour guides for all of knowledge.

—Patrick Ness

We have almost 800 students on our campus. It's a very large elementary campus by our district's standards. When I first began trying to figure out how I was going to teach that many students and have enough supplies on hand to conduct each lesson, I became very concerned about the cost of purchasing enough paper, pencils, glue sticks, crayons, and so forth for each student each week. I also had to think about how to keep track of that much paper. In the classroom I used writing notebooks and reading response notebooks for my students to record and collect their ideas and evidence of their thinking, but I couldn't justify purchasing almost 800 notebooks each year out of my library budget, so I sent an e-mail to each grade level's team leader and asked them all to discuss the possibility of donating a spiral notebook or composition notebook from the students' school supplies to keep in the library. I made sure teachers knew that the notebooks would be used to support the literacy instruction they were providing in the classroom. The teachers agreed, and once I had them on board I just had to figure out how to manage them.

In the beginning I had students keep their journals in their classroom. My thoughts were that I wanted them to be able to refer to the information in their journals as it pertained to classroom lessons. This became a way of collaborating with the classroom teacher. I could have students record information that was helpful to research, passwords and usernames for district databases, and ideas for writing that could then be used during their reading and writing workshops. However, it became obvious pretty quickly that remembering to bring their journals each time they came to the library and keeping up with them from week to week without losing them was a bit too much both for the students and the teachers. I didn't want to add any more responsibilities to the teachers' plates, so I began brainstorming a way to store the notebooks in the library.

I managed to get my hands on three filing cabinets, and they work perfectly to store students' notebooks. I have them organized by the day they come to the library and then by grade level. Each student in first through fourth grades has a notebook dedicated to library lessons. They stay in the library, but I have had teachers request that the students bring their library notebooks back to class to use the information contained in them to assist them in a classroom lesson. These notebooks are used for students to write and to take notes on library database access, for reading response, and for student response to the minilessons that we do in the library. I mentioned before that only my first through fourth graders have these notebooks. There are no spiral notebooks or composition notebooks on the kindergarteners' supply lists, so I do purchase tablet paper and construction paper for them to use while in the library. Most of what we do in kindergarten is done as a whole group, and on chart paper, but I often have them respond to what we've read through illustrations and words they are able to use. We call it writing because that's what they are doing. I allow students to take these papers with them each week instead of trying to store them in the library.

Something magical happens when you ask students to write in the library. At first they were confused. They weren't used to having to do classroom type activities during their library time. They certainly weren't used to having someone other than their classroom teacher ask them to write. They treated writing as they would in the classroom. They were timid about making spelling mistakes and didn't trust me yet to accept anything that wasn't perfect. Once they realized that I didn't care about spelling (I only had to say it a million times before it began to sink in) or perfect writing, that all I wanted was for them to get their ideas down on paper, they began to open up. Some of my students even asked to take their library journals home so they could continue working on a piece of writing. This was just the encouragement I needed to continue this journey of writing with students in the library.

Figure 8.1. Filing center for our library journals.

My younger students weren't quite as shy about writing. First and second graders don't really have expectations of what their library time should be like, and most of them are still open to trying new things. Most of my students embraced the activities I presented them with because they were getting to write their own thoughts. I didn't have an agenda beyond having the students think about literature and solidify their thoughts by getting them down on paper. Once this environment of trust and safety was established, I began to see my students let loose, and the library notebook became a bit of a keepsake for them and for me.

At the end of the year students take their notebooks with them. Contained in their pages are lists of books students want to read, ideas for writing, book reviews, writing samples, and much more. Often students ask to take their journals home because they want to use them over the weekend. It's rewarding to see the students get excited about an idea they developed while in the library.

Getting Started

Students begin by setting up their notebooks. This can be done however best suits the librarian, but I have found using the following sections helpful:

- Login Information: Students record usernames and passwords of library databases, the information retrieval system, commonly used Web sites, and so forth. They often refer back to these usernames and passwords in the library, in the classroom, and at home.
- Books I Want to Read: Students keep a running list of books they want to read. If they find a book they want and it's checked out, they can either put the book on hold or record the title and call number in the journal.
- Library Map: I like to have students draw a map of the library and give them a brief overview at the beginning of the year of where popular subjects are shelved. This gives them a reference to use whenever they want to browse shelves.
- Sight Word Lists: Younger students keep sight word lists in their journals and leave a few pages reserved for sight word games we can play throughout the year.
- Research: I ask my students to leave about five pages for this section so they can record questions that come to them about topics they are interested in. Additional pages are stapled into this section when we do focused research in the library.
- Reading Response: A good chunk, as much as a quarter of the journal, is reserved for reading response. I try to have some type of reading response activity each week. This also acts as a record of the books I have read to students. They often will check these books out during the year.
- Writing: Another quarter of the journal is reserved for writing. This space is used for writing activities, grammar minilessons, and free writing.
- Library Lessons: The remainder of the journal is set up for library lessons that we do throughout the year, such as Internet safety, digital citizenship, using and citing sources, and evaluating library materials.

Managing Journals

I mentioned that I purchased three filing cabinets to hold the journals, and that they are organized according to the day the students visit the library, as well as by grade level. I usually begin our library time together by reading to students and then follow that with whatever our minilesson is for the day. This activity is done with students sitting on the floor in a reading nook. I find that separating our activities by area of the library increases student focus. When read aloud time and the lesson are completed, students get their journals from their filing cabinet and make their way to the library tables, where they work individually and in small groups on the activity that day. When they are finished with the activity they can hang onto their journals while they search for books they'd like to check out. This allows them to add titles to their "Books I Want to Read" page in their journals, jot down questions they may have about topics they are interested in looking into, and access usernames and passwords in case they need to use a Web site or library database.

Students are trained to put their journals back in the proper drawer of the filing cabinet when they are finished checking out books and no longer have a need for them. They are also allowed to take them home, or back to the classroom if they need the information, as long as they bring them back the next time they come to the library. This system requires a lot of procedural training in the beginning of the school year, but the effort is well worth it as students learn to use their journals and understand their value.

9

Library Minilessons for Reader's Response

A library takes the gift of reading one step further by offering personalized learning opportunities second to none, a powerful antidote to the isolation of the Web.

—Julie Andrews

I have found the best way to teach lessons that actually impact student learning in the library, given the limited time I have with students, is through minilessons. My typical hour with students will include a ten- to fifteen-minute read aloud, a five- to ten-minute lesson (longer if the lesson and activity are done as a whole-group activity), and then about ten to twenty minutes for students to respond to the lesson independently. I try to spend about forty minutes of their one-hour visit reading to them, doing the lesson, and then having them respond. That leaves students with about twenty minutes to find new books to check out and read. Library schedules will vary from school to school. Your lesson structure will look different based on your schedule. My suggestion is to give students a minimum of fifteen minutes to check out and read their books. Use whatever time you have beyond that to read to them and do your lessons.

When identifying skills to teach during minilessons, looking to the scope and sequence of each grade level is always a good idea, as is collaboration with teachers. Collaboration is a great way to find out where classroom teachers are in the scope and sequence and to identify areas where you can support the curriculum in the library. Librarians often support curriculum through collection development, leading staff development, pulling resources for classroom use, and so forth. Another way that librarians can support the curriculum is through direct instruction, or coteaching along with classroom teachers. Collaborating with teachers is the best way to find out in which areas you can best offer that support. Depending on your situation and schedule, collaboration may involve attending grade-level or department meetings, setting aside time after school specifically for teachers to use the library and utilize your services. It may mean setting up shared files online using a tool such as Google Drive that both you and the teacher can access and edit, and to which teachers can upload requests for instructional support, or identify areas in which you may be able to provide direct instruction in the library.

Scaffolding One Lesson Across Grade Levels

In a single day I see every grade level from kindergarten through fourth grade. For planning purposes, and to save my sanity, I had to come up with a way of scaffolding my lesson across all of the grade levels. What's interesting about scaffolding a lesson this way is that I can meet all learners exactly where they are, because I become familiar with each grade level's standards and objectives. This gives me an excellent idea of the foundation each grade level has leading up to where the students are in the curriculum. With very few exceptions, I write one basic lesson plan for all grade levels and then customize it according to the specific grade level. I do best working from the top down, so I usually plan for fourth graders and then scaffold the lesson down to my kindergarteners' level.

Sometimes I plan a lesson around a particular book that I want to use, and sometimes I plan my lesson around a skill I want to teach. If I find a book I love and really want to share with students, I look for the teachable moments in the book. If there is a skill to teach, I find a book that supports that skill to read aloud to the kids. An example of this scaffolding is when teaching students to make personal and literary connections to texts. I use the vocabulary *personal allusions* and *literary allusions* with all of my students. Kindergarteners and first graders are incredibly adept at making personal connections to literature. They can almost always think of a story to share when something I'm reading to them has sparked a memory in them. Sadly, by the time they get to third or fourth grade they've been discouraged from sharing these connections out loud, and it's more difficult for them to make those connections because they've trained themselves not to say anything. There are so many time constraints placed on teachers that they don't always have time to hear students' stories. I love to encourage students to share these stories, and I always identify them as personal connections to literature. Eventually even my kindergarteners are using the terms. These connections are an integral part of the metacognitive process, and the sooner we get kids thinking about their own thinking, the better and sooner they will be able to think critically about literature.

My lesson plans for teaching personal and literary connections might look something like this:

Read *The Fantastic Flying Books of Mr. Morris Lessmore* by William Joyce aloud to students. While reading, model metacognitive strategies used so that students will see evidence of your thinking while you're reading. I like to point out that when I read this book I make a literary connection to *The Wizard of Oz*, because in the beginning there is what seems to be a tornado that transports Mr. Morris Lessmore to a very sad time in his life. The illustrations start as black and white and move to color as Morris discovers his place and purpose in life, and that reminds me of the *Wizard of Oz* movie. When Morris discovers the library and makes friends with all of the books, I share my personal connection to when I decided to become a librarian because I love books so much. Morris lovingly cares for the books as I do. Challenge students to think of their own personal and literary connections to the story.

Third and Fourth Grades: Students will write about their personal and literary connections in their library notebooks and share their thoughts with their small groups. *Second Grade*: In the whole-group setting, students will brainstorm their personal connections and share with the group. Create a class chart of each piece of literature that students are able to connect to Morris's story. Students will then write about their thoughts in their library notebooks and share their ideas with their small groups.

Kindergarten and First Grade: In the whole-group setting, students will share their own personal stories that they thought of during the reading of *The Fantastic Flying Books of Mr. Morris Lessmore*. With the teacher's assistance they will then think of other pieces of literature that can be connected to Morris's story. The teacher will model these connections using literature previously read in the library. The teacher will pull copies of *The Best Story* by Eileen Spinelli, *Dewey: There's a Cat in the Library!* by Vicki Myron, and *The Patchwork Quilt* by Valerie Fluornoy. Students will illustrate their personal connection on one side of a half sheet of manila paper, and one literary connection on the other side. They will write words and phrases to show their meaning and share their illustrations within their small groups.

If you have a lesson that you teach each year, you would need to select a different mentor text to use the following year. Another option is to scaffold the skill, but use a different text for each grade level. My goal is to craft my lessons in such a way that I can simplify the process for myself while exposing all of my students to the skills I'm trying to teach them.

Using Mentor Texts

It's a dream of mine to one day build a database that links mentor texts, authentic pieces of literature specifically chosen to illustrate a skill, objective, or idea, to the state standards, skills taught across the subjects, and by character qualities displayed within the texts. It would be so nice to offer teachers a way to easily search available texts according to what they will be teaching in class. Until that day arrives, I rely on my own knowledge of what is available in my library and on subject searches to find appropriate texts for teachers to use as mentor texts and to use in my own library lessons.

Using literature to teach a skill or a character quality is such a fantastic way to help students connect to the often abstract ideas we strive to teach them. The best way to become familiar with children's literature is to read as much as you can! The beauty of picture books is that they are quick reads, and you can almost always find some nugget in a book that you can use in a lesson. Librarians are a fantastic resource for locating mentor texts, but in a pinch Google is a great resource as well. I did a quick Google search for picture books to teach character qualities and found some really great documents that had already done the work for me. There are also some good professional books that will help you locate literature for lessons. *The Reading Teacher's Book of Lists* and *A to Zoo: Subject Access to Children's Picture Books* are both excellent resources for locating mentor texts.

Mentor texts provide great examples that can be easily integrated into library mini-lessons. The text will illustrate the lesson for you and can be referred to throughout the year. Students will remember stories and will connect your lesson to those stories. They serve as great reference points for both the library teacher and the student.

Minilessons and Informational Text

Young learners enjoy being able to predict what is coming next in a lesson, and establishing literacy habits will help you to engage even the youngest learners, as they thrive on repetition. These habits form the foundation of my minilessons. In *Making Thinking Visible*, the authors suggest that "the steps of the routine act as natural scaffolds that can lead students' thinking to higher and more sophisticated levels" (Ritchhart, Church, and Morrison 2011, 47). Creating literacy habits will allow students to build on prior knowledge and experience with literature and writing and will eventually move this knowledge from their heads to their hearts.

I try to alternate the genres I use in my lessons. One week I'll use an informational text, and the next week I'll use a narrative text. One of my favorite habits with informational texts is to use compass points, which I describe in greater detail in chapter 13 (Ritchhart, Church, and Morrison 2011, 93). Basically, I activate students' prior knowledge of a topic by asking them what they already know, what questions they have about the topic, what concerns or worries they have about the topic, and where they can go to find out more about the topic. This habit gets students thinking critically about the topic before I even begin reading from the text. The beauty of establishing these habits is that eventually they become part of the students' own process of learning and information seeking when they want to learn more about a topic.

Another approach I use with informational texts is to take the time to identify the textual features of the book we are using. I point out the table of contents. If we are reading a book about kittens, I ask students to identify which chapter is most likely going to give me the information I need to know about how and what to feed a kitten. I take note of boldfaced words, and if I find a word students might not know, we consult the glossary in the back of the book. By modeling this type of reading, I'm helping students establish their own routines to use when they are reading informational text.

I don't always read an informational text in its entirety, because I like to model real-life situations as much as possible. When I do research, I look for a direct answer to my questions. When students come up with questions about a topic, I help them narrow down exactly where we need to look for the answer to the question. Teaching them how to use the index to search for terms that will help them find the answers to their questions is an important life skill. I also like to have multiple texts on the same topic available in case we don't find the answer to each of their questions. In the earlier grades this involves a lot of modeling and whole-group instruction. As students get older, they are able to do more of this on their own.

It's important to let student interest drive some of your instruction. Ask your students about topics they are interested in and then let that drive your instruction with informational texts. It's fairly easy to do a quick poll at the beginning of a class period to find out what students are interested in, then grab a few books from the shelf to use in your lesson. Remember, you are teaching the skills related to using informational text; you aren't actually teaching about the topics themselves, so any informational text will work. It may as well be one that students find interesting and relevant.

Minilessons and Narrative Text

Just as I establish literacy habits with informational text, I do the same with narrative texts. I always introduce students to the author and illustrator of picture books and poems. I model my thinking out loud as we read through the text. And I hit on the six parts of hexagonal writing, described more fully in a later chapter, during and after reading. Hexagonal writing is an activity in which students think critically about literature by identifying any personal connections they make while reading, connections to other pieces of literature, the plot of the story, any major or minor themes in the story, and any literary devices within the story, and then form an evaluation of the story. Modeling my thinking teaches emerging and early readers how to go about analyzing literature as they read. It also sets a solid foundation for elements that need to be present when students write their own narrative texts.

Sometimes I let the theme of narrative literature drive my minilessons. Sometimes I teach minilessons based on literary elements such as setting, characters, plot, problem, and solution. Occasionally my minilessons are centered on making connections to literature or evaluating literature.

10

Making Reading and Writing Connections in the Library

Reading makes all other learning possible. We have to get books into our children's hands early and often.

—Barack Obama

I truly believe that it is perfectly acceptable for students to interrupt me when I'm reading. Often our youngest students make the best connections to literature being shared with them because they haven't yet learned not to interrupt the teacher while she's reading. I've also found that student engagement is at its highest when we are discussing the literature as we go along. One thing I've learned about increasing circulation in my library is that books kids are interested in are the books they will check out. Often students don't realize a book is one they would enjoy reading until I tell them a little bit about it and make it sound intriguing. I don't even have to read from books to get students excited about them. I can share the summary on the back cover and tell them why I'm looking forward to reading it, and that I won't get the chance to read it until summer because it will stay checked out.

I'm a browser. When I go to the library or a bookstore, I want a book to jump out at me. I'm embarrassed to admit that I've chosen a book on more than one occasion because something on the cover catches my attention and leads me to read the front and back covers. Students are the same way. They will read what they know they like until someone shares a book with them and encourages them to read it. Granted, I do have a few lovers of literature on my campus who will take a chance on a book. There are a few sophisticated browsers at my school, but for the most part, the students who use my library will stick to a genre, series, or author they know and like until something else catches their attention, usually because the book has been displayed or I do a book talk on it.

When I share my thoughts on a book or a story, when I make those personal connections from the story to my own life and share how I can relate to the story, and when I compare books to other books I'm familiar with, I'm showing students how to truly analyze a piece of writing as they are reading. If I model this reading behavior often enough, the idea of deeply reading literature will transfer over to my students. For this reason, I highly encourage my students to politely interrupt me and share their thoughts as we read. Young children are good at this because they have so many stories they want to share and haven't yet experienced any negative effects from sharing their stories. I teach procedures early on about how to share a personal connection to a book or story I'm reading to students. It's important to teach this procedure and practice it, so they learn how to share without detracting from the reading or preventing other listeners from hearing the story in its entirety. When students want to share a connection they've made, they simply raise their hands and wait for me to acknowledge them. I tell them from the beginning that I will always let them share their stories, but insist they wait for me to get to a good stopping point. I find that once one student shares, many others will want to share, and this is a good thing. Sometimes so many students want to share that I have to let them do so with a partner sitting next to them just so we can make it through the story before our time is up! I always point out that what students are doing is making personal connections to the story. I want them to understand that the story they are listening to is invoking emotions, inciting memories, and making them think, as any good piece of literature should.

My routine for sharing literature with students, no matter the genre, almost always consists of three parts. First I model my own thinking as I'm reading to them. Then I model making personal and literary connections to the text and encourage them to do the same, and finally I allow students to respond in some way to the literature.

Model Thinking

Teaching students to use metacognitive strategies, strategies that encourage thinking about one's thoughts, increases engagement and encourages critical thinking. I'm a firm believer in talking through a piece of literature I'm sharing with students. I love pointing out ideas I have and connections I make as I'm reading. If the story I'm reading to students reminds me of something from my own life, I always share it with students. Sharing my thinking accomplishes a couple of things: it serves to model how good readers interpret and connect with literature, and it encourages students to dig deep and make their own connections.

If I'm reading and I have a question about the literature, I'll ask the question out loud, or I'll say, "I wonder . . . ," or "I noticed . . . ," and what I'm seeing is that my students are using these same strategies when they are reading. The language of this type of critical thinking is becoming prevalent among my readers, even the youngest students. It's not uncommon to hear a kindergartner say, "I noticed that the little girl's dress is red and the rest of the picture is black and white." This student is applying metacognitive strategies. She is thinking about her thinking and taking note of what she notices, what she wonders, what she wants to investigate further, and what she wants to share that she has connected with.

Another thing I'll do while reading is jot down notes on a white board that I keep in my read aloud area. Many teachers use the "stop and jot" strategy. This strategy allows me to show students that I had an idea or thought that I want to explore further.

When I finish reading I make sure that I comment on the thoughts I wrote down while reading. Sometimes I'll make a note about something fairly obvious in the story so that students can reply to my questions.

Making Connections

Learning, critical thinking, and creativity occur when we make connections between seemingly unrelated things. These connections cause new pathways in the brain to form and existing pathways to change direction. Encouraging children to relate to literature is one of the greatest gifts we, as educators, can give our students, and the best way to do this is to model, model, model.

There are two types of connections that I teach as part of my literacy routine in the library: personal and literary. I refer to them as personal allusions and literary allusions in keeping with the hexagonal writing verbiage discussed more in the next chapter. These allusions, or connections, allow students to respond to literature using higher-level thinking, a skill inherent in young learners: they love to share their thoughts on literature and tell their stories, but time constraints and peer pressure often diminish this desire to share and change the way students think about writing. If we want them to continue making these connections, we have to allow them time to discuss the connections they make.

I was lucky enough this year to have beloved children's author Patricia Polacco visit my school. Her stories are easily relatable, and I've been teaching them for years. One of my favorite Polacco stories is *The Keeping Quilt*. I love reading the story of the quilt to students and then sharing with them the stories of my very own grandmother and her quilts. Few of my grandmother's quilts have quite the same historical value as Polacco's Keeping Quilt, but the sentimental value attached to them is priceless. When I share my story I make sure to use the term *personal allusion*. I say to the students, "I was able to think of a *personal allusion* to this story. My own grandmother made quilts, as did her mother before her. I treasure these quilts more for the fact that they were lovingly and painstakingly made by my grandmother than for their stories, but to me they are just as important as the Keeping Quilt was to Anna." I then ask students if there is anything in their family passed down from a grandparent or great-grandparent that they love or that their parents have told them stories about. If some are reluctant to share, I stretch the question to include any special gifts given to them by their grandparents. I allow students to share with the whole group, and after a few have shared I encourage them to turn to a partner to share any stories they haven't told yet. I want to make sure that anyone who made a connection has an opportunity to share.

Later, when we read Polacco's *The Blessing Cup*, I modeled making a literary allusion. I told students, "This reminds me of *The Keeping Quilt*. I have made a literary allusion, a connection to another story. In *The Keeping Quilt* Anna reminisces about weddings that have taken place in her family throughout the years and how the traditions associated with weddings evolved from generation to generation. She talks about how they placed gold, flowers, bread, and salt in the bouquets: "Gold so she would never know poverty, a flower so she would always know love, salt so her life would always have flavor, and bread so that she would never know hunger." In *The Blessing Cup* Anna's family is fleeing their home in Russia. They take this treasured family heirloom with them because the tea set comes with the wish, "Anyone who drinks from this will have blessings from God. They will never know a day of hunger. Their lives will always have flavor. They will know love, joy, and they will never be poor." These wishes remind me of the bread, the salt, the flowers, and the gold placed in wedding bouquets for the very same reasons. Alluding to other pieces of literature is sometimes difficult for the youngest learners, simply because their exposure to literature is slightly more limited than that of older students. However, I make sure they know that literature includes poems, nursery rhymes, songs, movies, and other stories they've had read to them. We talk about how song lyrics and movie scripts are texts and tell a story, and therefore they count when we are making connections from one text to another.

Students pick up on this skill easily, but they need to see it repeated over and over again for it to become part of their own literacy routines. My goal is that any time students are reading or are being read to, they will automatically think about memories the text triggers of things that have happened to them or that they have seen or heard in their own lives, as well as memories of other stories they've heard. I want this to become ingrained in them. I want it to be a natural part of their reading process.

We recently hosted a school-wide "Dogs vs. Cats" campaign in my school through the library. We read many books about dogs and cats. I shared novels, picture books, and nonfiction books with students and asked them to make literary and personal allusions to the stories and informational text we read. This theme was a good one for really teaching these types of connections, because almost every student has had some type of experience with cats and/or dogs. Most students have a (strong) opinion about these animals as pets.

My second graders wrote a persuasive piece on cats versus dogs as pets and which was the superior pet. I had them use stories from their own lives to persuade their readers one way or the other. My kindergarten and first-grade students illustrated their preferences by writing and drawing about the things they like and dislike about each animal. One kindergartener made me giggle when he wrote, "What I like about dogs is everything. What I like about cats is their tail." This astute six-year-old was already laying the groundwork for a persuasive piece. He had made enough connections to know that he feels dogs are superior to cats in the pet department. Later we voted for cats or dogs based solely on book characters. I had read part of *Because of Winn Dixie* to students as well as as *Clifford the Big Red Dog*. I also shared *Pete the Cat, Chester*, and *Bad Kitty* with students. The challenge came when students had to decide which team to vote for, cat or dog, with no reference to their personal feelings for these animals as pets. They had to rely only on their connections to the stories. Dogs won by a landslide. I'm guessing that students struggled to separate their personal and literary allusions. It was an interesting experiment for sure!

Reader's Response

Giving students an opportunity to reflect on what they've read is a very important task, whether in the traditional classroom or in the library. This has become one of the most crucial parts of the literacy routine I've established in the library. What is one of the first things you want to do when you read a book you really love? That you truly connect with? You want to share it. You want to convince others to read it. If you're like me, you have to document it in some way, whether it's through journal writing, writing a review on Goodreads, or pinning images on Pinterest that reflect your thoughts on the book (something I had to do after reading *The Fault in Our Stars*—so many beautiful quotes). When students are allowed time to reflect on literature, they make deeper connections to it.

Older students in my library, second grade and up, complete their reading response activities in their library journals. By the end of the year they have a scrapbook of the various books they've read and the reactions they had to them. First grade and up will complete their reading response in their journals and younger kindergarten students will do the task on paper or orally.

Sometimes I give students a task to complete in response to the literature, as I did with the cats versus dogs stories we read. I also like to ask students to write about what they were thinking as I was reading to them. I ask them to start off with a metacognitive thinking stem such as "I noticed," or "I wonder." At other times I hand them their journals and writing supplies and tell them to just go with whatever comes to mind. I allow my prewriters as well as my experienced writers to draw pictures if they like. Giving students freedom to express their ideas in different ways is a powerful tool in the literacy tool belt.

Just like allowing time for students to share their connections during the reading, I think it is invaluable to give them time to share their thoughts after the reading. It is so important to give students an opportunity to voice their thoughts with their peers in a safe, nonjudgmental environment. Providing discussion time with peers, giving students a voice, and having them share their reflections opens them up to new ideas they may not have heard otherwise.

Suggested Activities for Reading Response

- Write a book recommendation for this book. The librarian can even choose one to place on the shelf with the book. Recommendations can also be written on sticky notes and placed on a recommendation board for the book. Younger students can use smiley face and sad face icons to explain whether they recommend a book or not. They can also draw pictures to illustrate their thoughts. If you receive particularly well-written reviews, these can be added to the online library catalog to be accessed by students searching for books.
- Make allusions. Record any personal or literary allusions you made while reading. Explain why this book invoked those memories. Younger students can do this in the form of simple text combined with drawings that illustrate the connections they made.
- Write a letter. Students can write a letter to one of the characters, to a friend telling him or her about the book, or to their teacher explaining why they recommend or don't recommend this book for future students.
- Draw illustrations. Students can illustrate a stanza from a poem, the main idea or theme of the story, or a diagram from a nonfiction text.
- Make lists. Students can make lists of new words they heard in the text; emotions the text made them experience; or people, places, or events they thought about while reading the book. One of my favorite activities to do with young learners is to record a list of words from the text they know how to read. As students see these lists grow throughout the year, they can track their success.
- Create character diagrams. Students can draw a picture of one of the characters and think of personality or physical qualities that character possesses.
- Analyze the story. Students can divide their papers into two columns and list their likes and dislikes about the book, story, or poem. Pre-emergent writers can draw pictures and use icons to record their thoughts.
- Mimic the story. Students can respond to literature by mimicking some part of the story or illustrations. For example, after reading *The Neat Line* by Pamela Duncan Edwards, students can respond to the story by creating an illustration that starts with a neat line.

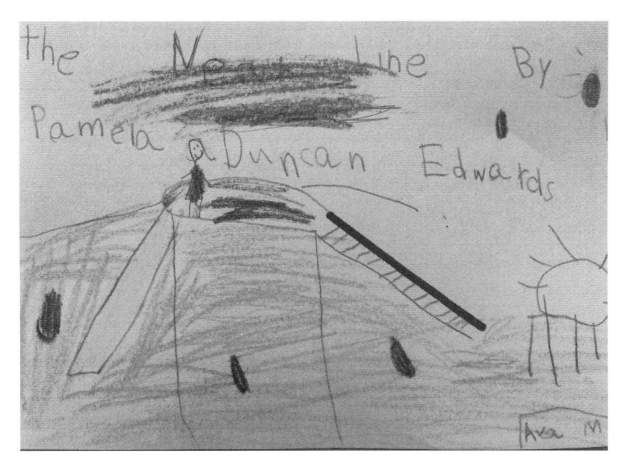

Reading response doesn't have to be a lengthy activity. I usually project the book title and author's name onto the screen in the library so that students can record that information in their journals or on their papers. The main purpose of reading response in the library is to get the students habitually thinking and talking about what they read.

11

Modifying Hexagonal Writing in the Library

When I was young, we couldn't afford much. But, my library card was my key to the world.

—John Goodman

Hexagonal writing is one of my all-time favorite tools to use with students to help them analyze literature. I first learned about hexagonal writing when I attended Abydos literacy training in my district. It quickly became a favorite activity to use in my classroom, and I knew that when I moved to the library I would have to find a way to incorporate it into my teaching, since it packs an immense academic, analytic, and evaluative punch.

Hexagonal writing is a prewriting strategy developed by my coauthor, Dr. Joyce Armstrong Carroll, and is used to write about literature. The six facets of the hexagonal touch on different levels of Bloom's Taxonomy, making it a quality strategy to use for analyzing literature. Carroll's hexagonal strategy requires the reader to compose a summary of the literature being analyzed, make personal allusions to the literature, make literary allusions to the literature, identify the theme of the piece, analyze the writing for any literary devices, and evaluate the writing. The process of hexagonal writing is quite time consuming. In the classroom I would usually spread it out over two or three days. Eventually my students were familiar enough with the tool that it became their main reading response activity.

Since I had not taught kindergarteners prior to becoming the librarian, I wasn't sure I would still be able to use hexagonal writing as my main reading response strategy, but they pleasantly surprised me with their ability to discuss its six facets. I don't discuss all six parts of the hexagonal for each piece I read to students. Instead, I focus on one or two areas for discussion and for independent response. I mentioned previously that I model personal and literary allusions almost every time I read to students. This has become part of our literary routine in the library. I discuss those two facets of the hexagonal approach and encourage discussion among peers as they come up during reading. Sometimes I have students focus on personal and literary allusions during their reading response time, while at other times I simply use it to drive discussion during and after reading.

Besides personal and literary allusions, my next two favorite parts of hexagonal writing, which lend themselves perfectly to book talks in the library, are theme and judgment, or evaluation. Students love to share whether or not they liked a book, story, or poem. Even the youngest learners are often eager to share their thoughts on the merits of a piece of literature. I do make a point of using the terminology when I am intentionally teaching this skill. If a student points out that he really liked *Pete the Cat: I Love My White Shoes* because Pete doesn't let anything bother him and his songs are funny, I make sure I tell him that I appreciate his evaluation. Not every student will immediately connect the word evaluation with her opinion of the text, but I'm laying a foundation for understanding that this is one way to analyze literature. I want the students to experience me using the terms. Plus, it makes them feel important when I tell them they are evaluating!

Theme is often a difficult concept for students to grasp. One of my biggest goals for teaching literacy in the library is to encourage my students to think like writers when they are reading and to think like readers when they are writing. When we read *The Fantastic Flying Books of Mr. Morris Lessmore*, I pointed out to students that sometimes the theme is so important to the author that he doesn't want to risk leaving it open to interpretation by the reader, so he will come right out and say what the theme is to make sure the reader really gets it. I explain that this is the case in Mr. Lessmore's story. The author, William Joyce, doesn't beat around the bush when it comes to the theme of his story. He comes right out and tells the reader, "Everyone's story matters." Again, I want to use *big words* (for vocabulary development) with my students, so I explain to them that when the author comes right out and tells you the theme, it's *explicitly* stated. When the author makes you use your brain, it's *implicitly* stated. If they hear these words enough, and I explain them well enough, even my youngest learners will begin to own them. If I use these phrases over and over again, by the time they are fourth graders they will have a very good understanding of what it means to find the main idea of a piece of literature and how to make sure they have a focused theme in their writing.

I received some fantastic responses when I asked students to illustrate the theme of *The Fantastic Flying Books of Mr. Morris Lessmore*. I was very impressed with students' understanding of the message the author so fervently wanted to convey. I was also impressed with the ability of my youngest students to grasp the importance of the statement, "Everyone's story matters." I wish I could tell you that I wasn't at all surprised by the deep thinking that took place among my kindergarten and first-grade students, but I was. It was thrilling as a teacher and a librarian to witness them grasping this great big idea and making it their own. I would have missed out on those insights had I simply read the book to them and then sent them on their way to check out books.

The last two parts of hexagonal writing, analyzing the literature for literary devices and summarizing the story, I usually do exclusively as an oral activity. I don't want older students to get bogged down in writing summaries, and this isn't practical for students who are still learning to write. Literary devices must be taught, repetitively, and my time

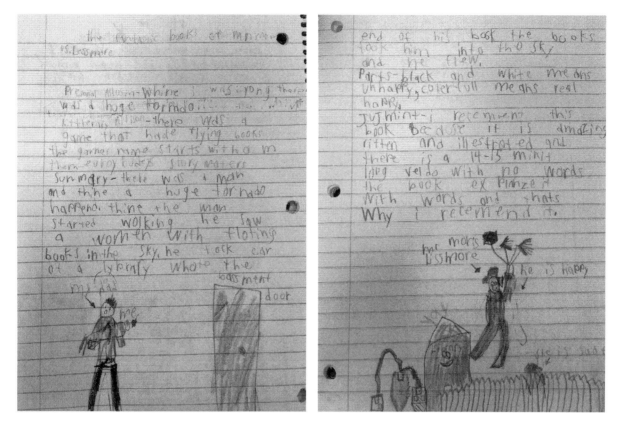

Figure 11.1. A second grader's hexagonal writing.

is so limited with my students that it is much easier and more effective to simply discuss these as they come up, which brings us back to modeling.

Modeling the Hexagonal Strategy

Modeling the hexagonal strategy is vitally important if I want it to become part of my students' literary routines. It is so easy, and takes very little time, to discuss the six parts as I'm reading to students or after reading to students. I typically don't ask students to respond to one of the parts of the hexagonal approach in writing until we have done it together, orally, many times. Because I am so passionate about students making personal and literary allusions while reading, I tend to focus on those two parts of the hexagonal from the very beginning of school. They lend themselves to being perfectly integrated into any lesson on almost any genre I might read to students.

We keep a running list of themes that we've discovered in literature and refer back to it often. This helps us start creating categories of common themes found in literature. This anchor chart also helps students who might struggle to identify the theme of a piece of literature in their general education classroom. Second, third, and fourth graders keep this list in their library journals and can refer to it when they are asked to complete a reading response activity that refers to theme.

Time Management

Due to time constraints in the library, I can't effectively address all six parts of the hexagonal strategy for every piece of literature I read with students. I model using the different parts from the beginning of the school year, and about midyear I choose a piece of literature to do all six parts with, but I split up that lesson into two or three library class sessions. I do want students to see the hexagonal approach completed for at least one piece of literature so that they can witness how the parts create a very good basis for a complete analysis of the literature. It's important to break this up over several sessions so that it doesn't seem like a chore; I want students to enjoy what we do in the library, and I break up the lesson into small enough pieces so that each part is effectively considered.

Time constraints also create wonderful opportunities for collaborating with teachers. The teacher and librarian can work together to complete the parts of the hexagonal strategy between library and class time. This collaboration reinforces the effectiveness of using hexagonal writing as a literary analysis strategy.

During the first reading I have students come up with a summary and make a personal allusion. I have prewriting learners take a piece of manila paper and fold it in thirds. I then ask them to illustrate the beginning of the story, the middle of the story, and the end of the story. On the back of their papers they illustrate a personal allusion they made to the story. This typically takes about ten minutes, because before I asked them to draw their pictures, we will have orally discussed both parts. Students who are able to write using words and phrases are encouraged to add them to their illustrations.

After reading the story again when students return for their next library class, I ask them to illustrate the theme and any literary devices we were able to find in the story. When they return for the third reading, I have them illustrate and write about any literary allusions they were able to make and evaluate the literature. Again, this writing and illustrating take place after we have discussed what we noticed in the literature. I never ask my students to come up with an idea on their own. I make sure that every learner feels successful and has heard several ideas before I ask them to do any independent work.

Some stories are simple enough that three parts of the hexagonal approach can be covered in one sitting. In that case I break the task into two class sessions and allow about ten minutes for students to respond to the literature.

Notecard Houses

It took some experimenting to find a way to incorporate hexagonal writing in such a way that it was manageable in the library setting while maintaining the integrity of the strategy as Carroll intended it. Carroll's hexagonal approach is actually completed on six pieces of multicolored triangles that fit together to make an actual hexagon. That's a lot of cutting when you are trying to teach 800 students to use the strategy. I still wanted a visual way of using the strategy so that students would have something concrete to look at once they put all of the pieces together, and the idea of the notecard house took form.

Once we get to the stage where I believe all students have a firm understanding of the six parts, we put it all together and record the writing and illustrations on notecards. I don't have to cut notecards, and it's handy to keep a supply in the library. It reminds me of my high school days and research projects, but despite those laborious tasks, I still love notecards! They are also just the right size to be easily managed when I have to keep up with 800 sets. Once all the parts are documented, each on its own notecard, I show students how to cut slits in the bottom and top centers of each card. Younger students will need help with this. I might draw lines on the cards where cuts are to be made (now we're reinforcing cutting skills!) Some students may need me to make the cuts for them. This is one of those activities that requires a lot of moving around the library and monitoring. I then have them stack the cards with the summary and personal allusion forming the base, the theme and literary devices in the middle, and literary allusions and evaluations forming the top.

These houses form a nice visual for students to see the level of thinking that occurred in each part of the hexagonal strategy. The cards rise as the level of the critical thinking skills utilized rises. The notecard house also gives shape to a very well rounded (or in this case boxy) analysis of the piece of literature. The houses are easily stored in library journals, can be taken back to class to show their teachers, or can be taken home to help students tell their parents all about the book they read in the library.

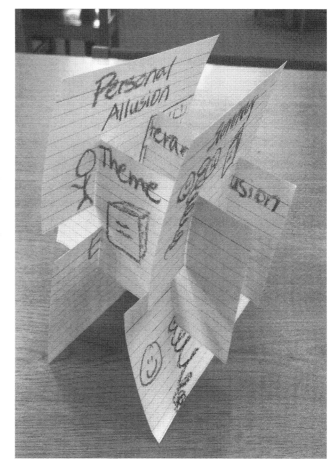

12

Establishing a Writer's Workshop in the Library

Libraries are the reason I'm a writer today. I spent hours after school at my local library, poring over books and doing research. About what? Anything I wanted! That was just the point. I knew that someday I wanted to see my books on those shelves.

—Jennifer Keishin Armstrong

Libraries are progressing beyond simply being places for students to check out books and conduct research. They are evolving to include maker spaces, flexible learning areas, and places for students to hang out and collaborate with peers. It makes sense to me that our school libraries could and should also be places where students come to write and to search for inspiration for writing. After all, we stock some of the best examples of writing in our libraries. Every year, at the beginning of the year I issue a challenge to my students: write something great, and we'll publish it! I sway them with promises of putting their works on the shelves, barcode, MARC record, and all, in order to make them feel like real writers. I originally expected that if any student ever took me up on this offer, it would be one of the older third- or fourth-grade students. To my surprise, it was a first grader who braved the waters of the publishing world for the very first time in my library.

Mackenzie came to me one day with a story she had written about rainbows and the day-to-day life of a first grader. I was so excited that I quickly grabbed one of the blank books I had on standby and told her to rewrite her story in her best handwriting and to illustrate it. I held my breath, not sure if she would remember or even be motivated enough to actually do it, but several days later she proudly returned with her book. As promised, I slapped a barcode label on it and entered a record into our information retrieval system. She was officially an author! She was so proud of her work! Her book has been checked out several times (once she even checked it out herself), and her classmates were so proud of her.

I wish Mackenzie's story was typical, but it seems students aren't so eager to take the risk of putting their writing out there for all to see, so it's a passion and mission of mine to give them every possible opportunity to feel success as a writer. Establishing a writer's workshop in the library doesn't look the same as it does in a typical classroom.

Finding a space to store materials while making them easily accessible to students can be difficult, but I was still determined to set up a writer's workshop in the library to encourage young writers to write and to publish their writing.

Managing Materials

There really are very few materials needed to begin a writer's workshop. You could easily start by simply making available paper and something to write with. The more materials students have access to, the greater the likelihood that they will want to make use of the space and actively write. Kids love being creative and love school supplies almost as much as I do. These are some materials to have in a writer's workshop space in the library:

- Paper: construction paper, colored copier paper, blank books, notebook paper, plain white paper, sticky notes, chart paper, butcher paper, index cards, and so forth
- A variety of writing utensils, such as crayons, makers, pencils, colored pencils, and so forth
- Scissors
- Glue: regular white glue and glue sticks
- Tape
- Dictionaries (these could also be available as apps on handheld devices)
- Access to writing software such as Word, Pages, and so forth

These materials should be stored in a location in the library where they are easily accessible to students and where they have space to write. Ideally the writer's workshop would be held in a relatively quiet section of the library. The space should be well lit and inviting to students. You want a space that encourages creativity.

You also need some system for storing student writing, unless you feel your youngest students could handle taking works in progress back and forth from their classroom to the library. One idea for organizing works in progress is to have files "checked out" to students who are currently working on a piece. I have filing cabinets in my writing space where we store the library journals for second, third, and fourth graders. I have extra space in these filing cabinets to hold files, and they are organized by the rotation day on which the students visit the library, then by grade level. These folders do not have names on them. Students simply store their writing in the folder until they return again to the library.

Another idea would be to have students use folders that they keep in their classrooms and bring with them each time they visit the library. This would allow them to continue working on their writing in their classroom as they have time. If your school or district provides online drives such as Google Drive for students to use, storing their writing online is another option. This would require additional time for teaching students how to log into their drives, but it is a solution if space is an issue. However, I prefer having younger students write on paper.

Making Time for Writing

Given the limited time we have with students, time management is important when first establishing a writer's workshop in the library. There are a couple of ways to work writing into the day. It could be part of the library lesson, and the workshop center could be open for students to use as they have the need for it, or the writer's workshop station could be set up at all times, and students could come and go whenever they have some free time in class, similar to the scheduling of maker spaces in most schools. Procedures will have to be taught to make sure students know how to use the materials in the workshop area and how to store their works in progress.

In my library, as I have mentioned, we write during just about every library visit. I work writing time into my library lesson in the form of response to reading, free writing, prewriting exercises, and book recommendations. Keep in mind that I have students for a one-hour block every six school days. I have the luxury of a decent amount of time with students, which allows me to have them write often. The benefit is that students have many opportunities for structured and free writing while they are with me. The downside is that my library is run on a fixed schedule, which is not ideal for libraries. If your library runs on a flexible schedule, you may not have a large chunk of time with students when they visit you, but you have the freedom to set up a writer's workshop that is more in line with what is actually happening in the classroom, and students are free to come more often, as the library is not scheduled. You can collaborate with teachers on writing projects and assignments and by allowing them to send students to the library to publish. Publishing is often a difficult task to complete in the classroom, especially in the upper grades, as there is so much content to teach. This is a great way for the librarian and teachers to work together, and it seems very natural to have the students publish their works in the library.

Prewriting Activities

Many prewriting activities are discussed in this book. One of my favorites to use during library time is making lists! I love to have students make lists of their favorite books, favorite words, characters and character qualities, places to visit, and so forth. Younger students make lists using pictures and illustrations. It's fun to have them go back to these lists to look for ideas they can expand on when they get ready to write something.

In addition to lists, I have students use any hexagonal writing we've done in the library to write well-thought-out book recommendations. Everything needed to convince someone that a story is one they would like to read is present in the hexagonal writing. Kindergarteners can use their hexagonal writing to create video recommendations or book trailers. There are many options of easy software that can be used to create videos and short films. If you have handheld devices like iPods or iPads, iMovie is a very intuitive creative software to use for book trailers. These can be played on the screen in the library on a running loop or during the morning video announcements on your campus.

Journaling is another good option for prewriting in the library. If students are using library journals, they can make a notation on each day that they come into the library and collect these entries for further writing later on. Students can also free write, or whenever inspiration strikes, they may even feel led to write their own stories. The idea is to get them writing as much as possible.

Publishing

When a student completes a piece of writing and has edited it until she is happy with the final product, I encourage her to publish her writing. I keep blank books in the library for students to use for publishing. These were purchased fairly inexpensively from a library supply store. Once the final product is complete, I barcode the work, enter it into the information retrieval system, and shelve it in the local authors section of the library. Right now that section is a shelf near the door of the library. It is a prominent display to encourage other writers to publish their writing. I hope that one day we will have so many student-published works that they warrant having their own shelf!

13

Research Should Not Be an End-of-the-Year Lesson

Libraries allow children to ask questions about the world and find the answers. And the wonderful thing is that once a child learns to use a library, the doors to learning are always open.

—Laura Bush

Research was a term that struck fear in my heart as a student, especially in high school. I had to research an American poet and write a dreaded research paper on his works and life. While some may find that interesting, it was torture for me. I was being forced to research a person in whom I had very little interest, and I was forced to use a formulaic method of filling so many index cards with questions and answers. I learned next to nothing about the topic I was researching. This exercise taught me that I didn't like research.

However, when I became a parent of a child with autism, I guarantee you I did better research than the Federal Bureau of Investigation, and I enjoyed the hours I spent poring over articles, case studies, and blog posts by other parents who were experiencing the same heartache I was. I was ecstatic when I found out that changing my son's diet could drastically affect his behavior in a positive way, and even more overjoyed when the outcome was one I'd hoped for.

What was the difference in these two research experiences? The difference was that I was researching a topic that was relevant to me and to real life. I was researching because I wanted to, and I discovered information that helped my child but that my child's doctor never mentioned to me.

It was during the course of my son's initial diagnosis that this idea of letting students choose the topics they research finally came to me. If I wanted them to learn how to search for information and do something with the information they found, I had to let them choose topics in which they were interested. It still took me a while to realize that what was most beneficial was to teach them how to research as a means of learning content.

While I was taking courses to earn my library science degree, I had the privilege of studying under Professor Marilyn Joyce at the University of North Texas. Our textbook for the class on research was titled *Making the Writing and Research Connection with the I-Search Process,* a work Professor Joyce coauthored with Julie Tallman (2006). I was immediately intrigued by the title of the book because I had been using the term I-Search for a couple of years, as a take on the popularization of sticking an "I" in front of anything Apple style. However, I had never heard anyone else use this term, and it was really interesting to hear someone finally explain that students are discovering information for the first time. *I-Search* is such an appropriate term for what they are doing, as *re-search* suggests they are searching again for information. Another idea that I latched onto right away was the notion of making the connection between the writing process and the research process. I had never thoroughly considered a connection beyond the actual writing of a research paper. Tallman and Joyce describe the role of the librarian in this process:

> If librarians desire to help students become readers and writers in their discipline, then the process they teach must make those connections and not be isolated to information literacy skills and strategies. The same applies to K-12 media specialists and their attempt to help students create their own successful reading/research/writing process. The process models for both writing and research provide a foundation for development of a research process that connects with the writing process. (2006, 12)

For the first time I encountered a respected librarian and professor suggesting that the librarian play an instructional role in the teaching of writing in the library. Research, or I-Search, isn't a new concept to libraries. Librarians have been aiding in the research process for years. After all, libraries are information centers, and they are also the learning centers of the school. However, now the librarian can move beyond helping students locate information and go one step further, to helping students know what to do with that information and how to form problem-solving habits that will extend beyond the classroom.

Elementary school curricula often place research at the end of the scope and sequence. It is a unit taught at the end of the year, after all of the literacy elements crucial to standardized testing have been taught. It's sometimes an afterthought. This is no fault of the teacher, school, or even the districts. There is so much to cover in a school year. But what if research wasn't taught as a unit at the end of the year, but rather I-Search was taught as routine for learning in any content area being taught?

Project-based learning or inquiry-based learning is a relatively new buzzword in education today. As the library morphs into a learning commons environment, in which information gathering and collaboration with peers are the norm, project-based learning lends itself beautifully to being a joint learning process between the classroom teachers and the librarian. Imagine the implications if students were taught to investigate the curriculum topics designated in the scope and sequence using the I-Search method. Students would become accustomed at an early age to being seekers of information instead of relying on a teacher to stand in front of them and lecture on the content they need to know. They would have the tools necessary to find the information for themselves, evaluate information for relevance, work collaboratively with peers, and take that information and create a product to be shared with others. Now we're talking about life skills! It would be a shame to relegate these skills, so lacking in the workforce today, to a unit at the end of the school year.

David Wray, professor of literacy education at the Institute of Education at the University of Warwick in the United Kingdom, saw firsthand the power of inquiry-based learning when one of his classes focused a study on six-year-olds learning through questioning. What he found was that through the process of inquiry, students learned how to evaluate, read, and write informational text when their learning was centered around an inquiry approach. Traditional classroom teachers are often bound by the demands of a rigid curriculum to teach content. Often there is very little time for students to experiment with inquiry-based learning by choosing topics that truly interest them. In the library, however, I am not bound by those same constraints. I can allow students to pursue topics they are passionate about. Research is sometimes thought of as a skill for older students. However, Professor Wray's study of young students led him to argue that "students should be introduced to nonfiction texts and taught how to learn from them from their earliest days in school" (Wray 2006, 21). School libraries serve all learners at a school. Imagine the difference we could make if librarians took on an instructional role, not just for teaching students how to locate and evaluate information, but to use that information to teach students how to read and write informational text as well.

I have a student who is crazy about dogs. I'm pretty sure she has read every dog book in our collection. Her approach to learning about dogs was to begin with the generic "How to Care for Your Pet" books, and then she moved on to breed-specific research. I showed her how to use the library databases to look up articles and find pictures of dogs. This obsession went on for the better part of the school year. She wouldn't have had time in class to dedicate to her passion, but in the library I was able to teach her not just how to find information about dogs, but how to find information on any topic that might interest her in the future. I have no doubt this foundation will empower her in the future when she is called on to inquire about topics both assigned and of personal interest. This young student, whose interest began when her family brought home a new dog for a pet, ended up publishing her own book about her dog and how to take care of it. She learned how to use information she found from other sources and her own personal experience to teach others about a topic that was of great interest to her. In the process she learned how to find, evaluate, and share information on any topic.

To make research meaningful to students, to get them to a point where it is a method of learning and not a task to be completed, we need to give them opportunities to inquire about topics they are interested in. How do we, as librarians, create this culture in our schools? What is our part in the research process and in making research more than just a lesson at the end of the school year?

The Question Jar

Keep a question jar in the library and let students ask questions about any topic they are interested in. Occasionally throughout the year, pull a question from the jar and do a mini I-Search study on it. Pull books on the topic. Locate articles in the school subscription databases. Make it clear that students can ask any question on any topic as long as it's appropriate for school discussion. Every now and then if a question comes up during our reading and I don't know the answer, I'll write it down and put it in the question jar.

When students have extra time in the library, they can pull a question from the jar and research it. One idea is to keep a fact wall in the library. Students can tape the question from the jar onto an index card and write their findings below it. The index card can then be taped to the fact wall. If another student wants to do further research, she can copy the question onto another index card, and when she is finished gathering information, she can tape the new index card to the original.

Method

One question pulled from our question jar was, "Are whales endangered?" This question came from a second grader, but I decided to use it to teach a strategy from *Making Thinking Visible* called Compass Points (Ritchhart, Church, and Morrison 2011, 93). On a piece of chart paper I put the topic in the center and circled it. From there I labeled the cardinal directions with N, S, E, and W. "N" stands for what we need to know about the topic. What are students' burning questions about whales? Some students wanted to know how big whales can get. Some wanted to know where in the oceans they live. One student wanted to know if more people are hurt by whales or if more whales are hurt by people.

Students brainstorm what excites them about the topic on the "E" side of the chart paper. What do students already know about whales that they find interesting? What facts do they know? What opinions do they have? Here we came up with some very interesting statistics about whales that I had never heard before. Some of our facts were quite obviously untrue, but I still put them on the chart paper. It's a big aha moment when you dispel a myth during research.

What worries or concerns students about the topic is documented on the "W" side of the chart. Whales are huge, scary animals. This was a big concern for younger students. They wanted to know if they ate people, so we wrote that down. Young students, obviously influenced by movies and cartoons, were also concerned that whales could capsize boats when they breech the water. I had a sweet little kindergartener who was worried that whales might become extinct, so we added that to our list.

The final section on our chart was the "S" section. Here we listed which steps we would take to gather our information, what resources we had available to us that we could use to confirm what we already know and to answer questions and concerns that we had about the topic. I made a list of all the library's resources and showed students the books I'd pulled and how to look up information on the library subscription databases. With younger students this research was done orally and over the course of several weeks. The writing that was done was largely dictated by students and transcribed by me onto a class chart. Modeling the method for gathering information and disseminating it teaches students a skill they will use throughout their lives.

Using Compass Points has become a habit any time a new topic of interest is raised in the library. Once I read the book *Little Owl's Night* by Divya Srinivasan (2011) to a group of kindergarteners. One student mentioned that she had learned about owls when her family went on vacation to a national park and she participated in a ranger-led program about owls. This personal allusion prompted other students in her class to begin sharing their knowledge of owls, and several students had questions. I took this teachable moment to record their questions, concerns, and the information they already knew about owls on a Compass Point anchor chart. We then used the book *Owls* by Gail Gibbons and the library databases to investigate the students' questions about owls and find out if their prior knowledge was correct. From this point on Compass Points became a habit for us in the library any time students

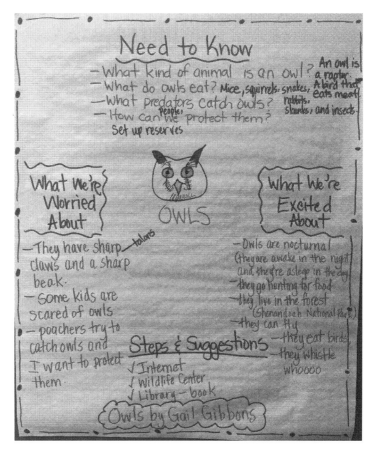

voiced an interest in a topic. Not only am I helping students form research habits that will serve them throughout our lives, but I'm acting on topics of genuine interest to them and creating novelty in my lessons, which makes it even more fun for me!

Resources

There's more to a library than just books! The Dewey Decimal System leads students to books that help them find the information they need. Students need librarians to teach them how to locate information using the other resources available in the library, such as the school's subscription databases. Another way librarians can help young students find information is to locate people in the community or in jobs related to their topic who can answer their questions.

Subscription databases require schools to pay for a site license to give students access. Some popular subscription databases for elementary students are Gale, World Book Online, Encyclopedia Britannica, and National Geographic Kids. These databases offer students access to thousands of articles on thousands of topics. The great thing about these kid-friendly resources is that most offer the ability to have text be read aloud and be translated into other languages, and they even supply a citation for students to use when presenting their information.

When students have looked through books available in your collection and have found all of the relevant articles in your subscription databases, yet they still have unanswered questions, you might then help them turn to an expert to get the answers they need. Students love sending e-mails to people in the community or in jobs related to their topic, in the hopes of getting a reply that answers their questions. This also teaches students a valuable lesson about going outside the walls of the school building to search for information.

This is also a good time to teach students how to locate information on the Internet and how to evaluate Web sites for accuracy and credibility. Our students have grown up using the Internet. Even our youngest learners know that you can find out anything on the Internet, so if we teach them early how to identify quality and credible sources, we can make the search for information more meaningful. Modeling Internet searches and pointing out characteristics of good sources will help students better differentiate among the many returns they'll get during an Internet search.

14

Give Students a Voice

Libraries are the future of reading.

—Courtney Milan

No More Quiet Libraries

It's a fact that libraries are changing. It's more important now than ever before to advocate for library services and for how libraries support education and student achievement. In order to do this, librarians are being called on to meet the needs of all stakeholders on their campuses and to create a library program that supports student learning. School libraries should be about more than just checking out books. Libraries should be seen as the center for learning on their campus. This vision is easily achievable when librarians collaborate with teachers and play an instructional role on their campus.

Libraries should support all types of learning. There should be quiet spaces for students to work or read independently, spaces for students to collaborate with peers on projects for class or simply a shared interest. There should also be instructional spaces in which librarians can do minilessons that support the curriculum and the vision of the school. Librarians are teachers first, and embracing that teaching role will demonstrate the importance of quality library programming.

Whether your library schedule is flexible or fixed, it is possible to establish this type of culture in the library. You may even be setting a new precedent for your campus that greatly impacts the collaborative environment among both staff members and students. Ideally, students would be able to come and go as needed. There would be times for classes to visit the library for literacy and library lessons. Teachers and librarians would work together to coteach lessons or units from the curriculum. The library would be a hub of activity.

Promoting Collaboration and Communication

In order to promote this type of library environment, librarians may have to advocate to school administrators, to classroom teachers, and to the community they serve. In addition to having appropriate spaces for multiple types of learning, librarians need to have a platform for sharing what is happening in their libraries. Set up regular meetings with school administrators to share what is going on in the library. Use social media sites such as Facebook and Twitter to help get information about library programs out into the community.

Share research on the impact of quality library programming on student achievement scores on standardized testing with other librarians in your school district or educational region. Become involved in professional organizations in order to collaborate with other librarians and share ideas with one another. It's imperative that school districts realize the benefits of excellent libraries, so that the possibility of doing away with libraries can't be considered.

One of the best ways to advocate for library programming is to get the students involved and excited about what you have to offer. Give students a voice! Give them opportunities to show off what they have done. Host poetry nights and allow students to share their writing with the community. Display student writing in the library and around the school. Designate an author's chair in the library, a special chair set aside for any students who have published a piece of writing and would like to share it with their classes.

Providing students with opportunities to collaborate through inquiry, sharing writing, and during reading response activities builds confidence, encourages a mentorship environment in which peers learn from each other, and strengthens social connections and self-esteem for all learners. In an article published in *Knowledge Quest*, teacher librarian Buffy Hamilton states, "The possibilities of the library as a learning space disrupt traditional precepts of the library as a data warehouse and instead establish the library as a site of participatory culture" (2011, 35). This culture of collaboration involves a skill set necessary to succeed in today's business culture, one that is sorely lacking in our society. Librarians have a part to play in establishing this culture on their campuses, and teachers and students will benefit tremendously.

In an article for the National Council of Teachers of English, Dr. Joyce Armstrong Carroll identified four types of "talk" used throughout the writing process: alchemistic talk, analytic talk, evaluative talk, and closure talk. Alchemistic talk occurs early in the writing process when students brainstorm with peers, record their thoughts, and then discuss with peers again to narrow their focus. Analytic talk allows young writers to further sharpen their focus by sharing their writing with peers and gaining feedback. Evaluative talk occurs after some revising has been done and the author shares her thoughts with peers, gains additional feedback, and then conducts further revision. Closure talk takes place when students discuss the writing process after it is complete, and it allows students to verbalize their own process, how they feel about their writing, and what insights they might have gained while writing (Carroll 1981, 100–102).

When these four types of talk are made into literacy habits, students learn that collaboration is the way to go! Sometimes young students need to verbalize their thoughts out loud, and hear the responses of their peers, to make sure their intended meaning has come across. I know that when I talk to peers about my writing, or about a book I'm reading, it never fails that I learn something new or change an opinion. The same is true for our students. Making collaboration and talk a habit is important, and beginning with our youngest learners is the best way to make sure the habit sticks.

Conclusion

Imagine with me for a moment any library in any school, in any state. In one nook students are seated in floor rockers silently reading a book or excitedly discussing the latest book in a series they love. Several groups have gathered at tables to work on a presentation to teach their classmates about naked mole rats. They read about naked mole rats in a Mo Willems book and didn't believe the librarian when she told them they were real animals. They had to find out for themselves, and now they want to share their findings with the rest of their class. A couple of other students sit off to the side, putting the finishing touches on their illustrations for the book recommendation they've written. The librarian told them she would display their recommendation on the shelf next to the book they are so excited to review. Yet another small group of students works on their reading response to a book the librarian read to them that day. Students are talking, sharing, discussing, laughing, drawing, reading, writing, and learning! The library isn't quiet, but it is making an impact. Students look forward to their time in the library. Yes, they are excited to check out their next favorite book, but they are equally excited about learning, working together, and establishing literacy habits that will build critical thinking skills they'll use for the rest of their lives.

It's a beautiful vision. One that makes me smile. One that validates my decision to trade my traditional classroom for a much larger classroom that impacts every student on campus. This vision isn't a dream. It's a possibility. It's a reality in many libraries already, and I am so thankful that I get to be a part of it.

Part II References

American Library Association. 2007. *Standards for the 21st Century Learner.* http://www.ala.org /aasl/standards/learning.

Bridwell, N. 1985. *Clifford the Big Red Dog.* New York: Scholastic.

Bruel, N. 2005. *Bad Kitty.* New Milford, CT: Roaring Brook Press.

Buzzeo, T. 2002. *Collaborating to Meet Standards: Teacher/Librarian Partnerships for K–6.* Worthington, OH: Linworth Publishing.

Carroll, J. A. 1981. "The Language Game: Talking through the Writing Process." *The English Journal* 70 (7): 100–102.

Carroll, J. A., and E. E. Wilson. 2008. *Acts of Teaching: How to Teach Writing.* 2nd ed. Portsmouth, NH: Heinemann.

Clements, A. 2007. *Dogku.* New York: Simon and Schuster Books for Young Readers.

DiCamillo, K. 2000. *Because of Winn Dixie.* Cambridge, MA: Candlewick Press.

Edwards, P. D. 2005. *The Neat Line.* New York: Katherine Tergen Books.

Fletcher, R. J., and K. Kiesler. 2003. *Hello, Harvest Moon.* New York: Clarion Books.

Flournoy, V. 1985. *The Patchwork Quilt.* New York: Dial Books for Young Readers.

Gibbons, G. 2005. *Owls.* New York: Holiday House.

Green, J. 2012. *The Fault in Our Stars.* New York: Dutton Books.

Hamilton, B. J. 2011. "The School Librarian as Teacher: What Kind of Teacher Are You?" *Knowledge Quest* 39 (5): 34–40.

Hand, D., S. Grissom, and J. Briggs. 2015. "School Librarians Are Teachers First." *Texas Library Journal* 91 (1): 4–5.

Joyce, W. 2012. *The Fantastic Flying Books of Mr. Morris Lessmore.* New York: Atheneum Books for Young Readers.

Kress, J., and E. Fry. 2015. *The Reading Teacher's Book of Lists.* San Francisco, CA: Jossey-Bass.

Lance, K. C. 2002. "What Research Tells Us about the Importance of School Libraries." *Knowledge Quest* 31 (1): 17–22.

Lance, K. C., and D. Kachel. 2013. "Achieving Academic Standards through the School Library Program: Administrator Perceptions and Student Test Scores." *Teacher Librarian* 40 (5): 8–13.

Lance, K. C., M. J. Rodney, and B. Schwarz. 2010. "Collaboration Works—When It Happens! The Idaho School Library Impact Study." *Teacher Librarian* 37 (5): 30–36.

Litwin, E., and J. Dean. 2010. *Pete the Cat: I Love My White Shoes.* New York: Harper.

McGhee, M. W., and B. A. Jansen. 2005. *The Principal's Guide to a Powerful Library Media Program.* Worthington, OH: Linworth Publishing.

Myron, V. 2009. *Dewey: There's a Cat in the Library!* New York: Little, Brown.

Polacco, P. 1988. *The Keeping Quilt.* New York: Simon & Schuster Books for Young Readers.

Polacco, P. 2013. *The Blessing Cup.* New York: Simon & Schuster Books for Young Readers.

Ritchhart, R., M. Church, and K. Morrison. 2011. *Making Thinking Visible: How to Promote Engagement, Understanding, and Independence for All Learners.* San Francisco, CA: Jossey-Bass.

Spinelli, E. 2008. *The Best Story.* New York: Dial Books.

Srinivasan, D. 2011. *Little Owl's Night.* New York: Viking Children's Books.

Tallman, J. I., and M. Z. Joyce. 2006. *Making the Writing and Research Connection with the I-Search Process: A How-to-Do-It Manual.* 2nd ed. New York: Neal-Schuman.

Thomas, R. 2014. *A to Zoo: Subject Access to Children's Picture Books.* Santa Barbara, CA: Libraries Unlimited.

Valenza, J. K. 2007. "You Know You're a 21st-Century Teacher-Librarian If." *Teacher Librarian* 35 (1): 18–20.

Watt, M. 2007. *Chester.* Toronto: Kids Can Press.

Wray, D. 2006. "An Inquiry-Based Approach to Library Instruction." *School Libraries Worldwide* 12 (2): 16–28.

Part III

Guided by Meaning
Through Early Literacy

Kelley Barger

15

Balanced Literacy

Literacy ought to be one of the most joyful undertakings ever in a young child's life.

—Don Holdaway

Planning and implementing an emergent literacy classroom is like a puzzle. Each piece becomes integral to the whole. As we open the box of our literacy puzzle and investigate how it is designed, we decide how to plan our attack. In the early 1800s our nation firmly believed decoding was the only way to teach young children to read. In the mid-1800s, with Horace Mann's research, America embarked on a new wave of reading instruction. Mann introduced the idea of learning words by sight. Throughout the next 100 years the country swung toward instruction using sight word vocabulary, with years of *Dick and Jane*, controlled vocabulary books written for young readers. From that revolution, we learned from Ken Goodman to utilize picture cues and context clues to figure out unknown words, and he started the movement we know as whole language. The controversy raged over phonetics and decoding or sight words, and teachers had to choose upon which side to stand. Around the middle of the twentieth century researchers began to explore forming a bridge between the two paradigms by introducing both methodologies together to help all learners. In 1998 a panel of reading researchers was created, the National Research Council, which published a controversial report, *Preventing Reading Difficulties in Young Children*. The report calls for young learners to experience both phonetics and sight words while learning to read. Then in 2000 the National Reading Panel released a report that put phonics out front as the best way to teach reading. This report mentioned comprehension and fluency as second to decoding. It went on to extrapolate that reading difficulties stem from lack of explicit instruction in phonemic awareness and phonetic segmentation. The report grossly oversimplified phonetics, and a firestorm of opposition ensued. In the years that followed many scripted phonetics programs rose to popularity, unfortunately at the same time that standardized testing increased in importance to the White House. A divide continued between the phonetic segmented, heavy decoding basals and the whole language camps as a springboard for several diverse methodologies and a new academic freedom in the classroom. As districts argue over which way to teach young readers, we are all winners, as the conversation is loud and very public, inviting teachers to take a stand. The arguments and debates

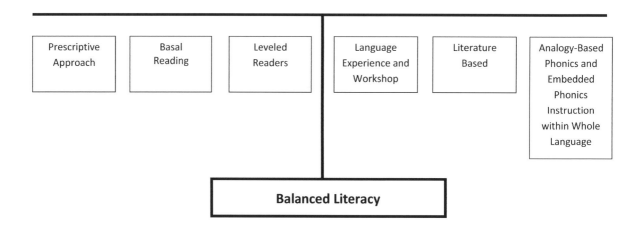

continue and will do so for as long as we are teaching, but we have empowered teachers in the discussion to commit themselves to use any and all methodologies available to meet every reader's unique way of learning.

Prescriptive Approach

This approach touts a skills-based approach based on decoding and phonetic segmentation. This is a bottom-up methodology in which individual letters are taught first, then words, then sentences, and then the reader is invited to read a whole text. The teacher prescribes the lessons synthetically.

Basal Reading

This methodology uses prescribed text and leans heavily on a sequence of lessons aimed at different grade levels. There are phonics-based basal systems, which are scripted, and there are anthology-based basal readers, which focus on embedding skills in rich literature.

Leveled Readers

These programs are published utilizing trade books that are leveled for different readability and teach literary conventions and reading instruction contextualized in the book. Leveled books and multiple copies of titles are sold as part of this system.

Language Experience Approach and Workshop

These philosophies follow continuous activities such as individual- and group-dictated stories, the building of word banks/walls of known words, creative writing activities, oral reading of prose and poetry by teacher and student, directed reading-thinking lessons, the investigation of interests using multiple materials, and keeping records of student progress. This is an interactive approach to reading instruction.

Literature-Based Instruction

This instructional method focuses on meaning, interest, and enjoyment; teachers encourage their students to personally select their own trade books. All objectives are taught in context within a student chosen book.

Analogy-Based Instruction

This instructional method focuses on using prior knowledge of letters and sounds via **"onset"** and **"rime"** to decode and pronounce words rather than only individual sounds. For example, *warehouse* is a compound word, and instead of sounding out each letter and decoding from scratch, the emergent reader sees the word in chunks. The first chunk is *are* inside *ware*, so the student adds the *w* to *are* and says *ware*, then the second chunk is *house*, and she found that on the word wall as a sight word. She has used her prior knowledge to decode this word. Using letter patterns assists the reader in reading fluency and builds confidence as readers extend what they know in the context of a story or sentence (Cunningham 1987, 2013; Cunningham et al. 1998; Goswani 1986; Moustafa 1997).

Embedded Phonics

This instructional method is holistic and meaning-centered at its heart. Readers learns to use semantic and syntactic cues to navigate the orthographic decoding as they read. They use picture cues, context in the story, and their inferences from prior knowledge of life and reading to attack words. The National Reading Panel (2000) posited that the approach is not linear or systematic enough to cover all needed skills; however, the holistic nature of the approach opposes that opinion.

Whole Language

This instructional method is really a belief system that turns the traditional bottom-up classrooms upside down. Whole language posits that classrooms should be centered on the child and what they bring to the classroom. The child learns to read focused on the whole word embedded in text. So students begin with books and stories, and through their prior knowledge of the world they engage in meaning making. This constructivist, top-down philosophy includes all the pieces of language. The students engage in orthographic discovery, semantic and syntactic cues, and pragmatic-centered lessons about their lives and interests (Goodman and Owochi 2002; Goodman 2014). Whole language is often associated with Cambourne's conditions of learning

Cambourne's Conditions of Learning

Immersion in the print, non-fiction, poems, songs, chants and children's literature as they read and write gives students unlimited possibilities to create connections with their world.

Engagement of the students in the classroom full of meaningful experiences with stories, poems, chants, songs, as well as writing invitations and quality children's literature and non-fiction books.

Expectations are held high for each student to read and write each day whether independently, shared, guided, or interactively.

Responsibility for a child's development as a reader and writer is shared by the teacher, the parent, and the students. Each has a role in the classroom learning environment either by inclusion of rich literacy experiences or a print rich environment, but the child is also expected to take responsibility for their own learning through choices.

Response is key in any classroom. We listen to students' stories and approximations and welcome their curiosity about literacy.

Approximation refers to the trials our students will come across and the errors that are bound to be made, but the power lies in the scaffolding that comes after an error and how to try again and again until the students learn to self-correct.

Employment is the idea of giving the child time and freedom to explore literacy in the classroom. When they explore and play with language they engage many areas of the brain together. The teacher can observe and invite the many unique qualities of each learner with the gift of time.

Demonstration represents the instructional strategies teachers can employ to guide, scaffold, and engage students' approximations in the classroom. Demonstration is a way to link hands as we learn from the teacher to the child. The child can then link concepts together that form connections as we read and write in the classroom.

(Cambourne 1988, 1999; Rushton et al. 2003). Cambourne believes that emergent literacy learners take in and hone their strategies and skills of reading and writing when certain conditions are present.

Balanced Literacy

This is a combination of instructional strategies. A good teacher knows her students and their unique needs and picks from all the options available to teach them (Smith 2005). In the early grades reading is more focused on learning to read; this shifts as they move up to middle school and high school, into reading to learn.

Literacy Components

Reading	Writing
Independent Reading	Independent Writing
Guided Reading	Guided Writing
Shared Reading	Shared Writing
Read Aloud	Interactive Writing

When starting our literacy puzzle, laying out all the pieces is a great strategy to be able to see what we have to work with. My strategy is to lay out all the edges until I am left with the intricate job of matching the colors of all the pieces together in the center of the puzzle. The classroom puzzle follows this approach, with the teacher being the puzzle creator. The emergent literacy classroom edge pieces to be laid out include both reading and writing components, which line the classroom with strong literacy boundaries. In his seminal work, *Models of Natural Learning in Literacy Development*, Holdaway (1992) lays out a design that invites demonstration, participation, performance, and practice or role-play within the sharing of writing and reading. Each edge piece is the foundation of literacy that must occur each day in the classroom. So let's lay out the edges of a successful literacy classroom puzzle.

Reading: Independent Reading

One of the most important components of guided by meaning is putting reading first. To learn to read, we must read. Children should choose their own books for their free reading or "ludic" reading time. The word *ludic* comes from Latin and alludes to play or being playful. Students should be playful with reading (Nell 1988.) Emergent readers also have a hand in choosing a book, from a list that is selected and handpicked for their independent reading level, whether in learning centers, "Drop Everything And Read" (DEAR) time, or as take-home reading for pleasure. Teachers monitor and conference, keeping records of their interactions with the texts. During this reading time, the teacher garners every moment of the student's learning by observation. "Kidwatching" is a great way to observe what a child chooses and reads, and how he or she interacts with a book (Goodman and Owochi 2002; Routman 2002) Goodman defines "kidwatching" as continually observing learning with an eye to instructional planning. In other words, as teachers listen to and observe the reading and reading decisions of children, they make plans for how to move them along to the next level in their growth. What children do today impacts what they do tomorrow. Recording these observations can take the form of anecdotal notes (Goodman and Owochi 2002; Routman

2002; O'Keefe 1996). Anecdotal records are notes about observed learning that are written down verbatim, in other words, without opinion. Interpretations or instructional decisions are made about growth during that period of time, and plans are made for instruction. Documenting without opinion invites teachers to see a clearer validity in the growth at the end of the observation period. While the teacher sits with each child and listens to that student read, he or she observes reading behaviors and makes notes for future minilessons to teach, as well as learning about the child's interests.

One afternoon a group of kindergarteners was working in the home center and Esmerelda, apron on and arms elbow deep in the sink full of water, turned to Joey and told him to make sure to add dish soap to the shopping list. I watched as Joey went over to the refrigerator and took down a piece of paper that was taped to the fridge door, then went to sit at the dining table, all while holding a baby doll wrapped in a blanket. He picked up a pencil and wrote, "dis sop." I leaned over his shoulder and peeked at the list. What a shopping list it was! Joey and Esmerelda were planning to purchase Mt, ceees, spgti, diprs, and of course dis sop. I asked the young couple, "I see you have lots on your grocery list. Are you planning a big dinner?"

"Oh yes, Visnu, Bobby, and Stephanie are coming for supper," Esmerelda told me as she was putting her clean dishes on the table, and she suddenly turned to tell Joey to write down Lemonade.

"Oh I love Lemonade! Can I come?" I asked.

"We only have five chairs!" Esmerelda said, looking around.

"Well, maybe tomorrow. Do you ever write things down on the list?" I asked.

"I put the paper on the 'fridge' with tape!" she said, pointing to the note taped on the wooden, child-sized refrigerator.

"Who wrote meat, cheese, spaghetti, and diapers?"

With one hand on her hip she pointed to Joey.

I learned many things about Esmeralda and Joey in that center time. I picked up my clipboard with Post-its™ attached and wrote Esmerelda on one of them. After her name, I wrote:

> Esmerelda
> was playing in home center washing dishes and planning for a dinner party with three friends. She directed Joey to write down items for the grocery list. As she was setting the table she called out to add lemonade to the list. I asked her if she ever wrote the list and she responded that she created the list but told Joey to write the items down and put it back on the frig.
> (*understands there is a purpose for writing* ☑; *dictating a list* ☑)
> **Writing a list in her hand; "kidwatch" for her using her constructed spelling process**

I learned that she understands why we write grocery lists and that there is a purpose for writing and reading in our world. Esmerelda also understands that she can tell someone else to do it for her by dictation. This anecdotal record is coded for my observation and progress notebook. The words in boldface indicate a factual record of exactly what happened to capture the moment without interpretation. The italicized words are for my progress records to show new understanding and/or transfer of knowledge. The words in bold guide my instructional planning for a future mini-teach on writing a list in her own hand with constructed spelling. I put a þ when a student has mastered a checkpoint on our scope and sequence/grade level expectations, and a « when the concept is ongoing and to remind me to keep an eye for transfer of the concept in her writing (Clay 2000).

I also made notations for Joey:

Joey

was playing in home center taking care of a baby (baby doll wrapped in a blanket) when Esmerelda called out to him to make sure to add dish soap to the shopping list. I observed Joey walk over to the refrigerator and pull down a taped piece of paper and take it, baby and all, to the dining table. He wrote dis sop on the bottom of the list. As I looked at the note, I noticed the words "Mt, ceees, spgti, diprs." After he added dish soap, he taped the note back up on the refrigerator.

(understands there is a purpose for writing ☑*; took dictation from another student about an item on a list* ☑*; confidently sat down to write and used constructed spelling* ★*; uses 90% consonants in his constructed spelling* ★*)*
"Kidwatch" for usage of vowels in his writing/constructed spelling

I learned that Joey is a confident writer who doesn't hesitate to write using constructed spelling. He is still primarily using his consonant sounds, but occasionally inserts vowels. I will continue to watch for his progress with his sound to symbol progression. The anecdotal notes will be filed in my observation and progress notebook under the designated student's name, and I will share these notes at parent conferences and refer to them when assessing for report cards. Anecdotal records assist the teacher with ongoing assessment of understanding in authentic situations.

During this time of reading, the teacher also interacts with the emergent readers. Reading conferences give the teacher a chance to listen for the lessons already taught to see if the child is transferring the knowledge to real-life reading (Avery 1993; Gallagher 2015; Atwell 2007, 2014). Independent reading is foundational due to the guided sense of the reading choices and practice.

Reading: Guided Reading

As children practice reading, they also need strategy instruction and assistance as they move forward. Guided reading replaced traditional reading groups and became a standard literacy practice after the publication of research by Fountas and Pinnell (1996) on their work in reading recovery. Guided reading structures the explicit teaching of skills and strategies good readers need. For example, while "kidwatching" during independent reading, I noticed Precious standing with two friends, Emily and Casey, with their heads in a book. I asked them to hurry and pick their books so they could have time to read. After Precious picked her book, I leaned down next to her to listen as she read. I use whisper reading to listen to my young readers: I lean down next to them, and when they see me positioned at their side close to their heads, they begin to whisper the reading, so it is between the two of us. I do this to prevent their being embarrassed by reading in front of peers. Precious opened the book she was currently looking at and started to read the book she had chosen. As she was reading I noticed a skill to build a future mini-teach on. I learned that Precious doesn't use the picture cues to figure out a word. She prefers to sound out the word, and if she can't get it, she skips it. I noted this on my clipboard under her name and wrote on my future mini-teach list: "Using Picture Cues while reading." After listening to all three young ladies, I noticed that they all struggled with what to do when they became stuck on a word. We had had a few mini-teaches on how to figure out a word in context, but these three girls needed a refresher or reteach. During guided reading time I pulled the three girls together and took a big book and three small books to the table.

> Teacher (**T**): I have a great story here for us called *The Little Mouse, the Red Ripe Strawberry, and the Big Hungry Bear* by Don and Audrey Wood. What do you notice about the cover of the book?
>
> Emily (**E**): There is a big strawberry on it.
>
> Precious (**P**): Look at that mouse on a ladder!
>
> **T**: Look at the title at the top of the book. (Pointing to the title.) Do you see the word Strawberry in the title? What sound would Strawberry start with?
>
> Casey (**C**): /S/ the letter S.
>
> T: Right! Do you see a letter S that makes the sound /S/?
>
> E: That is the word /s s s s/ /t r a/ /b e r e/ strawberry.
>
> T: It sure is the word strawberry. How did you figure that out, Emily?
>
> E: I looked for the s because I know s says /S/.
>
> T: Precious, you noticed the mouse also; can you find the word mouse in the title?

I continued priming the students to read *The Little Mouse, the Red Ripe Strawberry, and the Big Hungry Bear*, being careful to model how readers identified words using picture cues. I also added four other cues that helped us figure out words we didn't know. I

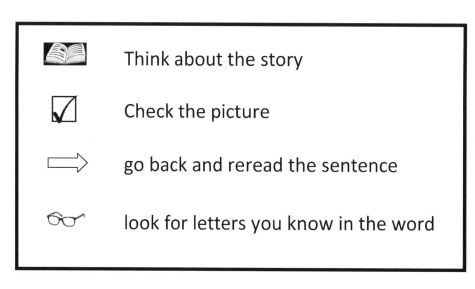

gave the girls a regular-sized copy of the book and a bookmark with graphics showing the five ways to figure out a word, with a picture cue before each one. As they used their bookmarks and cues to figure out words, I monitored their reading and leaned down to listen to them whisper read. So the small guided reading group was formed when I found students who had similar needs and did a mini-teach.

The teacher supports the reader through small, *flexible* groups, like my four girls who needed help with figuring out a word. In the group the teacher directly teaches reading strategies, which the reader uses independently while reading. These strategies could be decoding, with lessons on phonograms or word families, main idea, visualizing, inference, and so forth. Reading instruction happens before, during, and after the reading to cement the concepts explicitly taught, ranging from word work (Cunningham 2013) with decoding to making connections from the reading (Caine and Caine 1998; Keene and Zimmermann 2007).

> *Before the Reading*: In a small group of readers who have similar needs, the **teacher chooses a book to teach a strategy** explicitly and introduces it to the group with their own copy.
>
> *During the Reading*: The teacher models the strategy and then the **readers practice the strategy** with the group book in their hands.
>
> *After the Reading*: The teacher monitors their practice by listening to them whisper read and looking in their reading notebooks.

In this foundational edge of our literacy puzzle, the teacher assesses progress through leveled reading boxes created with trade books aimed at different readability levels for the many types of readers in the classroom. Each child has his or her own box or bag of leveled readers/books, poems, stories, and songs.

Reading bags are created to include materials for individual readers. They include books, poems, stories, and songs that are written at the child's independent level of reading to build confidence and fluency. The bags might also include materials that are written at their instructional level to challenge the reader, but the bags are always in keeping with the interest of the child.

Conducting informal assessments designates students' instructional level, frustration level, and independent level reading aids in the creation of the leveled reading material for each child. This might include giving them a basic reading inventory as an informal assessment in the classroom. Another form of assessment for young readers entails retelling the story. The market has been inundated with supportive manipulatives such as story cubes and sequence pocket charts to accomplish a retelling, as well as designs for creating storytelling gloves and flannel boards. A rubric also helps in determining the quality of the retelling.

Emergent readers thrive on tools like wall charts and mnemonics for remembering what to do if they get stuck on a word or idea in the story. One such mnemonic is a hand, on each finger of which is an option for helping them figure out the word, like the bookmark used above in the mini-teach. Readers think about the story, check the picture, go back and read the sentence again, look for word parts they know, or ask themselves if the word looks like another word they know. The more ways we find to remind students about strategies that good readers use, the more we can give our students tools for success.

Word work (Fountas and Pinnell 1996; Cunningham 2013) explicitly teaches how guided reading can create a foundation for young readers to grab onto the orthographic system of reading as they come to words they don't know. To support decodable texts, bring out magnetic letters and boards and manipulate the word structures. For example, put the phonogram /ug/ on a magnetic board and then slide the /h/ in front of /ug/; the child will read **hug** and the young reader could replace the /h/ with r, m, d, p, and then venture into blends with /sl/ and /pl/, to make slug and plug.

This quick word work lesson can detangle a word by dissecting the parts into word chunks, phonograms, or word families. Once you model how to create words that follow the patterns in the decodable text, let the reader practice making words using the same patterns with other letters. When a small group of students is working in the same book, take the group through word work with the words found in the book to start with the whole story, then isolate the words to work with them, and go on to the key stage of replacing them back into the story to finish the lesson. For decades, American schools prescribed using a letter of the week and isolating the sounds in teaching. We now know that emergent readers need to control the letters in the context of story. Our brain is wired for story (Haven 2007, 2014). Taking letters out of context and teaching them in isolation can distort the assimilation of a working schema for reading (Donaldson 1979; Wilde 1991; Goodman 2014). Using quality children's literature allows the teacher to highlight word work and literacy conventions and invite social construction.

Guided reading is foundational in our puzzle, but to accomplish small group work in the emergent classroom, a teacher employs classroom management strategies like learning and/or literacy centers to encourage engagement as the small groups are pulled aside. Literacy centers are independent activities that are self-checking and supportive of the strategies and skills being taught to large groups as reading/writing connections. Literacy centers are not worksheets and are not worksheet driven. Interactive centers are designed to be one on one or two on two micro groups focused on a task aimed at the social construction of meaning with literacy. These centers include things like "read the room," "alphabet soup," writing center, and big books. As the children are engaged at their centers, the teacher pulls a guided reading group together to work with them. I put up small cards that have pictures of the center and a label on them with small dots on the bottom. I have as many as six to eight options for the students during literacy time: rebus story, sticker story, word families, build a sentence, songs, letter writing, poems and chants, read the room, environmental print stories, listening center with audiobooks, flannel board, and puppet stage.

My students love to write rebus stories. Rebus means the story is represented in pictures and words. I put out a box of pictures I have cut from magazines and old books and games, then the young writers pull out the pictures they want in their stories and write using the pictures to represent the words when the graphic representations are in a story. This helps the writers represent the item or concept graphically and alleviates the need to construct the spelling for every word. The pictures often represent concepts or items that are integral for the story but more advanced in spelling construction. As my students are engaged with their literacy centers, I pull out my guided reading groups as one of their options and rotate the groups and centers.

Reading: Shared Reading

As in independent reading, children practice reading alone and with peers. Shared reading is an activity in which reading is shared between the child and the teacher. Holdaway (1979) first introduced us to shared reading as a "shared book experience," opening a world of reading to all children. The emergent reader, with the assistance of the teacher, could READ a story, song, chant, poem, or rhyme by sharing the text with the teacher. The theory of shared reading stems from the teacher reading the material first and using repeated readings with the children as they join in on repetitive or predictable text, or the whole story as the text becomes more familiar. This experience often uses a big book, but don't discount any type of reading materials. Picture-driven text is the most supportive of young readers. Brain research teaches us that we all house mirror neurons that help us mimic behaviors, emotions, and expressions (Ramachandran 2012). We actually learn by observing. Children watch the teacher read, and as they learn the text, they join in with their voices. They learn by collaboration through their mirror neurons.

Each week in my balanced literacy classroom, I brought the kindergarteners around the circle rug facing my rocking chair and big book easel. One Monday I opened a large copy of *The Cow That Went OINK* by Bernard Most. The students began to lean into the pictures, and their faces lit up as their eyes scanned the pictures of a cow and a pig. I asked them what they saw on the cover, and they all called out, "cows!"

"Do you see that little cloud next to the cow right here?" I asked as I pointed to the cow standing all by itself.

"It means he is talking," Luke called out. I wasn't surprised, as he loved comic books and thus was familiar with speaking bubbles.

"You are right, Luke. Can you read what it says?" I pointed to the work OINK, and we sounded it out together, with my voice leading in timber.

"O I N K?" They laughed and shook their heads, looking at each other.

I laughed with them and said, "Well, we better open this book right now to find out about this funny farm." This particular cow only oinked. The other animals laughed at her, except the pig, who went MOO. As they started teaching each other their language, the children laughed and called out the words they were saying as I pointed to the talking bubbles. We chanted the animals' laugh: "Rippet Ha, Tweet Ha, Cook a Doddle Ha, and Gobble Ha." After we read the book, I told the young readers that the book would be in the library center all week with pig and cow puppets so they could act out the story.

Shared reading is rooted in experiential learning. In other words, children learn to read by reading. The procedures illustrated in the example are suggested below, but remember that your students' needs should guide the structure that you use in your classroom.

- **Introduce the story and prime the students:** Activate prior knowledge, ask for predictions, and talk about the author and the cover of the story.
- **Read the story:** Share the text with the reader while asking questions to check comprehension and invite predictions. Chorally read the predictable text and point to repetitive portions.
- **After the story:** Together, read the repetitive parts of the story and discuss the ideas within the story, or extend the story with creative dramatics, chants, and songs, or even sequence with the high points.
- **Reread** the story together as long as they enjoy it.

Some teachers do repeated readings over a period of time, and some do them on the same day, but I caution that you should know your students and what their attention span is, as repeated readings can be overdone in a compressed time period. Each time, invite the children to join in the text and input dramatics, music, movement, and joy. As the children watch your verve, they mirror the emotions, expressions, and behaviors to emulate your reading.

Reading: Read Aloud

Read aloud is a strong edge piece in our puzzle. The joy of story is the core of reading. The teacher picks a book for read aloud that is on any level, as long as it is content appropriate, and then adapts the time limit based on the students' attention span. The goal for read aloud is to introduce stories so students can find themselves in books through rich characters and interesting locations. The pure essence of story emanates from the reading into the classroom with a read aloud. Haven (2014) states that our brains are wired for story, and it pulls us into what is happening as the logic unfolds in the story structure. The characters come alive with the human voice speaking the author's words.

In my classroom, we highlight an author a week and enjoy at least one book each day. On one occasion, I was starting circle time with a classic by Bernard Most about dinosaurs. I was reading *Dinosaur Cousins*, and one of my friends stopped me by raising his hand and saying, "STOP! What did you say?" I repeated the part I had just read, and he said, "That sounds just like that other book we read a long time ago." I asked him what the other book was about, and he told the class that it was all about how animals that are cousins often stay in the same areas of the zoo.

"Oh you mean, *A Visit to the Zoo* by Aliki?" I asked as I walked over and found the book in our library center. "That is it, let me show you!" I put him in my lap in the author's chair, and he found exactly where the book talked about how animals that are alike are put close to each other in the zoo, just like in the wild. I smiled and told him he was a great listener. I was excited that he had made a great text-to-text connection with *Dinosaur Cousins*. I hoped the other listeners would make those connections; it is terrific to hear them when they do.

"Well, thank-you friends, we seem to know a lot about animals of all kinds," I said. The students were beginning to understand that real people write books, just like they do. On another occasion, as we read *The Important Book*, I stopped and struggled with a word and invited the students to help. I talked about the important things and asked questions about the text out loud as I read, to model how good readers read books.

Teachers can use "think alouds" (Dole et al. 1991) as they read to *model how reading is done*. Teachers explicitly model by stopping and discussing how they figure out a word or idea as they read, or they can implicitly model as they stop and ask questions (Hoyt, 2008), such as, "I wonder why Ruby wanted to learn how to read and write when other girls in China didn't?" In *Ruby's Wish* by Shirim Yim-Bridges (2015), little Ruby was growing up in China and wanted to take classes with the boys when the other little girls were expected to learn how to cook and do needlework. Her grandfather allowed her to go to school with the boys as long as she kept up with her cooking and needlework lessons. As children listen to the teacher read the story, they also might be wondering why only boys learned how to read and write in China during that time and why Ruby wanted to do both when the others did not. By stopping and asking the students, as well as asking herself, the teacher is providing a great example of implicit modeling of internal questions, which helps children form inferences as they read (Dole et al. 1991). This helps the children use their mirror neurons to learn how to question a text as they read independently. As I read, I share my thinking with the listeners so they can see how to handle a word they might not recognize. Through this process, the children can gain insight into things a good reader can do to figure out the word in context. The teacher might say, "Oh I know that word . . . it starts with a B and I see a picture of a ball, so it must be . . . BALL." This type of implicit modeling can show children how to use great strategies as they read.

Our reading foundational puzzle edges are complete, so we now move on to writing to round out our literacy puzzle.

Writing: Independent Writing

Our balanced literacy puzzle continues with the writing foundational pieces. Once these four pieces are set in place, our puzzle activity will be focused on the center, while bringing in all the colorful and creative complexities of an emergent classroom. Just as independent reading is the forefront of our reading, so independent writing is central in our writing. Writers choose to write about topics of their choice, from dinosaurs to setting up a lemonade stand. The variety is exciting to watch as they write, research, illustrate, rewrite, and publish stories and how-to books. One of my kindergarten students, Ian, loved his pet turtle so much that he and his mom came up to me after school one day and asked if he could bring it to school. I smiled and told him, "Of course, as long as you bring him first thing in the morning and sit in the author's chair and read a story you have written about how to care for a turtle." His grin spread from ear to ear; his mom wasn't smiling. She leaned in toward me and whispered, "Ian is a *non-reader*!" She didn't want Ian to find out! I knelt down to Ian and asked him, "Ian, do you need to go to the library today to read about turtles to get some information before you write your book?"

"Oh yes, I do!" he responded. "I know right where to find a great turtle book about how to take care of a turtle like my Maximilian, but we just call him Max."

"Don't forget to ask the librarian for help; she can show you lots of great books about caring for a pet."

"Yes, ma'am, can I write my story during center time?"

"Absolutely!" I said as I smiled at his mom. Ian ran off, happy in his adventure of planning, while his mom just looked at me. I assured her that he would create a great book and that both the librarian and I would assist him, "You will be amazed at what Ian will read and write when he is motivated by a Max visit!" Ian did go to the library that day, and he and the librarian found three great books. You see, we have one of those librarians who, rather than showing my kindergarten students only picture books, asks, "How can I help you find something great?" Ian went directly to the writing center during center time and worked the whole time on his creation. At author time, he came over and, just like his mother, leaned in to whisper, "I am almost done, but I am saving it for tomorrow when everyone can see Max while I read."

"What do you have left to do?"

"Just the illustrations, and I can do those at home."

"Ok, I can't wait to see Max and hear your story. You have been a hard-working researcher today."

Ian did bring Max in the next morning and read his amazing story about turtles. Yes, he used constructed spelling! Yes, he had illustrations and lots of description in his story. He sat up so proudly in the author's chair as the class watched Max strutting around inside our circle of friends. Oh, and by the way, he also brought a note from his parents: "Thanks for inviting Max to class and our son to show us he is a reader and a writer! We will be by to pick up Max at 9:30."

Allowing children to have control over genre and topic invites writing rather than page after page of, for example, the same pilgrims and turkeys on your wall at Thanksgiving. I watched Ian as he wrote and observed his process, and I aided in his approximations of letters and sounds, but the writing ownership was right where it belonged: in Ian's hands. During independent writing time, teachers monitor and conference with the writers and take anecdotal notes. Just as an art teacher in an art studio observes the students' painting and interacts with them as they paint, the teacher in a balanced literacy classroom moves about the classroom, learning about the potential of the children as they learn from their own language.

The language experience approach (LEA) (Veatch 1979) is associated with pedagogy that stems from the child's language. It was originally introduced as a reading methodology, but has evolved in my classroom as a language methodology, as it engages reading, writing, speaking, listening, and viewing. When a child is guided by meaning, he or she enters the process with unique experiences and language. If we celebrate rather than try to fit their writing into a predetermined mold of correctness, we won't miss the possibilities of what students can do. Lucy Calkins's words ring in my ears as I work with children of all ages: "Celebrate what they are doing rather than what you wish they were doing" (1994). Look deep into their constructed spelling and dig out what they are thinking. Then I look at the standards, scope and sequence, and benchmarks and match those up to find out how to move that child forward.

For example, Hadley, a first grader in St. Louis, is learning through her language construction and approximating how we use root and compound words. As I celebrate her ingenuity and use of resources, I can also see she is putting words together to form larger words as well as isolating the sound /w/, as she looks at the word wall under W for the word *where*. Has she spelled it incorrectly? No; she has approximated the word and constructed her meaning from it. The word wall guided her meaning, and it was crystal clear. This teacher tells me she is using all the wonderful resources in our classrooms to assist the young writer.

The language experience approach remains a dynamic teaching pedagogy for our time working with ELL (English Language Learner) students who are learning to write and read and children who won't let convention stop their creations.

Writing: Guided Writing

In the guided writing puzzle piece, I support the writer through small, flexible groups. In the group I directly teach writing strategies that writers will use independently while writing their own pieces. This is where I can use all the information they gathered through observation during independent writing and my anecdotal notes to support the progress of the young writers. The groups remain flexible, as they are created by need. For example, if you have a group of young writers that might need a lesson on how to use the resources in the classroom, like word walls, individual dictionaries, or word banks, pull the writers together for a quick mini-teach (Carroll 2007). This lesson can send them on their way to then practice it in their independent writing. Word banks are great resources for the classroom, as they create a visual dictionary for the students based on what they have been reading.

During the mini-teach, I model the strategy and then the writers practice. After the lesson I monitor their progress and note the transfer of the information into their process of writing. The writing notebook is a great way to observe the ways the writers

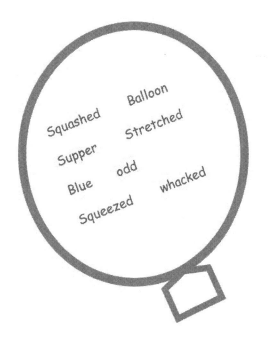

This word bank is from *The Blue Balloon* by Nick Inkpen. The students knock on the floor as I read when they come to a word they don't know or they think is really cool. We spell it out and write it on the word bank, and it becomes a visual dictionary in the room for future reference by young writers who want to use one of the words in their stories. The brain is alerted to the memory of the book, the topic, and the color.

have used the information. For example, Hadley, a young writer, wanted to write a letter to an author to tell him about something she had noticed in his latest book. After I asked if any of the other students were thinking of doing that as well, four students were gathered who were interested in writing a letter to an author, and a mini-teach was organized by priming the students about letters. As a model, they were asked to help me write a letter to the author who was being studied in the class that week. So the class wrote a letter to the author, using their voices as the letter was written on a large chart paper so they could see the writing and hear the think aloud as the letter was written in the correct format. After the lesson, Hadley began writing a letter to Tomie DePaola. A copy was put in her portfolio to show that she had transferred the information to other writing.

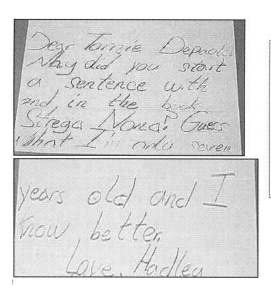

January, 2004 1st grade
Hadley wrote a letter to Tomie DePaola about his book *Strega Nona* and his sentence structure. Hadley has a great understanding of empowerment in writing what you feel. She is an author and she sees it as her duty to let another author know his mistake so he can fix it.

Writing: Shared Writing

The shared writing puzzle piece is as integral as the shared reading piece, because they represent a window into the child's thinking processes. Just as you share the reading in shared reading, you should share and celebrate the writing in shared writing. Many teachers use strategies such as morning message (Graves 1994; Graves and Kittle 2005; Wells 2009; Wasik and Bond 2001), in which they take advantage of the morning entry of the students to involve them in writing. In the sample below, you can see that the teacher had an easel set up with chart paper filled out with a message for her students to read when they entered the classroom. Depending on the age or ability of the students, I read the morning message with the students using the shared reading method and share the pen with them so a student can write in the blanks. Sharing the pen is a method wherein the teacher and the student both write on the chart. The teacher leaves underlined spaces on which the student can add words that have been learned (Tompkins 2003). The students then fill out the graph below with their names.

This morning message is prewritten with lines for the students to fill in. The bottom has a graph on it for the students to interact with their pen. The more authentic the writing the more the learning so write with the students as much as your students can handle.

Shared writing is a collaborative approach to writing instruction that helps broaden children's understanding of written language. Through shared writings, children develop confidence in their abilities as writers and an inventory of skills and strategies to use during their independent writing. I scribe in front of the children with shared writing so they can model prewriting strategies and write aloud (Higgins, Miller, and Wegman 2006), such as listing ideas, making pictures, and using different genres of writing. For example, my kindergarten class was writing a story about penguins because the local zoo had opened a new penguin and puffin house, and all the young writers were

very excited to go research it firsthand. So as a class, we took up the pen and began to think of characters for our LEA group story. They had all seen the movie about penguins and how happy their feet really are, so this writing helped to dispel some of the misconceptions that we had acquired in our previous experiences. We had read *Tacky the Penguin* by Lester, *Little Penguin's Tale* by Wood, and many fact books about penguins to supplement our knowledge. So the students were most interested in writing about the emperor and little blue penguins. We drew a large Venn diagram and listed all the characteristics of both kinds of penguins.

As you can see, they really had a lot of great facts to share. This type of shared writing experience involves the students calling out things and the teacher writing *verbatim* exactly what they are saying in order to retain their voice. This is a beautiful example of a language experience story and learning about prewriting through a child's voice. We went on to think about a story map for the story and brainstormed via chart paper for our setting using blueprinting (Stillman 1991; Carroll and Wilson 2008), which is a prewriting strategy that involves the students drawing a map of a place and then labeling it with ideas for a story. We drew the habitat of the penguins and then filled in the picture with action shots of what the penguins in our story would be doing. Whether you take the prewriting to a full class story as we did, or stop with prewriting ideas for them to write about, shared writing promotes the writing process by showing students the functionality within the enjoyment of writing by modeling. Those mirror neurons will be firing as they approximate the text while creating a story that is miles above their emergent writing abilities. This demonstrates the process in action and enhances participation in all stages of the writing process: brainstorming, writing, revising, editing, and publishing. Shared writing provides opportunities to plan, organize, and construct texts. It also includes exploring the conventions of spelling, grammar, and punctuation in a meaningful context of story. This component of a balanced literacy classroom is especially helpful with young writers and ELL students who are new to the language, as it is supportive of their voices and is guided by meaning.

The LEA stories brought to my students confidence as writers and ownership of the story. What they might not be able to construct with their own hands, I helped them write from their voices onto paper. I also like to bring down fifth graders to help with

LEA stories for my kindergarten students, as they write their words down verbatim in their own hand like a pro. Many emergent writers can tell stories that are so elaborate and creative the mind boggles, but they lack the fluency to get all the twists and turns of the story onto paper in their own hand. Dictated stories in the LEA tradition help them feel ownership of the story while utilizing a helping hand. Vygotsky calls this the zone of proximal development. He defines the concept in his seminal work *Thought and Language* (2012, 110): "[W]hat a child does in cooperation today, he can do alone tomorrow." For example, in shared writing a child can tell a story that is complex and descriptive, but once she tries to write it out, her language fails her and she becomes frustrated. She begins to think, "why even try, it is too hard." So she simpifies the story down to choppy little sentences that tell half the story, without the rich language and description in the telling. However, a more advanced writer can dictate the story and still own the story with all the unique qualities of authorship. Now, there is a time to pull away from the coauthor when the child progresses in fluency and can attempt the story on his own. If the child is left too long with the scribe, he can rely too heavily on her and fail to attempt his own construction of the text. Shared writing can provide the same experience via a dictated group story.

Now back to those kindergarten students intent on a penguin story. We brainstormed about our setting in blueprinting and brainstormed the characters in a Venn diagram and learned about their enemies in the stories we read. My students were ready with their great creation, and I was ready to transcribe it verbatim. Below you will see the penguins' story, rich in dialogue and descriptive action, packed with the adventure of the great frozen icebergs they call home.

Transcript:

The seals swam around and around. They watched the penguins play on the icy land. The seal is the enemy of the penguin. One brave king penguin waddled down to the water and told the seals, "You have to help us." The big seal looked up and swam cloooooer to the penguin. "MMMaah," said the seal. Then two little penguins waddled up and clapped, "Quiet!!" Everybody looked at the new penguins. The little blue penguins clapped on their lips, "We have to hurry, the hunters are rough and tough." The little blue penguin could hear thump, thump, thump. "RUN!!!" The seal ran. The penguins waddled. The hunters couldn't find the pretty little blue and King penguins so they took their maps and traps and thumped home.

As you can see, the class revised the story by adding adjectives and changing out a tired word. The shapes on the sides are the story map pieces we did to get ready to structure our story so we could make sure it contained all the story parts. The keys at the end are the keywords we added to our word bank for the penguin story. I spend about half the year with LEA group stories, starting on day one to build students' understanding of story and confidence in writing. We continue on with these stories throughout the in interactive writing and guided writing to help learn lessons, and at the same time that we write LEA group stories, we also do independent writing.

Writing: Interactive Writing

In interactive writing as a foundational puzzle piece, the teacher interacts with the students to refine their writing. This component of writing involves the teacher working one on one with an emergent writer on his writing to think through the construction of a concept or word. As we observe students' independent writing and shared writing, we assist them by explicitly instructing in guided writing. The teacher takes the writing and explicitly teaches the young writer to get closer to convention. Word construction while making letter-sound connections, conventions of print, and writing for an audience are just some of the possible refinements a teacher and writer could work on. Interactive writing differs from shared writing, as it is targeted on refinement. For example, I was teaching a third-grade writer, Miyana, at a local elementary school, and she began with the creation below.

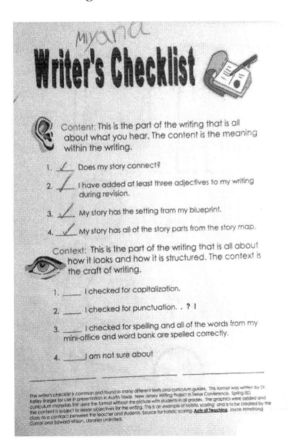

In the Content portion of the Writer's Checklist, the first item on Miyana's list to check in her story is to make sure the story sounds the best it can sound.

Does my story connect?

Miyana looked back at her story and read over it again with her bridges in place and said, "Yes, Yes it does!"

She checked that item and moved to number 2.

Miyana now understands that a story needs to connect all the way through so readers of the story understand as they read.

Her story sounds the best she can make it sound!

She created a basic story map with the parts of a good story. The story map included characters, setting, story problem, events, and story solution.

She mapped out her story by placing the parts of the story in an order she felt dictated her meaning. She took small icons of the story map and put them in an order down the side of her paper to remind herself of how she wanted to structure her story. The important thing is that Miyana decided on the structure of her parts. Once she had finished her first draft, she came to read it to me:

T: Will you read me your story?

M: SURE.

(As she read the story she stopped between each section of it where the paper had white spaces.)

T: Why did you stop reading and pause here and here? *(pointing to the white spaces)*

M: I don't have anything written there!

T: I see that, why is that?

M: I don't know.

T: Sometimes when authors are writing their stories, they have white spaces also. They have to build bridges to connect the pieces of writing. Have you ever been on a bridge?

M: Yeah, I went on a bridge at the zoo.

T: Why did you walk on the bridge?

M: To get to the other side. The Monkeys were on the other side of the water and I wanted to see them.

T: Well, that is exactly why authors use bridges in their writing. As they are reading, they want to get to the next part of their writing. So they create a bridge between two pieces of writing.

M: Oh . . . like here! *(pointing to the first white space)*

T: Exactly! I have these Post-its® that will serve as our bridges, and we can place one in each place you think you need a bridge.

T: Great places! The bridge at the zoo was for walking, but these bridges are for writing, so what do you think needs to be on the bridges?

M: Writing?

T: We have bridges placed there, so let's take these bigger Post-its® that match and write what we want on the bridge. First let's read what is on either side of the first bridge.

Miyana read both passages before and after the bridge.

T: Okay, if we were going to connect your first writing about Chucky Cheese and who was there, what would we need to say to help the reader get from this sentence to this one? *(pointing to the first sentence and then the second, reading them out loud)*

Miyana looked at me and shrugged her shoulders.

T: Why was everyone at Chucky Cheese?

M: We went there for a birthday party.

T: Ahh, I didn't know that yet. I bet the readers of your story are wondering, and if the reader is wondering, then that is a great clue to write more so they understand the whole story!

Miyana quickly picked up her pencil and began writing on the Post-it®.

So as she elaborated on her bridges and then incorporated the new text into her writing, she read it to me again as we went over her Writer's Checklist.

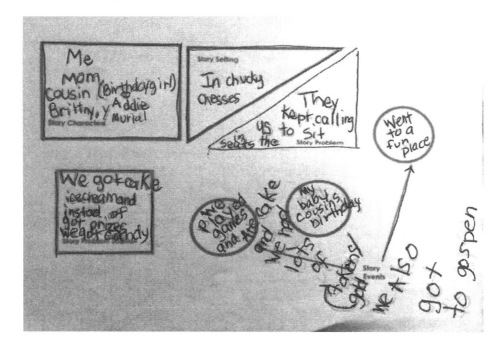

Miyana's story is only one example of the things we can do during interactive writing. Hadley might need an interactive writing conference, in which we can refine her word, "Wherehouse" so she can see the difference between warehouse and "<u>wherehouse</u>." The key remains the number of interactive writing conferences we do with young writers. As teachers, we place great value on our words and tread lightly, as students' learning through their writing will motivate them to move forward in their quest to become great writers.

16

Components of Literacy

When I say to a parent, "read to a child," I don't want it to sound like medicine. I want it to sound like chocolate.

—Mem Fox

Now that we have crafted our learning environment puzzle, we will scaffold our emergent learners through reading, writing, speaking, listening, and viewing. Our classroom should invite each student to experience a literacy-rich, developmentally appropriately tailored, learner-centered classroom filled to the brim with learning opportunities. How will the child develop and hone literacy practices for life? The educator moves within the environment to nudge, stimulate, and celebrate young children and their literacy achievements. While crafting the elements is our first step, the academic organization and delivery is the scaffolding we work from. How we teach and guide our students becomes that scaffold children need to wind through, step up on, stand and view, and even hang onto as they grow in literacy. We take each strand within our scaffold of language and build a strong base for all learners to ascend. While we investigate the individual strands, keep in mind that for a scaffold to be strong, each rung must be attached and interlocking, to hold a person upright. Thus our literacy scaffold must be integrated, built on prior knowledge, developmentally appropriate, and holistically garnered.

Reading

In the teaching of reading, educators have many options to choose from for instruction. I teach all strands of language through quality children's literature and learning centers. Reading is a service subject that all other content and strands lean on. We learn through interacting in an environment that is full of print, so our classrooms must mirror the environment and burst to the seams with print. The children enter the classroom and are immediately bombarded by images and print to scaffold learning. They find out how to find books, where to place their backpacks, directions to the restroom, how to make the snack for the day, where their desks are located, and words, words, words. Rebus-style charts work best with this age group because they support the emergent reader, who can then put together the text symbols and picture cues. A rebus chart is a visual chart using words and pictures to represent concepts. They can be procedural, like the one shown here, guiding the students in the listening center to use a tape recorder. They could be center rebus charts created by hand or the computer, such as the feely cup activity in the science center (Clay 2000).

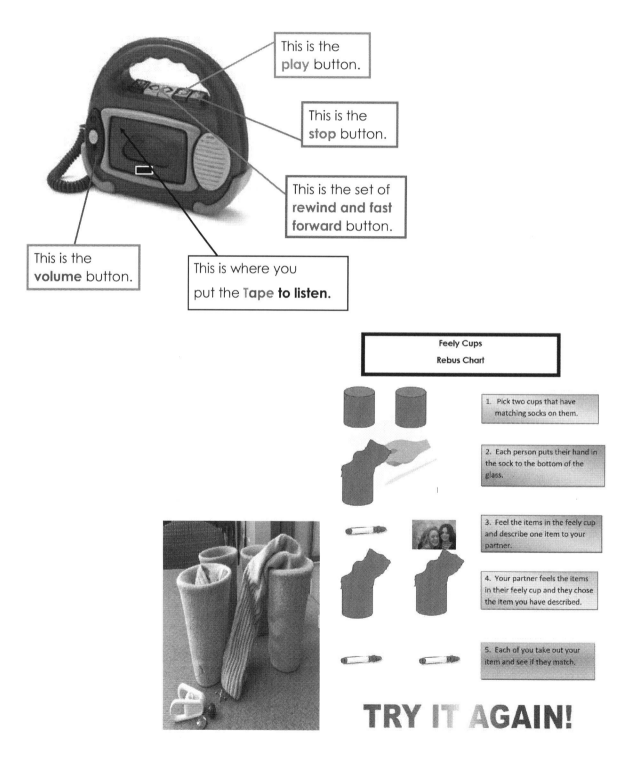

How to use the Tape Recorder

Rebus Chart

This is the **play** button.

This is the **stop** button.

This is the set of **rewind and fast forward** button.

This is the **volume** button.

This is where you put the Tape **to listen.**

Feely Cups

Rebus Chart

1. Pick two cups that have matching socks on them.

2. Each person puts their hand in the sock to the bottom of the glass.

3. Feel the items in the feely cup and describe one item to your partner.

4. Your partner feels the items in their feely cup and they chose the item you have described.

5. Each of you take out your item and see if they match.

TRY IT AGAIN!

My classroom is designed around the learning centers. The activities and materials in the learning centers are tied to what we are learning. Piaget (2001) teaches us that play invites the child to utilize the things they are experiencing and learning. As you can see in the following illustration of my classroom, centers are the backbone of the space. The tables in our classroom do double duty as center setup and workspace.

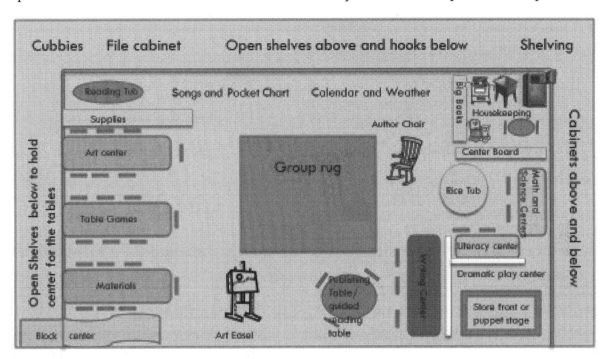

In centers like dramatic play, the center hosted a Chinese restaurant in February as we extended our study of the Chinese New Year and the Moon Festival into practice with cultural events and even food. I used the stove from the home center and put a small table and chairs in the center for the children to role-play either working in the restaurant or eating there. Back in the kitchen were lots of yarn "noodles" and felt mushrooms, broccoli, carrots, and shrimp to put into a wok on top of the stove to create a great lo mein for the customers. I taped above the stove a line of rebus charts to guide them in how to make each dish listed on the menus that I created for the restaurant. My local Chinese restaurant donated chopsticks and fortune cookies in return for our putting a sign in our Chinese restaurant with that restaurant's name on it. After the activity I sent a letter from our class and enclosed a picture and a thank-you note written in LEA style. Now we get lots of fortune cookies each year.

The centers also included lots of pictures of Chinese restaurants and the dishes displayed that students could create, just like when we go into a restaurant and see the pictures in the menu or on the wall. I placed books about food and China in the center so they could learn about the culture as well as the food. I had ticket books for them to take orders. I created the ticket books with the pictures of the dishes they could choose from and the prices. We put a cash register in the center and then placed wallets and pocketbooks FULL of play money in the center also. The menus were easy and fun to create. I created the felt food options, took pictures of them, then went to my desktop publishing program and created a menu. Once the Chinese restaurant let us borrow menus from them, and I just put the pictures on top of theirs and tried to re-create the menu. I have found that the more friends I have around the craft table, the faster the felt food flies out of my felt craft kitchen. I have put the felt food items in the art center, and the students have worked on the items for the center.

How to Make Lo Mein Rebus Chart

1. Put your vegetables in the wok.

2. Stir fry your vegetables.

3. Put in your noodles.

4. Put in your shrimp.

5. Put the Lo Mein in a bowl with chopsticks and take the dish to

your customer!

I had a little boy in my class named Tex. Now Tex was, of course, from Houston, Texas, and he was the smartest five-year-old cowboy I have ever met. He came in the first day with his cowboy hat and boots on and walked right up to me and said, "Hey teacher, you got someplace safe for my hat?" I shared a special place on top of my file cabinet with him, and each morning he would walk straight there, pull the step stool up to the file cabinet, and place the hat carefully on top. Tex needed lots of air for his brain to cool down when he was thinking, as he had ideas pouring out. He was in the art center one day making felt shrimp, and he looked into the bucket of felt pieces and said to the three friends sitting with him, "You got any ribs in there?" One of the little girls looked at him and then at the others and said, "What are ribs?" For the next ten minutes she heard about the very best way to cook them, how to eat them, and whether to use dry rub or marinade. Tex ended with a piece of paper and a drawing of ribs on a grill. He wrote at the bottom: "MMMM good!" Of course we had a BBQ center soon after that, and he was in charge of the planning. Tex exhibited speaking, "some listening," viewing, reading, and writing skills. I took him over to the computer, and we looked up some pictures of all kinds of BBQ. When we created Tex's BBQ center later that month, his mom brought in ribs for the kids to try on Friday and gave each student a recipe for ribs, or as Tex calls them, "r-iiiiii-bs" in three syllables.

Growing Symbolic Mastery with Play

1. *Play detaches from the real-life conditions associated with it.*
   At this early stage children play with materials that are directly represented by the actual object or situation. For example, Lily and Rosey would sit at the table during dramatic play, and the conversation while ordering from the Chinese menu would contain action things they had heard their parents say when they ordered at restaurants, or they would only use the utensils they use at home.
   > Lily: "I don't want to order too much food, because I don't want to waste it."
   > Rosey: "Oh, I am hungry, so I will eat it all."
   > Lily: "Your eyes are bigger than your stomach!"
2. *Play becomes less self-centered.*
   In early play children perform all the actions and accomplish all the things that are happening. They must "cook" the food over the stove and take it to the customers, but later, as they become less self-centered, they might delegate parts of the play to others and let things just happen around them.
3. *Play includes more complex combinations of schemes.*
   At this stage children are beginning to understand that play represents actions and scenarios outside of the play. They begin to exhibit sociodramatic play, in which they know they are not in the Chinese restaurant, but also recognize that the center represents events and mechanisms of a Chinese restaurant. They start coordinating the roles and their play with peers.

(Berk 2011, 322)

Learning centers are a central curricular focus for all strands of language. In all strands we use the children's authentic language and build the classroom together. The room was changed every three weeks as the centers changed out. At my school, we were a team of four kindergarten teachers, so we rotated centers and shared some centers. My class housed housekeeping and dramatic play, so I welcomed a student from each of my colleagues' rooms to interact and sent my students out to their rooms, where Play-Doh™, the science or discovery center, painting, the reading bathtub, and the reading tent resided. This type of sharing helped keep the center creation down to a completely new center every couple of months, but new centers rotated every two weeks with those centers that were previously in other classrooms. This is key, as the students ran into the room every other Tuesday as we previewed the new centers in our room. They were on the edge of their carpet squares, anticipating the role-play in the center. The teachers role-played the shared centers in their rooms, and we showed both correct manners and disrespectful manners in the center. The kids laughed as we threw food on the floor in the restaurant when the cleanup song was sung and ran out, leaving it a mess. They called us out on it, and Tex or "Tex-like" friends told us exactly what we should do. They viewed the role-play, spoke their minds about how to treat our materials, and wrote down which center they wanted to go to first, and then we read about the theme that day. It was worth the academic time we spent to preview the centers, because we could see how the students interacted and practiced their literacy inside the small, hand-designed worlds they loved to play in.

We each had a book or library center filled with books of all kinds. Each had a special library shelf with the "Author of the Week" books displayed as well. The library center should host big books, small books, pop-up books, nonfiction, fiction, leveled books, and multiple copies of books to share with friends. I placed books like *I Know an Old Lady Who Swallowed a Fly* and *Wheels on the Bus* in a flannel board center as well, with felt pieces that students could use to sequence and retell the story and sing it with friends. Young children love puppets, and there was a center next to the library where the students could reenact the story behind a puppet stage or do readers' theater. This is where I kept my rocking chair, which we called the author's chair when we read from our own work. I took a small pillowcase and cut half of it off, then sewed it back across, and it slid down perfectly over the back of my rocking chair. The students decorated it for me, and we wrote "Author's Chair" on it. When that chair case was placed on the back of the rocking chair, the students would sit in a circle on the rug and await one of their friend's newest best sellers.

Writing

When young children come to the empty page, they see possibility. They want all that is in their heads to be put on the paper. Sometimes they look at their papers and what they see doesn't resemble books or pictures they have experiences with, so they get discouraged. They tell us, "You do it!" If a child has experienced lots of great read alouds in a loving lap, she often see books that have pictures that are keen and clear, with words that are bold and lie across the page in symbols. She might not understand, but she can approximate them. If a child has experienced lots of outings in the world, seeing animals in their habitat and people milling about doing life's work, he often sees events and episodes that are in focus and recognizable. If a child has experienced life from his home, he sees his mom and dad cooking and cleaning and hopefully loving one another. At this tender age, children are curious and investigate their environment. They want to illustrate what they see in their world. So when you give them a piece of paper, they take to the crayon or marker with abandon. After they finish they want to share their pictures and stories of experiences. In the beginning they draw pictures and sometimes approximations of symbols, which they "read" to us as the story. This is writing. This is *their* writing.

They continue illustrating their lives until someone tells them, "Hey, that doesn't look like a tiger!" Then the children put down the markers and don't draw a tiger again. They turn to you and say, "You do it!" How can we intercede and scaffold in that amazing time when they are curious and adventurous before they learn judgment? Educators can introduce LEA. At this emergent stage, when their ideas move through their heads faster than their little hands and fingers can portray them, we can step in and scaffold writing with them. Chapter 15 discussed LEA stories and how teachers can use chart paper and markers and make the children's stories come alive for them at their brain's pace. I want to explore LEA a bit more here to give you the process for beginning to use LEA in your classroom with writing. We invite the children to write on their own with their approximations and inventive spelling alongside our group stories, but in the LEA, we scaffold by modeling writing. The symbol system is daunting to young children, as well as to children learning English as a second language, and modeling how the symbol system works illustrates how orthographic, syntactic, semantic cues (Goodman and Owochi 2002; Goodman 2014), and pragmatic cues (Tompkins 2013) work in action. Language experience enhances their approximations and inventive spelling by showing the writing going from their mouths through the scribe and onto the paper.

I always start my year with a trip around the school to help students learn about the new building and what happens in all its individual parts. I read several books about maps and adventure-taking. *Scaredy Squirrel* by Melanie Watts (2008) is a story about a flying squirrel that is scared of leaving his tree, as it is all he has known, so he plans for all contingencies. *My Map Book* by Sara Fanelli (2001) is a wonderful nonfiction book about maps of all the places and things in one girl's world, using handmade maps. *As the Crow Flies: A First Book of Maps* by Gail Hartman (1993) illustrates bird's-eye views of various locations. Once I have read some of the books, we go on a fact-finding mission around the school and interview various people who work in the building, asking them about what they do and where they do it. We either audiotape or videotape the interviews on a phone or tablet as we listen or write down notes about their answers. Then we go back to the classroom and draw the school on a map, labeling all the places we have been. I print out the pictures of the people we found there and attach them to the map. Over a week or so, we add facts from our interviews and things we picked up from our adventures, until we have created a wonderful comprehensive map of our school. This is our first experience with shared writing and LEA. We also create one for our classroom, which we put on the computer and print out for the students to take home. This invites the family to talk about the child's day and experiences as the child guides the family through our classroom.

Soon we start working up to stories written on our chart paper. Remember the story about the penguins discussed in chapter 15? Well, that story is a great example of writing a story together as a class. In the beginning the stories are very simple, but as we work with them, they build up to very full and robust stories with dialogue and plot twists. I am scaffolding the students as they learn to write stories on their own. I think scaffolding is like holding their hands as they learn to walk. At first they need your hand as balance and leverage to stand up, and soon they are standing on their own. Then you hold their hands again as you move forward to scaffold that all-important first step. They bounce back on their bums and laugh, and you try again and again until one day, they move their feet forward and place them securely down on the floor, and you jump up and cheer, scaring them back down on their bums. We celebrate this milestone, this baby step into

The Grochies Get Mad

One day the children went out to play and one grouchy man came to grouch up the children. They get scared. They get the grouchies. The gouchy children hit the good children. The children get grouchy again. Someone very nice came to the children and the grouchies ran away.

The End

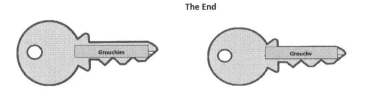

walking. Why can't we celebrate their first step in writing the same way—an approximation! Below is a baby step story my kindergartners wrote early in the year.

This "grouchy" story came from the early genius of my students and shows a very early attempt at a narrative. The story has characters, a setting, a story problem, a story solution, and events. Now the plot is simplistic and the events few, but we have approximated a good story. The two keys represent the keywords we discussed in the last section. These words stayed on the bottom of the chart paper story, which was hung up after we worked with it. After a week I put the chart paper story in our class dictionary. The keywords were the beginning of a word bank from their writing, as opposed to words taken from books others had written. If the students want to write about a grouchy person, or if they get the grouchies in a future story, they will know to go to our class dictionary, which contains all our stories with keywords and hangs on a chart stand, look for the grouchy story, and see how to spell grouchy or grouchies.

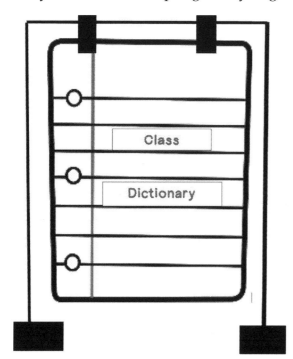

After each word bank is created, it is posted in the classroom for one week and then added to the back of the chart stand which holds all the word banks behind a chart paper with class dictionary written on it. This stands in the classroom to be used as a classroom dictionary, just like the picture dictionaries and traditional dictionaries.

By the end of the year, we had about fifty stories, recipes, maps, morning message charts, graphs, and memos on that chart stand, and I held a drawing to find each entry a forever home with one of the kids in the class. A mom came up to school in September one year and told me that her daughter had put a class story on her wall at the foot of her bed, which she had read to her family each night since she had taken it home at the end of kindergarten. I laughed and told her, "I bet that was a long summer!" To which she replied, "SUMMER! My child is in second grade now!" Now that is ownership shifted from the class to the individual student.

Steps to a Successful Language Experience Approach (LEA story)

1. The LEA can be done with a small group for specific instruction, with an individual child for dictation of their ideas, or with the **whole class on chart paper**. Gather the materials needed. (markers of different colors, large chart paper)
2. **Talk** and brainstorm with the class about what our story of the day will be about. (Alternate genre options: recipes, how to, maps, poetry) Bring out a lot of ideas.
3. When the idea is set, begin guiding the students, "We need our first sentence." With every sentence the students share, the teacher writes the sentences in different colors to highlight sentence structure. This makes it easier to notice punctuation and capitals. (In an LEA, highlighting and color coding can be done for anything like quotation marks in red, key words in a certain color, etc. Take a cue from your minilesson content.)
4. During the story it is key to keep the **enthusiasm HIGH** and interactive. Ask questions like: "What do you think will happen next?" "I am looking for a friend sitting respectfully to share the next sentence." The teacher leads the activity, but the students share the content. This is a challenge because not all students will be on task completely at all times, so being very engaging with language helps to pull out the story one sentence at a time. This activity is great to use for several weeks before beginning Writing Workshop to lay the foundation for the writing process.
5. After the story is complete, the teacher comes back the next day to the chart paper and takes the students through concrete revision and editing techniques like Hamburger Revision (see Hamburger Revision) or Ratiocination (see Acts of Teaching, Carroll and Wilson, 2008). The younger students need **concrete experiences** with the **Writing Process**. This is modeling for the process for students to learn by doing before they begin working through the process independently.
6. When **publishing**, the chart paper can serve as part of a large chart book of story like an anthology hung on a chart stand for the students to read at will, or the words can be transferred to a book. When this is done, the students lead also the process of deciding which section goes on a page and it is marked or cut. The teacher can write those sentences on a page or glue them and then the students split into groups and illustrate each page.
7. When the book is completed, it is placed in the library with the other books and stories. **Celebrate**

As the year progresses the stories become more complex, like this twisting and turning story about a sassy baby monkey and a bag of cheese popcorn. As the students gain more and more confidence as writers, we move through the writing process to revision and editing, as we did in this story.

We come back to the story the next class day and read it again together as part of repeated readings. To model revision in action, I use a concrete strategy to help bring the wonders to my emergent writers. "Hamburger revision" is used to guide them to add new words and exchange tired words in their writing (see box below). Working with my kindergarteners on revision, I noticed that exchanging words was tough for them. They are at a stage of development when they are still playing with irreversibility. Children can't reverse actions, causing their thinking to be solid after the fact (Berk 2011). The young author relies on what is in front of her and can't transform it after it is set. These children are in the preoperational stage of learning. Once their pieces are written, the possibility of reentering the text is unfathomable. Irreversibility refers to the lack of ability to follow steps and then review thinking to relook (Berk 2011). To give a concrete example, I told a story that activated their story-wired brains (Haven 2014) and gave them a way to transform by using a concrete example of the revising stage in the story. I brought in a felt hamburger in a bag and told them the story of how I had picked up a hamburger from a local place and decided to have a juicy hamburger with lots of lettuce and pickles on it instead of a bare-bones hamburger with a bun and a piece of meat (see box below for full teacher talk). Young children need to touch and experience at the concrete level to internalize new concepts. After modeling the action of revising the story with the felt props, I go back to our story and begin to revise by adding the adjective "baby" to the noun "monkey". We also add cheese to popcorn. The next day we come back to the story and exchange out our tired words, such as changing *nice* to *lovely*, as seen at the end of the story. The concrete nature of the strategy brought the wonders down to the students' level and helped them grasp the concept so they could do the action.

Teachers teach in all parts of the world, so different foods work just as well. My university students taught hamburger revision but tried different area foods (see hamburger revision manipulatives box below). My students tried Chicago using hot dogs and made them juicy with pickles, sauerkraut, and so forth. They tried using an ice cream sundae and even a healthy salad. For each alternative, you will want to choose an "orange slice," as in the hamburger revision story, to show how to ensure internal cohesion within the text and take out the off-topic, extraneous information.

We come back on another class day and read over our LEA story again with our new revisions. As we are reading, I stop at the end of the first sentence and ask, "What do you see at the end of this sentence?"

Betsy raises her hand, and when I call on her, she says, "a dot."

"Yes it is. Do you know why it is there?"

The first time we talk about the end punctuation, the students rarely know why the "dot" is there and usually don't notice it. I tell them it is a period, and that a period tells the reader the sentence is ending.

"See how we changed the color of the next part to red? We start with a capital letter to tell the reader we are starting a new sentence. Let's circle the period and the capital

Hamburger Revision

"I went to McDonald's last night and ordered a hamburger for my dinner, but when I got home, I found I had only a bun and a piece of meat."

"This hamburger would taste all right and I could eat it, but it would taste so much better if we could juice it up. How can we juice up our hamburger?"

Add onions, cheese, lettuce, etc.

"What do these things do to this hamburger? Our story is like this burger…It is a good story. . .Do you think we could juice up this story like we did our burger?

Add things/words.

The teacher and students together find places for descriptive words or action words.

"Last night I worked late and on my way home, I stopped at McDonald's again. I ordered another hamburger, and when I got home I took out my burger and look what I found—an orange!"

Hold up an example from the felt hamburger.

"I like oranges, but not on my hamburger. . .I think I will put this orange slice on my napkin and save it for desert."

Hold up example.

"Do you see / hear an orange in our story? Do you hear a sentence or thought that we need to save for another story?

The teacher and student reread the story and target the orange.

"Well, boys and girls, I'm going to McDonald's tonight with some of my friends and I'm tired of the same taste. I still want a hamburger. How can I change the taste without changing the burger?"

Change the cheeses.

"Okay, so tonight I will order a hamburger with Swiss cheese instead of American cheese."

Show example of the two cheeses with the felt hamburger.

"Friends, is there a word or words that are tired in our story? Can we make any exciting changes in our story, but still keep the same story idea?"

The teacher and student exchange tired words or thought with new exciting, jazzy ones.

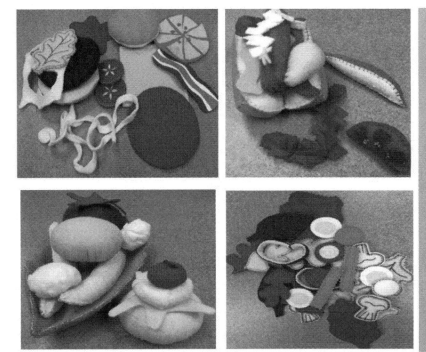

The left top is a hamburger that is traditional in the story and the orange is the extraneous information piece. The Chicago style hotdog is to the right on top with coconut as the extraneous piece. The bottom right represents an ice cream sundae with whipped cream and the orange could be the extraneous with the sundae or the salad on the bottom right.

letter so we remember what we just learned. Let's see if we can find other periods and capitals."

This editing stage is a first step into editing at this stage, but it helps guide the students through the writing process and lets them start to see how we need to think about the reader when we write. During the next class period we publish our story and add it to our class library with all the authors we enjoy. We use a writer's checklist (see the section on interactive writing in chapter 15) to check out writing to see if we are ready to publish.

The LEA provides a visual component to writing a story. Teachers can tell students how to write a story, then nudge them in their own inventive spelling and approximations revolving around their own meaning making. Language experience approach stories like the ones outlined above *show* them how a story comes from our ideas and imagination and is crafted in writing. The modeling is authentic, as the story is coming from their voices. I use LEA all through the year to supplement students' own writing experiences during reading/writing connections and book extensions in the classroom as an extra view into literacy. We write recipes, maps, poems, directions, and even notes about things to remember.

As I write this, I am thinking of the space shuttle with a teacher aboard, as it is the thirtieth anniversary of the shuttle *Challenger* disaster. I remember so clearly the students huddled in my Houston classroom around the TV to watch the first teacher go up into space. We all collectively gasped as everything just blew up in the air. All the emotions had to go somewhere in those young brains and hearts. We sat down with a large piece of chart paper and began writing down our questions and thoughts for the astronauts' families. Writing is a natural outlet for all ages and stages of humans. That lesson taught them to write out their ideas, thoughts, and emotions. They drew pictures with their inventive spelling approximations, and we mailed them to NASA, as the children knew at this tender age that words written down have power. They knew that because they had been immersed in writing since the first day of school.

Viewing

On the first day of school my students, no matter their age, walk in and immediately look around the environment to view their new surroundings. Their eyes scan the tables, book centers, posters, and art supplies. Viewing is an integral part of our learning as we take in everything, but for young learners this strand of literacy takes precedence as they take in their world. Knowing this key component of an emergent literacy learner, I display all that we are going to learn and have learned. The classroom is immersed in print. I use a checklist (see below) to remind me to keep a print-rich environment updated and vibrant.

Is my room Print Rich?

1. Are there books and writing materials in a reading/writing center and in various places throughout the room?
2. Are there places where children can share thoughts, questions, or messages for others?
3. Are there opportunities for writing and reading in each learning center?
4. Are there various types of print, such as maps, charts, globes, pictures, and books at child level in the classroom and in the learning centers?
5. Is there a wide variety of writing tools and materials, and do the students know where to access them?
6. Is there a wide variety of other items that encourage reading and writing, like flannel boards and flannel board story parts, listening center with books and tapes, tape recorder, literacy centers with lots of invitations to read and write?
7. Are there a lot of things to talk, read, and write about?
8. Are the word wall and word banks current, inviting, and at child level? Are there resource books in the learning centers?
9. Are there comfortable, accessible places that invite and encourage students to read and write for all children?
10. Are there books of all kinds displayed in such a way that students are invited to use them?

In my kindergarten class, I learned early that food was a hook and motivator for my new friends. They loved cooking in class, so I instituted Wednesday Cooking Day. Some days I would put our cooking experience in a learning center, and some days we would sit in a learning circle and cook together. In either methodology, I would plan the experience with the students the day before. I kept the cooking theme related to our units, like haystacks when we studied the farm and farm animals. We would make octopus chili when we learned about the ocean. During school year holidays and special occasions, we would cook for that celebration, such as marshmallow snowmen in January. My students especially loved our local dentist coming to the class with his giant toothbrush and those little red dots you eat after you eat a cookie. The students ate their chocolate cookies and then went to brush with brand new toothbrushes. They returned knowing they had done a fantastic job, and after they ate the red dots, they smiled to see how their friends' teeth lit up with red places where the cookies still hid after brushing. We talked about what they had learned about dental health and how a dentist is our mouths' best friend. One year we decided to create smiles on cooking day. So the next day the students eagerly came into the classroom, looking around to see if they could crack the secret cooking ingredients. We circled around a large piece of chart paper, and as I took each ingredient out of a grocery bag, they called it out and I wrote it down under ingredients on our chart (see illustration below). After the ingredients were listed, we put all of them in front of each child and built our yummy smiles. I wrote on the directions portion of the large chart the instructions in numerical order, just as recipes do, then performed each step until we had created a yummy smile. Of course then we ate it! The Yummy Smiles uses peanut butter, but if you have students with nut allergies in your classroom, you can replace the peanut butter with chocolate spread. After we ate our yummy smiles, we read over our recipe again, and then I put it on the wall behind our cooking center so the students could re-create a yummy smile there with the leftovers. They had to view/read the recipe and follow it.

As you can see in the rebus chart recipe below, you can also put the recipes on file folders for a smaller version when do the cooking experience in learning centers.

Viewing the steps inside the LEA-style recipe, the materials come together to teach students to create their yummy smiles. They experience the cooking with all their senses. We each have very active mirror neurons that aid in our learning. We view our world and learn from what we see. Have you ever learned something by watching a YouTube™ video or sitting next to a friend performing an action you wanted to learn? This is the theoretical support for modeling. As children watch the teacher write, they are learning through mirror neurons before they practice with their own hands. We read aloud to our children to model reading behaviors, meaning making, reading with expression, connecting picture cues to text, and the joy of story. Those small brains are viewing all, and the mirror neurons are stimulated.

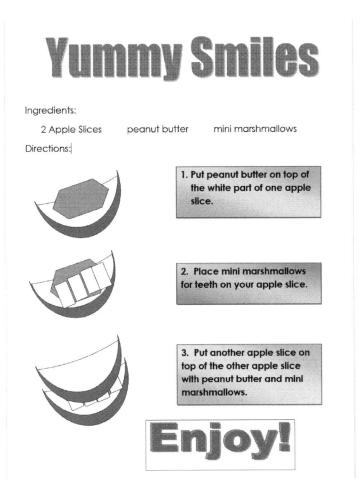

Yummy Smiles

Ingredients:

2 Apple Slices   peanut butter   mini marshmallows

Directions:

1. Put peanut butter on top of the white part of one apple slice.

2. Place mini marshmallows for teeth on your apple slice.

3. Put another apple slice on top of the other apple slice with peanut butter and mini marshmallows.

Enjoy!

In learning centers, children read and follow rebus charts like the Yummy Smiles. They can range from simple directions in the beginning of the year to more advanced at the end of the year.

Research tells us that viewing something can help us imitate it. For the optimal learning from our mirror neurons, the viewing needs to be accompanied by the interaction of setting a purpose for the viewing and extensions of debriefing and practice opportunities (Rodriquez, Lopez-Alonso, and Fernandez-del-Olmo 2013). This tells me as an educator that talking about the cooking experience the day before and then writing the recipe in tandem greatly energizes the learning potential. After we create our artifacts of cooking, reading, and writing through LEA, I post them in the classroom for a week and then put them in a special place in the room. For example, the LEA stories that have keywords go into a word bank and eventually a class dictionary of all the chart paper on a chart stand as a large class collection. I place the recipes together after their use in the classroom on a chart stand and then type them up for an end-of-the-year classroom cookbook for the kids to give their parents.

Cooking with Kids

- ☐ Cleaning up can be a teaching opportunity. After you cook with students, invite them to help with cleanup. They can put all the dishes in a dish bucket or take them to the kitchen. Use the opportunity to categorize the dishes by size, smallest to largest. Make cleanup a science and math lesson.
- ☐ Problem solving and working together on projects on both the planning and implementation is a learning experience to be shared.
- ☐ As a science connection, weighing and measuring and comparing the weights and measures, both standard and nonstandard, can teach concepts authentically.

Speaking and Listening

In my third or fourth year of teaching kindergarten, I met a new student whom I will call Billy. Billy ran into the classroom from his first bus ride to school, looked around the room, and promptly hung his backpack on the back of a chair and sat down. He was ready to start learning! I went over and asked him if he wanted to put his backpack on the closet hook. He looked at me with a very serious face and said, "I am not sure I am staying yet!" I smiled and replied, "Well, when you are sure, I can show you where they are." It took him two days before he was sure. Those two days were the only two days I remember Billy listening more than speaking! I resemble that type of young student, so I understood, but we did go through an adjustment about the times to talk and the times to listen. That is an important lesson for us all. I knew exactly when Billy had something to say to the group, as he had a big "tell." He would raise his hand and pump it up and down until I saw it and called on him. He would start off the same way each time, "Miss, don't you know. . . ." He would follow this with all kinds of information that 80 percent of the time was on the topic we were talking about. I learned a lot from Billy that year, but my favorite was what I learned during parent conferences when his mom and dad came. They sat and listened to how Billy loved block center best and would hurry his work so he could go there during every center time. He loved to build space rockets. His dad raised his hand and said excitedly, "Don't you know, we both work inside the space program!" I smiled and replied, "Well, I didn't know that, but it clears up lots of things!"

Speaking and listening are so interconnected that many states and our national standards combine them with early childhood. I also combine them in my expectations during read alouds. Each day we start and end our class with a read aloud. In the morning we read books from our author of the week. We celebrate all kinds of authors who write both nonfiction and fiction. Some authors take up two or three weeks. We talk about the author and show a picture of him or her. The Internet provides access to the world of authors for our children. We can show them more about their lives and books with pictures and extensions for their books. We can even watch them read their own books on video through the Internet. At the end of the day our helper for that day gets to choose a book from anywhere in the room to bring up to the rocking chair for read aloud. My students sat on the circle rug and snuggled up close to the rocking chair, demonstrating their love of story. It was their favorite time of the day. It was my favorite, too! While read aloud is a perfect time for listening, it is also perfect for speaking. The more the students interact in the story and predict events, the more they comprehend. Of course sometimes the speaking is "off topic," but for the most part, my students attended to the story, the pictures, and the adventure of read aloud. I still remember one time in fourth grade when we had a guest reader. She was a matriarch in our small town. Her outreach for the last decades of her life centered on reading books aloud to fourth graders. She had been a fourth-grade teacher when she was in her twenties and told us she missed those days. In my fourth-grade class she read *The Hundred Dresses* by Eleanor Estes. I was enthralled. I scooted up with every chapter until I was right at her feet, waiting for each word. The story and the experience are still one of the pivotal events in my career choice. The book follows a little girl who comes to school each day in a clean but wrinkled and worn dress. A set of girls, what we know today as "mean girls," make fun of her, and she tells them she has 100 beautiful dresses all lined up in her closest and 60 pairs of shoes. They laugh and dismiss her. The young girl lives in an area of town that is known to be a "bad area." One day the little girl doesn't show up for school, and the girls go after school to her neighborhood to find her, as she has told them she was going to show them the dresses that day. When they arrive in front of her house, they can see her family is gone and the house is empty. I won't tell you the end of the mystery, but I will tell you that they did see those dresses, and you will have to run to the library to pick up the book to find out how. That story and Mrs. Fielder's reading style changed my path in life right there on the floor at her feet. A story read aloud can do that. My regular teacher never read to us. The last time I had been read to in school was first grade. From that day on I missed it. I said to myself that day that I would be a teacher and read great books every day. I have kept that promise by reading to my young students and still read aloud to my college students. They love the stories, and we talk about how to extend them and what great predictions to bring out in their classrooms.

When you read aloud to young children, asking for too many predictions and checking for understanding too often can impede comprehension. I like to read through the book and find the best places for prediction. From the predictions the students make, I am making assumptions about their comprehension. I can listen to the conclusions they are drawing to make the predictions. To dig a bit deeper into the predictions, I can ask questions: What part in the story helps you predict that? This also helps model for students how to use the book to support their predictions and inferences. Also, they learn incrementally to build their stamina to listen to stories and to each other's interactions. I constantly watch my learners to see if they are actively listening to the story. Are they engaged in the action? Are they motivated to see the next page? What questions are they asking? Are they drawing logical conclusions about the characters? Can they predict the ending using support from the text and their prior experiences? Viewing and sharing speaking and listening is engaging for all if we remain attentive to who is doing the majority of the speaking and who is doing the majority of the listening.

17

How the Emergent Learner's Brain Works

Writing is thinking on paper, or talking to someone on paper. If you can think clearly, or if you can talk to someone about the things you know and care about, you can write—with confidence and enjoyment.

—William Zinsser

Inside the brain of emergent literacy learners we can find all of their unique connections to the environment and literacy experiences they have gathered throughout their young lives. Medical doctors study the brain, and neurologists scan and discuss brain functions and processes and can see inside the brain with high-powered scans, but educators observe and affect what goes in. Teachers are trained to design the environment and plan for learning experiences, but they have learned less about the physiological side of the child's thinking than we do from the expressions of learning. We can almost see their cognition some days as their eyes light up when they figure out a story or learn more about a character they love. Then some days we see them sit and ponder for an afternoon, watching a clear butterfly box as a chrysalis begins to crack and shimmer. We marvel at their statements as they verbally share all that they are taking in.

"It is shaking!"
"Look, color is running down the side."
"The caterpillar's house is getting too small for our butterfly."

They express what they see and ask many questions to take in what is happening, sometimes yelling it out at whoever might answer.

"What is making it shake?"
"Where did that color come from?"
"How did the butterfly get in there?"
"Will the butterfly crack the house so it can get out?"

I wish I could look inside their heads as they peer inside the lifespan of the caterpillar with an MRI (magnetic resonance image) to see how their brains are lighting up. If we listen carefully to the questions, we can almost see their processing. We read books about caterpillars and butterflies and all that comes between, but the experience of seeing the caterpillars, chrysalis, and butterflies in their environment is what causes the learning to stick for young explorers. We can hear and see these utterances, but we can't see how that learning is bouncing around inside their brains to gather or assimilate new information and create connections or accommodations to the previous learning. They have watched a tadpole become a frog in our aquarium and an egg become a chicken at a farm, and now this lifespan modifies what they know about how animals develop. No matter how much we would like to open their brains and peer in at the complicated processes of learning at this age, we must use our "kidwatching" to approximate the depth of their understanding. The unique challenge of teaching young children is their combination of expressive and receptive language (Morrow 2012). We are hobbled by their emergent level of language, which limits how they can tell us what they know and understand, so we stand close and lean in to observe what they share with us and ask us, and all that their faces tell us about what they are taking in. The frontal lobe is late to fully develop, so speaking what they know is later than understanding the connections they have made, and we must observe and ask how they use their new learning to see if they conceptually understand.

There are several things we can add to our understanding of how young children think and retain short-term and long-term memory. These things can assist us in our approximations of their understanding. In this chapter you will learn six essential things educators of young brains need to know and how we can help scaffold learning for our emergent readers and writers.

1.   What happens to our brains as they develop prenatally?

Each minute in utero 250,000 neurons, which are small cells that make up the building blocks of the brain, develop (Bergman et al. 2012). They will bloom and move as the child grows, as the brain is only 25 percent of his size at birth. The brain is thought to be fully developed around age twenty-five. Each minute in pregnancy is critical; how the mother cares for her body directly relates to how the baby will develop. This speaks to our need for prenatal care early on in the pregnancy and continual attention to the environment mom and baby are surrounded by. Research shows that abused or neglected babies have smaller brains, which resemble the brains of Alzheimer's patients (Teicher and Samson 2016). Positive and negative experiences dramatically affect synaptic connections in the brain. They function on the "use it or lose it" principle (Shaywitz 2003). Only those things we foster and use are retained at peak level. Some wither and die. We therefore greatly increase a child's chance of learning and growing with education as well as medical care during pregnancy. At birth the brain houses approximately 100 billion brain cells. To care for the development of those neurons, a mother needs to be dedicated to nutrition and safety as well as being immersed in good health and begin to build a loving relationship with the growing baby. As a community of educators, we can offer education, literacy opportunities for the family, and a safe environment to explore the resources available to families in the area.

2.   How are our brains built for learning?

The brain is part of the central nervous system and controls all our movements, emotions, and mental activity (Charlesworth 2014). Inside our brains neurons are busy at work making connections with our environment. The cell body is made up of a nucleus, or center of the cell, and an axon that is loaded with myelin, a sticky substance that protects and holds the new information. The myelin holds onto the information and helps our neurons connect to one another. These connections or synapses make up our understandings and develop the brain to make more and more of the connections. "Children's experiences provide increased connections. Any one neuron may be connected to as many as 15,000 other neurons" (Charlesworth 2014, 32). As children with rich experiences grow, they create many synapses, which results in neural plasticity. This plasticity is what makes it easy to learn new things at such a rapid pace in early childhood. Young learners make so many of them that they must prune the unused synapses while retaining the ones they use over and over daily. Another part of the neurons is the dendrites, small, hair-like fibers that help us receive information (Charlesworth 2014). As we grow our neurons they stay fairly consistent, but the dendrites and synapses can flourish and multiply. I like to think of this structure as being like a hand, as our arm supports the hand with long fingers that reach for things in our environment, like the neuron with the help of the axon and dendrites reaches for information in thinking. Think of a hand waving at a parade or clapping at a fantastic performance. The fingers are moving enthusiastically; students are actively engaged in the experience. If we can help stimulate our dendrites to move enthusiastically, think of all the connections they can make. We are gifted with a great responsibility as teachers to encourage and incite this engagement in learning. While the movement shows growth, the inverse is also true. The lack of movement and engagement can also cause great changes, in the form of dendrites failing, withering, and dying. This dendritic deterioration symbolizes a dearth of learning and lessening of the potential for learning.

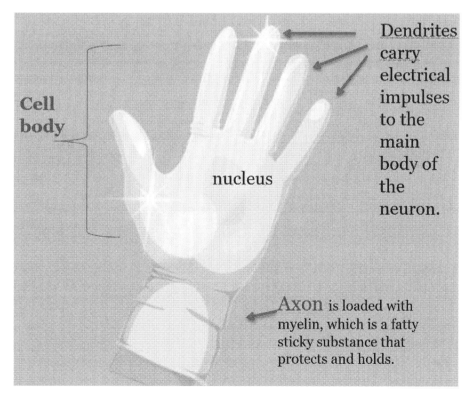

We have long understood how a lack of movement can cause apathy and atrophy of muscles; teachers are beginning to see that lack of learning can actually cause a lack of potential for learning with this process. Research is being conducted on dementia, Alzheimer's disease, and other neurological deterioration in the medical field into how physiological and behavioral changes in lifestyle can instigate a change in the brain's function and capacity (Ciaramella et al. 2016). These studies have a correlation with what is happening in some classrooms today with the overuse of worksheets, teaching to the middle, and lack of recess and movement during the day. "Synapses are eliminated through pruning and experience. What you don't use is usually eliminated in the competitive neural world" (Jensen 2005, 130). We know active learning is key, as we know that play is integral in the lives of young children. "The result of the various interrelation of humans shaping environment and environments shaping humans is that there is no fixed human brain, it is always a work in progress" (Jensen 2005, 11). As children play, they process the environment and learn from language and interaction with friends, objects, and situations. So we can infer that our brain circuitry, like electrical circuits, becomes stronger when they are active, and when they are not active they are pruned (Charlesworth 2014).

3.   How can we enhance synaptic connections?

Synaptic connections are defined as the spaces that connect dendrites to one another, where they stimulate a chemical and electrical reaction and light up a connection with thinking for the brain (Jensen 2005; Haken 2016). The word *synapse* comes from the Greek and means to clasp, connect, or join (Carroll and Wilson 2008). This clasping or joining is done neurologically between dendrites as we connect thoughts, pictures, and experiences. In a synaptic connection we can see the chemicals running back and forth and how close they get to one another. It is as if energy is flying back and forth. Chemicals carry the energy as neurotransmitters, and once they move from one neuron to another, they alter the electrical charge to the edge of the new neuron (Jensen 2005; Haken 2016). As these chemical reactors carry the energy, they can be affected by an influx of chemicals into the bloodstream. Addictive drugs can damage the connections, as they mimic the neurotransmitters and falsify the synaptic connection and do permanent damage to the connection. Stress can also affect our processes, as well as threats or fear (VanDycke and Fox 1990). We can enhance the synaptic growth in complex, rich environments in our classrooms while we share social interactions, children's literature, songs, rhymes, and chants in active learning situations. Classrooms in which intimidation, worksheet packets completed on a stopwatch, raised voices, and high-stakes testing pressure are present can affect our connections and potential for learning for a lifetime.

4.   How does mirror neuron response help us teach?

Have you ever been in the middle of a conversation and know exactly what the other person is talking about, yet you can't remember ever learning about it? Well, it just might be that your mirror neurons have kicked in. Mirror neuron response is the process whereby we make connections within our neurons that are formed from observations (Bonini 2016). When we experience things, we take in all the particulars of the experience and make connections with the input, as explained above, but in addition, the brain is always taking in information (Jensen 2005). When we stand in the bleachers of a soccer game, go to an open house, or even watch a cooking show, the brain is stimulated to learn. We make connections with what we knew before plus what we just observed. Even when we are not the one performing the action, the brain takes it in (Altman 2002). My little kindergarten friend who always asked me, "Don't you know?" was cataloging in his brain all we did and observed. He was telling me all he knew, and it certainly was important. A little girl can see her sister pull her hand back from the stove and scream, "It's hot!" The little girl knows even without touching it that the stove is hot and she can get burned. She has inferred from the observation that a stove can burn, and her mirror neurons help her to remember that rule the next time she gets near a stove.

Coaches have long used this knowledge with their players as they teach using films of game play. They point out what the players did to react to a situation to show them how they can improve upon their responses the next time. They also point out the things that they have learned to do instinctively at certain points in the game. We can learn from watching ourselves play and experience, but we can also learn from observing others play and experience. Thus, mirror neuron response becomes the theoretical support for modeling in our world. Have you enriched your knowledge by watching others as they are doing something or by asking them questions? One cooking day in my KDG classroom, I brought out a box of sandwich cookies, long black licorice strings, a white tube of icing, and micro chocolate chips. Chavon yelled out, "Oh, I can't have that, they have 50 calories and will go right to my hips!" The others looked at me as if the cookie would fly from my package to their hips. I laughed and said, "Then you might nibble it slowly so you really enjoy it." No doubt her mom was watching calories and had remarked on the cookies in the store, but she had it in her brain ready to burst forth when she encountered the cookies. The others were happy to know the cookies would go the normal route into their tummies to get to their hips after we ate our "spider cookies." I used to tell parents the funny things that their kids had to say about things they had observed, and one parent told me that if I would ignore half of everything I heard about their lives at home, she would ignore half of what they heard about my life at school. I think that was a great deal! Mirror neuron response also acts as an emotional contagion when we read a story and our faces and bodies react to the words and the events they represent. As I read to my students, they mirror my actions and reactions to the story. They gasp when I gasp, they look sad when I read a sad section, they laugh while I laugh. I also notice that my students' attitudes vary in the classroom, and I can modify that with my attitude. Some days when you come into your classroom with a headache or frustrated with traffic, you enter with a scowl on your face and then wonder why your students are having trouble settling down. Is the problem your attitude, or theirs? Is it the atmosphere created by those mirror neuron responses? I learned quickly to take a moment outside my door to "leave it at the door" before I walk inside. I also teach my students to do the same. I kept a basket right inside my classroom in which we would drop our "baggage" as we walked in. Some days we would have to revisit the basket! I believe learning centers can benefit the most from mirror neurons as we go to the centers to experience life and events and learn from them, just like when we go to a cooking class or a soccer game.

5.   What is the neurological process of scaffolding?

"By age 5, the brain has learned a language, has developed sensory motor skills, and is concerned with active exploration" (Jensen 2005, 29). As most children enter formal schooling, they have already learned through interacting with the environment, so as they continue to grow, they need to continue to explore and observe. Young ones also learn best through hands-on experiences, as our brain processes and discovery are the best way to create connections. As we are learning, the glial cells, the protective coating like little peanuts in a package, protect the neurons and take everything in and hold it. They protect the new input like those little peanuts protect the package. It is believed that glial cells are the cellular support system and the foundation for scaffolding, because "by climbing the glial trail, neurons find their home" (Ledoux 2013). When a child learns a new idea or fact, it is taken in with the outside parameters of the experience. These outside factors help the new idea or fact to find a forever home. If we are reading, *The Hungry Caterpillar* by Eric Carle (1994), while we are watching the evolution of the butterfly from a caterpillar in a clear box in our classrooms, we scaffold students' understanding of the life of a caterpillar. We talk and write about what caterpillars eat and where they live. This full-bodied discussion is inspired by the book and becomes part of the learning about a caterpillar. This learning instigates connections about the climate of the caterpillars in a natural environment and then what they truly eat in the world. We are scaffolding their understanding, thus helping the event or fact be cemented into the glial cells and then travel to the neuron to connect other facts and events about life cycles and animal transformations. We are assisting in helping students form a trail they can follow back to recall the information at a later date. Do you remember little Hansel and Gretel, the two kids who were abandoned in the woods? They left little breadcrumbs on the ground so they would know how to get back. Of course they hadn't thought about hungry birds that would follow them and eat the crumbs. Thankfully they had some help getting home after a bit of drama in a house in the woods, so they didn't need to rely just on the breadcrumbs. Our students are like Hansel and Gretel; when left to their own devices, they can create faulty breadcrumbs and lose their way back to retrieval. So we are there to assist with scaffolding to help them build a lasting trail back to the information. Teaming nonfiction and fiction is a great tool for scaffolding ideas and events for your students. Rich, socially constructed experiences extend the learning and help the episodic memory follow that trail (Moscovitch 1995; Fuster 1995; Jensen 2005).

6.   What part does "flow" play in motivation and interest-driven learning?

I had been teaching about four or five years when I learned a valuable lesson about motivation and the importance of interest-driven learning. I was teaching in Houston, and our school was in an area where many different immigrants from the Middle East tended to settle. Our school served students who spoke over 100 languages. That was both a blessing and a challenge when it came to teaching. I found out that my small-town Texas upbringing had not given me the best prior knowledge of different cultures and their tacit and religious mandates. I was teaching kindergarten, and on the first day of class a tall five-year-old boy walked in, put his brand new school supplies on a desk, walked up to me, and declared, "Vishnu, Hindu God of Love!"

"Well, hello," I said and leaned down to his level. "So your name is Vishnu."

"No, Vishnu, Hindu God of Love!"

So I assumed I must have used my Texas accent and called him "Veees New." So I tried again. "V i s h n u."

"No, Vishnu, Hindu God of Love!"

"So your entire name is Vishnu, Hindu God of Love?"

He smiled and walked to his seat, happy to be in kindergarten. Now Vishnu, Hindu God of Love was a lovely student who worked hard every day. His work was wonderful. He was beginning to read and loved to share things about his Pakistani culture. He brought in kokam (a red-colored, sour fruit), curried rice, and sweets his mom made so we could try them as a class. October soon arrived, and the time came for parent conferences. In came Vishnu, Hindu God of Love's mom and dad. As I began showing them his portfolio and talking about what a great addition Vishnu, Hindu God of Love was to my class, his dad and mom started laughing and looked at Vishnu, Hindu God of Love. Suddenly he was interested in finding a book to read while we talked.

"Oh, he did that to his babysitter too!" his dad said, laughing.

"Is that not his name?

"Oh, it is his name and where his name came from. When we told him where his name came from, he thought he was the Hindu God of Love! So now he wants everyone to know it! You can call him Vishnu." The father's look at Vishnu was that look parents get when they have made a point more than once.

"Do you mind if I continue to call him Vishnu, Hindu God of Love, or is that breaking a rule or disrespectful?"

Dad looked at me for a long time. Mom, sitting behind him per their religious rules, smiled to herself and quickly hid the smile. "I guess you can if you want to. It is okay, but why do you want to do that when he was playing a game with you?"

I answered, "Well, each child brings his culture and family into my class, and Vishnu, Hindu God of Love brought that to our class. He was very proud of it and wanted us all to know the history of his name, and I respect that. I hate to burst his bubble. We all need to feel important sometimes." I am not sure if I earned Dad's respect, but I do know that my stock went way up with Mom and Vishnu, Hindu God of Love.

On the first day of school, kids bring with them their prior knowledge of the world, and the more open we are to finding out what they know and to incorporating their interests in our lessons, the more our kids will be motivated to learn. One way to integrate students' interests is to always put out great children's literature. I always put out lots of books about names and how names came to be given to people at the beginning of the year and have students tell a story about where their names came from. If they don't know their name's history, that is their first day's homework. This is a great way to start a conversation on the first day of the school ride home. It is so much better than "What did you do in school today?" and the response: NUTTIN!

Children's Literature That Highlights a Child's Name or Culture

Chrysanthemum by Kevin Henkes
My Name Is Yoon by Helen Recorvits
The Name Jar by Yangsook Choi
My Name Is Maria Isobel by Alma Flo Ada

I have seen many a child be inspired to pick up a book and find a new world to imagine and escape to. For example, students learn about how many cultures eat rice in the book *Everybody Cooks Rice* by Norah Cooley. Their faces light up when they see a book or idea, and then the bell rings and they go to MATH! We must find ways to enrich our content areas with great books to take the children deeper into the curriculum as well as motivating them with high-interest books. I have watched a child on his own search out the history of 9/11, the number of people affected, the money that was lost, and how people dealt with it. He covered the system of economy, math, social studies, culture, science, and history. This is when a child is in flow. Csikszentmihalyi (2008) says a person is in flow when he or she is flourishing inside learning and reaching his or her greatest potential. Like a ballerina in the lead role of *Swan Lake*, or Gabby in the Olympics, when she reached outside herself and won individual gold when she thought she was there only to help her team. She was in flow. We hope to keep our students in flow during the day and into all their learning environments.

18

Phonemic Awareness

What a child can do in cooperation today, he can do alone tomorrow.

—Lev Vygotsky

The quote above is one that most educators have encountered before, as it is a staple in our classrooms: the idea of our students assisting each other as they learn. This idea also revolves around the teacher as the guide and facilitator for the children as they learn. When they master or transfer the information or skill to their independent work, then we taper off, and they stand alone. I would like to take this quote to a new place in this chapter. I like to modify the quote for teachers and in the spirit of this chapter. What a teacher can do in cooperation in the classroom today, he or she can do in the classroom tomorrow. So with the help of the material found here, teachers can guide, scaffold, and encourage students to learn tomorrow.

As teachers we are also learners, in the sense that we observe what our students express and then assess the quality and design of their next instruction. We are learning about how they learn. In the early childhood classroom this can happen within minutes many times a day for each child. A base belief that all children can learn is essential to our mission, as they bring their approximations and understandings to school each day. With the help of benchmarks, checklists, and a standards continuum, we can determine the content and context of the next lesson to teach them. Teachers have the instinct to know when to nudge, when to step back and observe, and when to step back in to support. So Vygotsky's zone of proximal development (2012), represented in the quote above, is many faceted each day.

Experiencing and learning phonics is a progression of language acquisition. Each stage of the process moves the literacy learners further into independent use of the language. The more they learn, the more they can manipulate stories, sentences, words, and letters. The class goes on the journey and forms a safety net around the learners to hold them up when they fall and to bounce them back up to try again. How do we show children we trust their approximations? We serve as the net! The children show you they trust you when they approximate and wait for your reaction, afraid to share it with others until you make it real. The young learner looks to the teacher as the expert; if she says it is real, then it is real. You see their heads come up and their shoulders straighten, and they walk taller when you acknowledge their reading and writing. With this trust we nurture the approximations and nudge them forward. Focus on what children are doing rather than on what we wish they would do" (Calkins 1994, 41). When we celebrate their first attempts, we make them successful for the children. They are holding their breaths, waiting. Once the teacher shows this trust in their work, they will continue to work and learn through language in the stories you read, the paper you put out to write on, and the listening ear at the author's chair.

Young children come to us with all they have packed in their backpacks and their brains on that very first day. Open the door and welcome in all they have and celebrate the learning to come. For years in our country we followed the idea that children must learn their alphabet first and then read and write. We then moved as a nation to the belief that sight words are the answer to reading (Moustafa 1997). We must teach them all of the sight words, and then they will BOOM read. More recently, we have encountered the idea of leading children to bring meaning to a story using all they have to work with. Educators can give students experiences in rich children's literature from which they can infer, picture, create meaning, make connections, and READ. Educators can share paper and pencils on which to create meaning, imply, picture, guide, and WRITE. The key to unlocking literacy is not inside the methodology; it is inside the child. We are but facilitators on the journey. The classroom can become a resource from which the child can take all he or she needs to read and write. We have sight words on the word wall and word banks; we have books in the classroom with all kinds of letters, words, and stories; and we have our own stories hanging on the wall.

Phonological Awareness: The Deep-Seated Tradition of Oral Language and Scaffolds in the Sounds of Language

Sharing great stories in beautifully crafted children's literature models for the students how meaning is made inside the story and pictures. Writing stories together illustrates for the students how to put the ideas inside their brains onto paper to create meaning. My classroom always started with writing. Many classrooms choose the inverse. They start teaching reading and lead the students into writing. I propose that children come with the ideas already in their heads, and when we let those out first and do shared and guided writing with them to create stories, we are demonstrating how stories are made. This causes them to come to reading with an understanding of how stories are created from someone's thoughts. They are already authors, so they respect the author's attempts, just as our class respected their attempts in the classroom. As we are writing stories, recipes, songs, and chants, we are also reading books with all types of stories, both fiction and nonfiction. The students see letters, words, and sentences used in both reading and writing. They learn that these letters are a way to communicate ideas and are motivated to learn more and more of how to use them to get their ideas across.

In a classroom of children, some will come from homes where people read every night, some will come from homes that have the TV on at all hours as they run around the house, and some will come with only survival skills in their pockets. We start each year with songs and chants to help all the students share a common understanding of how language can twist and turn and carry meaning to all. We start with what the children all have in common: an awareness of environmental print.

Environmental Print: Environmental print represents written words or symbols that are found in the environment of the child. This is the print that you experience as you pass by in a car on the way to work or school and places you live near, eat at, or shop at. Steak and Shake™ is on my way to the kennel, so I see the black-and-white checkerboard and read the letters almost every day. Steak and Shake is in my environment.

Environmental Print: Environmental print is words or phrases printed in a font or design that is unique and causes us to remember the words from the environment of the print. McDonald's™ is written using large golden arches and is easily recognizable. The child will read the word McDonald's™ if it contains the golden arches, but might not be able to read it if you just write "McDonald's'.

Environmental print carries two meanings, as it refers to the environment of the print and the environment of the child. I begin my school year by sending a letter home to my students' families asking them to send in box covers, packages, or pictures of environmental print. In the letter I share with the families how these items represent words their youngsters can already "read." When the children bring in the items, we put them on the word wall or create a bulletin board of the items. These items become a visual dictionary for the children to use if they are writing and need the word, a nudge, or a model. Once we have started our word wall, we are ready to begin adding other high-frequency words to assist us all in writing.

As Penny and Jan sit at a table near the environmental print word wall, they are talking and pointing and then laughing as they write on a large piece of paper. I lean in and notice that they have written Honey Nut Cheerios above a picture of a table with four people sitting around it. Written under the table I see [s gd]. I ask the girls to read it to me, and they laugh and say, "Honey Nut Cheerios is good."

"Who is eating Honey Nut Cheerios at your party?" I ask.

"We aren't having a party, we are having breakfast!"

Jan and Penny used environmental print to draw meaning and used functional print to put across their meaning. They used inventive spelling to sound out /s/ is and /gd/ good, and that became functional print (Fisher 1997). If children are given authentic opportunities to write and read, they will use their learned behaviors to write and read. A person doesn't have to know all the letters of the alphabet to read or to write. Emergent readers and writers start to become aware of the phonetic scaffolding as they are engaged in reading and writing. They come to the learning of new concepts in phonological, phonemic, and phonics awareness because they need it to progress.

Phonological Awareness Continuum

Oral Language to Phonemic Awareness to Phonics Awareness

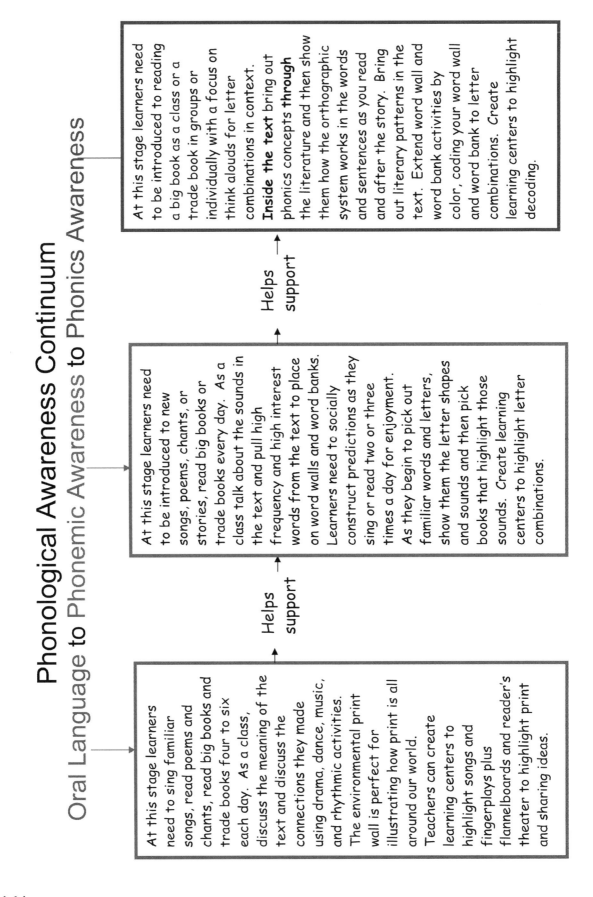

At this stage learners need to sing familiar songs, read poems and chants, read big books and trade books four to six each day. As a class, discuss the meaning of the text and discuss the connections they made using drama, dance, music, and rhythmic activities. The environmental print wall is perfect for illustrating how print is all around our world. Teachers can create learning centers to highlight songs and fingerplays plus flannelboards and reader's theater to highlight print and sharing ideas.

Helps support →

At this stage learners need to be introduced to new songs, poems, chants, or stories, read big books or trade books every day. As a class talk about the sounds in the text and pull high frequency and high interest words from the text to place on word walls and word banks. Learners need to socially construct predictions as they sing or read two or three times a day for enjoyment. As they begin to pick out familiar words and letters, show them the letter shapes and sounds and then pick books that highlight those sounds. *Create learning centers to highlight letter combinations.*

Helps support →

At this stage learners need to be introduced to reading a big book as a class or a trade book in groups or individually with a focus on think alouds for letter combinations in context. **Inside the text** bring out phonics concepts **through** the literature and then show them how the orthographic system works in the words and sentences as you read and after the story. Bring out literary patterns in the text. Extend word wall and word bank activities by color, coding your word wall and word bank to letter combinations. Create learning centers to highlight decoding.

Phonological and phonemic awareness have been studied for the rich backbone they create for later reading success (Wackerle-Hollman et al. 2015; Nyman 2014; Pannell 2013; Savage 2007; Castles and Coltheart 2004). Research has found great links between strong phonological experiences and successful readers. All children come to the first classroom with some experience in literacy. This could range from a rich read aloud background to an awareness of using communication to get across an idea. In the early years, we have the opportunity to greatly impact students' future reading success by including various hands-on stories and language. "Phonological Awareness is a broad term that involves working with the sounds of language at the word, syllable, and phoneme level; it is an umbrella term that includes rhyming, alliteration, segmenting and phonemic awareness" (Vacca et al. 2015, 132). During emergent literacy, when the child is just beginning to become aware of language and the sounds it creates, we can invite his curiosity with the sounds of language through familiar songs, poems, chants, big books, rich stories, talking, and singing stories. These include drama, dance, music, and rhythmic activities along with our environmental word wall. Take the story of an old farmer that most students have met through books like *Old MacDonald Had a Farm* by Carol Jones. There are many great versions, but this one is unique, as some of the pages have circles cut out of them so the reader can see into a small portion of the next page, which represents an animal on Old MacDonald's Farm. As they are singing E I E I O, students can be peaking into his barnyard and making predictions about another farm friend. The teacher turns the page, and they are rewarded with the answers to their predictions. They don't care if they were right or wrong, as it is just so much fun to find out what animal is awaiting them. We all sing loudly and joyfully chant the repetitive text:

> Old MacDonald had a farm, Ee-igh Ee-igh O!
> And on that farm he had a. . . . DOG! Ee-igh Ee-igh O!
> With a bark bark here, and a bark bark there,
> Here a bark, there a bark, everywhere a bark bark . . . ,
> Old MacDonald had a farm, Ee-igh Ee-igh O!

We sing and work our way through the story, and after we read the story in song, we add new animals to the end; the students draw pictures of the animals so we can add to the farm story. We know that Carol Jones just didn't have time to add these animals. Some of the students mimic the pages in the book by cutting out a circle and hiding their animal behind it, to draw out the moment of discovery. They have picked up on the magic of this version. Some use inventive spelling to approximate the chant, and some draw an animal and read the story in the author's chair as the full chant. All of the students are correct in their enrichment of the story. All attempts are celebrated, and we add our pages to the end of the book, then place it in our classroom library. When the students check out books from our classroom library, the books they want to take home first are the ones we have read, chanted, enriched, and loved, as they want to share that reading experience at home with their families.

One of my kindergarten students' favorite songs was about a wienee man. You might remember singing about a wienee man in camp around a fire or at scouts. I learned about the wienee man while cooking Girl Scout™ stew around a big pot on my camp-out. My Girl Scout™ leader, Jo, led us in a sing-around about the wienee man. I laughed that such a thing could happen to a simple wienee salesman:

> I know a wienee man.
> He has a wienee stand.
> He sells most everything from hot dogs on down.
> Someday I'll change his life.
> I'll be his wienee wife.
> Hot dog, I love that wiener man!
> Wienee Man, Wienee Man, OOOOOOOOO!
> Wienee Man!

When I shared this song with my students, they also laughed and had to sing it again and again. I pulled out a wienee man puppet that had feet and hands, and we danced. Over the years we sang this song so many times it became legendary in our elementary school. I spoke at a fifth-grade graduation many years after I left the elementary school, when my last group of kindergarten students graduated, and at the end of the graduation, the parents and the students stood up and sang "Wienee Man." I believe the song had staying power. Was it because of the fun lyrics? Yes! Was it because we danced with the song? Yes! Was it because singing and laughing long to be shared, just like language? Yes! There are songs I still sing loudly and dreadfully with my friends on road trips. We sing the ones we have memories of, the ones we know by heart, and the ones we know all our friends can sing with us. This shared experience illustrates the lasting power of shared language.

In my classes we put the words for the wienee man song on the pocket chart and then added sticky notes to the word *wienee* and wrote variations of the song. One student wrote ketchup on his sticky note, so we sang about ketchup man, and then we sang about mustard lady and had to add even more sticky notes. Each time we adjusted the song, the students experienced letters, words, and parts of speech as they revised the song lyrics. We used this strategy with other books, like *Brown Bear, Brown Bear* by Bill Martin Jr., and used the great resources at web sites built around the book and that Eric Carle offered, with pictures and extensions for the book. We placed the pictures in the pocket chart in all combinations and added and subtracted animals, leaving the predictable text on the pocket chart. We even created a classroom version for our principal: "Mrs. Frost, Mrs. Frost, What do you see? I see a custodian looking at me!" It was a great way to meet all the new people at our school at the beginning of the year. These games and books are great ways to share language as well as teaching your content and standards.

Flannel boards are also a great way to bring stories to life. They have been popular with early childhood teachers for forty years and remain a great hands-on way to sequence and tell a story. I use them for assessing retell and brainstorming a new story. There seems to be a renaissance for the flannel board in recent years, as homeschool cohorts have found them and are creating many great book sets online for teachers with directions and patterns we can use to create our own. I invited my students to create the story characters and scenery for their favorite books. I put lots of felt and accessories in the art center, and the students went over to get books from the classroom library or big book stand, then took them back to the art center and created things. I leaned over and observed Elizabeth as she took a piece of paper and drew out her characters one by one and wrote their names under each.

"I see you have all the characters in the book *Tacky the Penguin*. Are you going to do any scenery?" I asked.

"What is scenery?"

"Let's open the book and I can show you. All around here, where Tacky and his companions are swimming, is scenery. It shows the reader where the story is taking place."

"How do I do that?"

"Well, do you want to show the water or the icebergs, or both?" I inquired.

With a smile and waving her scissors, Elizabeth said, "Yeah!"

So during center time we cut a large blue shape of ocean out of felt and put it on the bottom of the flannel board, then cut out a large white piece of felt and put it on the right side of the flannel board, creating scenery for Tacky and his companions. I also learned from one of my students in an undergraduate class about a flannel board apron.

I asked her to bring it in, and I knew I had to create one. She had made a teacher-sized one with pockets and two student-sized ones for the students to follow along with the story. In the picture below, you can see how the teacher can tell a story with assistance from the students or can assess a story sequence or retell it with the students. For example, figure 18.2 is a teacher flannel apron with a story about Gary Ghost and how he can change his color. As the teacher tells the story, she puts a new ghost on her apron to represent the color he changed to. The child makes the same changes on his or her child-sized flannel apron. Later in a learning center, the child can retell the story with the flannel ghosts as the teacher assesses the retell.

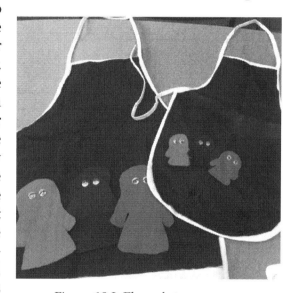

Figure 18.2. Flannel story aprons.

To make the aprons, I took canvas aprons from a local craft store and drew around the inside seam of the apron where I wanted the felt, then I cut out a pattern. I then cut out the felt, and with my sewing machine I adhered the felt to the apron. The pockets on the teacher apron are great for storing parts and pieces as you tell the story. Flannel boards also work perfectly for songs and poems. The students love to see their favorite stories depicted on the felt board, such as *Brown Bear, Brown Bear*. What do you see in the picture to the right? Figure 18.3 is a sample of

Figure 18.3. Flannel board sample.

the story on a flannel board with felt story pieces. The children can retell the story again and again in a learning center.

My students love "Wheels on the Bus," so we created the pieces for the things that happen and the people on the bus and then sang as the flannel board represented our song. I like to line up chairs in the shape of a bus, with a bus driver seat up front, and animate the song first so students get all the parts in their heads. Then we create the parts.

Fingerplays and transition songs are also great to stimulate oral language in the classroom. Fingerplays are rhymes that are accompanied by hand or body movements. An old classic is the one about the glasses:

> **These are Grandma's glasses.** *Make "glasses" over eyes with fingers.*
> **This is Grandma's hat.** *Place hands close together over head.*
> **And these are grandma's hands.** *Clasp hands together.*
> **In her lap.** *Place hands in lap.*
> *Recite this second verse in a deep, low voice:*
> **These are Grandpa's glasses.** *Make "glasses" over eyes with fingers.*
> **This is Grandpa's hat.** *Place hands farther apart over head.*
> **And these are grandpa's hands.** *Cross arms.*
> **In his lap.** *Place head on arms, as if sleeping.*

The students follow along, chanting as they mimic the motions. Mem Fox (1990, 2008) calls this creative dramatics; I call it fun. She reminds us that we all love to move and interact with language (Fox 1990, 2008). This fun fingerplay serves two purposes: first, it is fun and is interactive and shares language; and second, it also quiets down the room to get ready for learning. Transition songs or chants help us move from one place to another and are a fun way to get there. Whether we move as camels, with "Alice the Camel" (has three humps) or we clean the room after centers with the "cleanup song," we are enjoying the transition. Storytelling and reader's theater are also great ways to share stories and action. Storytelling is the act of telling a story without the book and follows a rich oral tradition of passing along information in story form. This learning activity stimulates speaking and listening and heightens the story in the telling. Students listen for the syntactic structure of the story to follow along. They derive meaning from the semantic cues they hear in the story without the challenge of orthographic decoding. I like to pick stories that have multicultural support, so the students can access their pragmatic cueing systems to fill in the blanks as they insert their prior knowledge. My students learn about different cultures and folktales from other countries. As you plan for a storytelling experience, remember to think about the complexity of the story, the number of characters, the actions, and music support or props you will use, and match all of them with your students' development (Hoffman 1985, 2011). Reader's theater is much like storytelling in that both scaffold oral language, but reader's theater puts the story into the hands of the students. Teachers can access a multitude of Web sites and teacher resources to find reader's theater scripts that are leveled; however, all stories can be adapted to the reader's theater format to engage students. To assist students in learning content, the teacher can adapt materials for curriculum-based reader's theater (Flynn 2004/2005). Older students can even be invited to write the script, create the props and characters, and perform the reader's theater to engage them in the full process, as this cements the retention of the materials they have manipulated.

Like storytelling and reader's theater, songs are powerful language magnets. Kids are attracted to their rhythm and love to sing along as well as write their own. I always had at least six song cards hanging on my chalkboard for us to sing each morning. We changed the six songs out every week or so as they mastered them. At the end of the year, we had learned about 300 songs. It is important that students see the music and the words to have an awareness of the print as we sing. The words come from song lyrics written down, and language is transacted. I wrote the song on the back of the quarter sheet of poster board to create the song cards, so I could be reminded of the lyrics as we sang. We sang old classics like "Miss Mary Mack Mack Mack" and "This Old Man," but we also sang contemporary songs like "I Like to Eat Eight Apples and Bananas" and "I Love You and You Love Me." The students became so excited by singing songs that they wanted to create their own. I put the quarter-sized poster board in the writing center and invited them to create songs that would hang on our chalkboard for a week, after which they could take them home. Garrett created one of my favorites during dental health month. I still sing the song some mornings as I brush my teeth to remember the steps and how important it is to brush our teeth to the best of our ability. Nancy also created a great bus-shaped song card for our class favorite, "Wheels on the Bus."

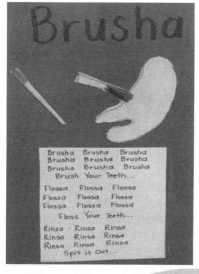

Alice the camel has five humps.
Alice the camel has five humps.
Alice the camel has five humps.
So go, Alice, go.

Alice the camel has four humps.
Alice the camel has four humps.
Alice the camel has four humps.
So go, Alice, go.

Alice the camel has three humps.
Alice the camel has three humps.
Alice the camel has three humps.
So go, Alice, go.

Alice the camel has two humps.
Alice the camel has two humps.
Alice the camel has two humps.
So go, Alice, go.

Alice the camel has one hump.
Alice the camel has one hump.
Alice the camel has one hump.
So go, Alice, go.

Alice the camel has no humps.
Alice the camel has no humps.
Alice the camel has no humps.
Now Alice is a horse.

Clean up clean up everybody everywhere. Clean up clean up everybody do your Share.

Clean up clean up everybody everywhere. Clean up clean up everybody do your Share.

Clean up clean up everybody everywhere. Clean up clean up everybody do your Share

Phonemic Awareness: How Phonemes Make Sounds That Blend to Make Words

As young literacy learners experience language in songs, chants, poems, and stories, they begin to notice and point out the letters and words they see. Some they recognize over and over, some are on our word wall, and some they just are attracted to by the way I read them or how they look. This is the perfect time to begin explicit instruction on how words are made by letters and letters make sounds. Our students are entering the phonemic awareness domain. For example, books like *Chicka Chicka Boom Boom* by Bill Martin Jr. and John Archambault are terrific for the way they use letters as characters in the story. The students yell out as they see them because, like good friends who live next door, they recognize them. As A and B work their way up the coconut tree, the students are carefully scanning all the features of the A and the B to make sure each really is their friend. This is a great opportunity to talk about A and B and their characteristics, just as we talk about other characters in books. We look around the room for examples of A and B and celebrate them with highlight tape. As we read further we meet their children, a and b, and we again search for them and welcome them to our classroom. We are playing with language and literally inviting language to play with us. This awareness of letters and their sounds sparks students' interest as they recognize that these sounds are what their teacher asks them to "sound out" as they write. When we read, we have letters in front of us to decode, but in writing we must encode onto the paper the letter sounds and then think about representing them on paper. This is much more of a challenge for new readers and writers. The more print rich the classroom, the more students assimilate the letters and play with them. They try them out in different situations on paper and in the books we read. Of course some words are easier to decode while reading, and some words are discrete sounds to encode when writing. These consonant vowel consonant (CVC) words are the easiest, as they are easier to discriminate. Consonants are sounds that allow air to flow through the mouth without any obstructions; vowels are sounds in which air is obstructed (Carroll 1998). Words that contain three sounds are the easiest to discern. For example, S in sat is a sound. A word like SAT makes the sounds of /s/ /a/ and /t/. As children learn these sounds, they tend to stretch them out so far that the word is not comprehensible. Thus, as we teach sounds in our English language, it helps young learners to put them into context. In a story we don't read about the CCCCCC AAAAA TTTTT, we read about the cat. Also when young readers are decoding and the words are stretched to their limit and beyond, this causes them to add other sounds, like the short u sound, so that word would now be CU AU TU.

We don't want our students reading this way, and we don't want them to assimilate the letter sounds this way. So we teach them to stretch them out to hear the individual sounds but to also make sure they stay together. I took out a blue rubber band to illustrate this concept with my kindergartners. As I stretch out the word c a t, I pull the rubber band, but not so far that it breaks (I pull it until it breaks), because then our word falls apart. The letters must stand together. So I illustrate again how c a t can stretch but not break the rubber band, and it comes right back together like the word should. This visual brings this very abstract concept to their level of thinking with a demonstration. A worksheet can't teach this lesson no matter how hard it tries. When I am "kidwatching" and I see a student insert the letter u into his writing, this is a red flag for me to listen to him. As you can see in Nancy's tooth book below, she is inserting a u into the words; she is stretching too far. She has taken apart BR, sounding out B and R so far they break apart. She again stretches r out so far in the middle that she again breaks the word. As I listen to Nancy read, she says BBBBUUUUURRUUUUSH, so I pull out a rubber band and stretch out the word as I say it. This brings BR together again as a blend.

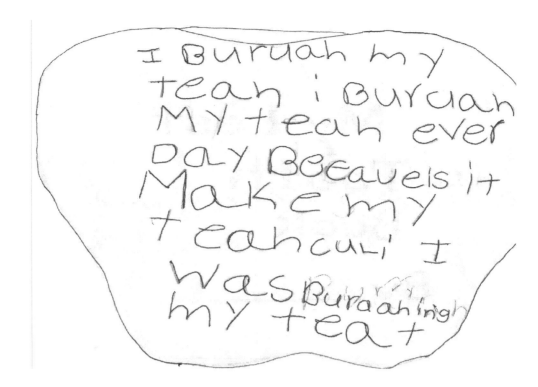

I also teach phonograms, also known as word families, as students reach this stage. As young children know about families, they can make the jump to word families (Carroll 1998, 70). Phonograms utilize both **"onset"** and **"rime."** Onset refers to all the letters that are positioned in front of the vowel, like C in CAT. Rime refers to the vowel and all the letters that follow, like AT in CAT (Carroll 1998). I draw a T chart on the board.

As the students can see, families have similar characteristics. They share a family name (last name), but each member has a unique first name. Word families have a unique onset but share a rime. One way to illustrate word families in the context of children's literature is to use the book *Sheep in a Jeep* by Nancy Shaw and create your own word family pocket. I begin reading the story, and

First Name		Family Name
Kelley		Barger
Kurt		Barger
Dot		Barger
Edward		Barger
	B ‖ AT	
	R ‖ AT	
	S ‖ AT	

every time the students hear the eep family, they say /eep/ out loud. This gets their oral language and creative dramatics into the lesson. After the story, using magnetic letters, I place the "eep" letters on the right side of a magnetic board and then with random letters try it out and see if I can make a family for eep. The first one I use is "sheep," as that was in our story. I put s and h together on the left of eep and slide them together to form a family. I ask the students if they think there are other members of the eep family. They call out "jeep," which was also in our story. We put up J and slide it to our eep family, and we have a new member of the family. We continue this activity until we have several members of the eep family. Then to cement the learning and to make it visual and constructive, I create a center to make word family pockets (see word family pocket rebus chart learning center direction sheet below, written for the students' independent work). Word families can be celebrated and practiced as many ways as you can dream.

Educational resources companies market magnetic letters that are designed by word family rimes, blends, digraphs, diphthongs, and individual letters. These work great for a word work lesson or a magnetic letter center to support the pockets and flip books. Another great way to support onset is finding beginning letters in books and stories we have written. We have even found them on our center board and chalkboard. I read *Some Smug Slug* by Pamela Duncan Edwards, and we laughed because we couldn't believe there are that many S words in the book. The book also hides the letter S on every page so the students could search out the hidden S. We read this together with a roll of highlight tape and highlighted every single **s** at the beginning of s words in the story, and that was quite often! After we celebrated them in the story, we went around our room on a scavenger hunt for the letter s words and highlighted the s in those also. Words like *songs*, *sink*, *sun*, and *slide* had a highlighted s on each word. We then wrote all the s words in a word bank of s words to put in our class as a part of our class word bank dictionary. As you can see in figure 18.7, a learning center can be created using the highlighting center rebus chart.

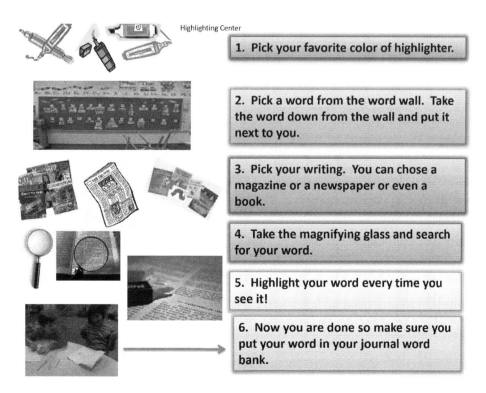

Figure 18.7. Literacy center rebus chart.

Now that the students have been playing with the orthographic nature of letters and words, they are beginning to show signs of more mature, inventive spellings using vowels. They are now hearing and noticing how words are unique in the way they are created. Their spelling is telling me to start teaching more technical lessons about phonics. When teachers blend those books that are built for word family practice and control the vocabulary to help students with CVC combinations plus high-frequency words, we give our students the gift of all the sounds in the English language at all times. If we rely only on contrived, controlled vocabulary books that manipulate the story to teach a concept, then we are hobbling our students with language usage. I use every resource I have available to teach what my students are showing me they need. As you see in Nancy's story below about butterflies, she is writing nonfiction. If I had not infused the classroom with nonfiction books as well as fiction books about caterpillars, she would have only written in one genre. Here she needs to tell others what she is learning as she reads and explores the butterfly's lifespan in our class's butterfly glass house.

Nancisommxay

Insects his 6 Less saiors his 8 Less
Butterflies, thelacewing saioRs is notainsects
Mostof the time thepuss.
Hairstreak theShiny papa
Butterfly tost withthentiny feet.

As you can see in Nancy's piece, she is learning all about how the caterpillar turns into a butterfly. She needs more precise language for this nonfiction piece. Simple words and high-frequency words are not enough. She has moved to needing the RIGHT word. So she begins to sound out words that she needs. You also notice she has corrected the over-segmented words and is now leaving out the inserted U letters and smoothly blending her sounds. Many of the words are conventional spelling she learned as she used her classroom resources in our word banks about butterflies and caterpillars and the books she has read and enjoyed. She is not copying a book for the text, she is creating and encoding as she goes . . . she is writing the text she needs. It is time to teach more advanced phonetic skills.

Phonics Awareness and Mastery: Manipulating Sounds and Symbols to Make Words and Meaning

As I have done in the discussion of the first two phases of phonics awareness, I also cover phonics instruction: teaching phonics in the context of children's literature. Inside a big book, a picture book, or even a classroom-written, shared and guided writing experience, I dig out phonics concepts through the language-bringing-out patterns in the text. I like to start off reading *The War Between the Vowels and Consonants* by Priscilla Turner (Carroll 1998; Smith-Barger 1999). The story is another one that characterizes the alphabet letters. In this story, the vowels A, E, I, O, and U, and the consonants, B, C, D, F, G, H, J, K, L, M, N, P, Q, R, S, T, V, W, X, and Z, join Y, who fights for both sides and is a spy engaged in war. The consonants are jealous that the vowels get all the attention, as there are fewer of them. The story is a humorous way to look at the function of each type of letter and how they have to learn to work together to stop chaos from ruling the world. After we read the story, I pull out a large bucket of foam letters, and we put the letters on two sides of the room with Y at the end, hiding. We then reenact how the letters came together to STOP the war. After we blend our word STOP, we go on to make lots of new friends in this peaceful world of words. The students can manipulate the blending action and feel the letters in their hands and actually pull the letters together to create words. This authentic blending lesson helps the young learners feel the experience of blending sounds to make words. For more practice, I put the book and loads of pipe cleaners in the reading center so they can make their own letter characters and make words together.

To go deeper into how we manipulate the sounds in our English language, we can revisit that old farmer and his animals and sing again the song he sang with the animal sounds. We are still using our love of oral language and singing the books, but this time we are switching the rhyme "Ee-igh Ee-igh O" and *replacing it with our five vowels*. I take a glove and write the vowels with a permanent marker on each finger; we sing the book, transplanting our vowel letters first as long vowels and then the vowel sounds as short vowels. The students love the manipulative glove and also how the vowel sounds change the beloved song and book. The short vowels can be tricky, and they love when the teacher misses one (Carroll 1998). As we are exploring vowel sounds and the unique ways they can change with the addition of other letters, we can try more advanced vowel combinations. Carroll (1998) illustrates using the book *Goodnight Owl* written by Pat Hutchins to teach the diphthong OU: "This term refers to a word that combines two vowel phonemes within one syllable. For example, OI is a diphthong in the word OIL. A diphthong is a vowel sound" (Carroll 1998, endpaper). This book is a great classic story of an owl who is very unhappy about not being able to sleep during the day in his forest when all the other animals are awake. The book uses onomatopoeia to tell the story of all the animal languages. The class picks characters for the story and then creates a sack puppet (figure 18.10). On the face of the sack puppet where the eyes go, the students place one large, wiggly eye and then draw one eye closed like the owl on the cover of the book, to show that the owl is trying to sleep (**O U**). The U forms the closed eye, and this is illustrated by putting eyelashes on the bottom (as seen in the picture below). The bottom one inch of the paper sack is cut off and is used to create the ears and beak. The students write OW over and over on the body to show feathers, and each time they write OW they say the diphthong sound /ou/. This provides oral practice for the sound of the OU diphthong. The class dons the puppet and acts out the owl getting angrier as each animal sounds off and keeps him awake. With all the owl puppets and animal sounds, the story comes to an end with nightfall, when all the animals are quiet and owl screeches loudly! The students love this story,

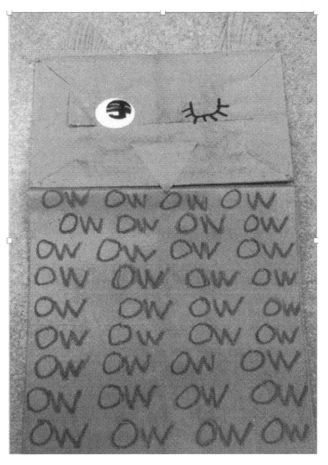

Figure 18.9. Student-made phonics artifact "owl puppet."

and the teacher can follow up with an explicit lesson on the OU diphthong in context at the beginning, middle, and end of various words.

As students progress through the phonological awareness continuum, they are refining and using everything that they have learned to read up to the present. They begin to hone their reading skills and grow in their ability to decode when they read and encode when they write. They learn to manipulate words and use phonics generalizations to break down words and put them back together in a new configuration. Making Words™ (Cunningham 2013) is a higher order thinking strategy that breaks down a secret word into the many smaller words that can be created using the letters that belong to the secret word. At this time the students are able to not only bring their prior knowledge of onset and rime, sounds they have learned as diphthongs, digraphs, and blends to decode a word, but they can also turn the process backward and encode words and manipulate the letters to make smaller words.

In the example, you can see the secret word was "feathers" and the students were given the letters e a h f s t r e on small sticky notes on a piece of paper. Some teachers use magnetic letters, letter tiles, or even printed letters on paper. It is important at this stage to keep the activity as manipulative as possible, so that the student can move the letters to form the words to try them out. If they try to make the word "seat," they see that they can make that word because each letter they move, they have at their disposal. They can't, however, make the word "seethe," because they only have two of the letter e. I have divided the learning activity in this specific example into categories of word size, like two-letter words or three-letter words, as this scaffolds them to find the final secret word, which contains eight letters. They often jump ahead; they find "feather," and some find the secret word "feathers." The teacher can choose which skills to put inside the secret word options to tailor the lesson to their individual students' needs.

This learning activity works great in a learning center as well. In this version, the teacher uses the format of writing down the smaller words to assess students' comfort with letter combinations and the diphthongs and digraphs they make, their use or lack of use, and their engagement in assessing their confidence in the joy of the puzzle. There are many Web sites and books written for Making Words,™ which teachers can utilize when planning for the strategy; however, the manipulative nature of the strategy is where the power is found.

During the first stage of our journey of understanding phonics in reading and writing, the students must experience language in music, rhymes, chants, and creative dramatics as they play with language in their world. These oral language experiences springboard students into phonemic awareness (Nyman 2014). Their time immersed in phonemic awareness supports and necessitates their learning of phonics. Their natural scaffolding through the stages of phonics progression has boosted their fluency in both reading and writing. They read and write with more flow and expression, and becoming more accurate and precise has given them ease in the processes of reading and writing.

Cueing Systems of Reading

As students are exploring the graphophonemic nature of decoding, we must also keep in mind all of the reading cueing systems good readers employ. As we have learned, there are many facets to language, and for decades researchers have debated whether they should be taught in parts or as a whole, heuristically or segmented, in isolation or in context. The psycholinguistic and sociolinguistic support of holistic exploration of language best suits young children. The psycholinguists believe we must have an understanding of the processes and function of literacy before we introduce them to young learners (Holdaway 1984). As emergent readers and writers, the students strive to make sense of what they are reading or writing. "Reading is not a passive activity; it is an active thinking process that takes place behind the eyes. Nor is reading an exact process. All readers make mistakes" (Vacca et. al 2015, 24). As readers are making meaning of a text, they can "miscue" or call a word incorrectly or incompletely or substitute and omit words based on the meaning, the structure, or the decoding (Goodman 2014). These miscues follow three basic information cues: orthographic or graphophonemic, semantic, and syntactic (Pearson and Jonson 1978). The orthographic cue refers to the physical print itself. The sounds and symbols carry speech sounds. As young readers and writers learn more and more about print and phonological awareness, they hone the skills of letter sound associations and generalizations. The semantic cue outlines how the prior knowledge of experiences and their world is used when students read. They know that the man in the picture is holding a baby, and the print says father, but they call it daddy. This is an example of a semantic miscue, as they are using their background knowledge to surmise that the man holding the baby is a daddy like their daddy. Since they call him daddy, they say daddy even though the first letter of father is f; they place their meaning on their semantic cues. The syntactic cue relates to the structure of the language. The more experiences the student has with language, the more she brings to what she is reading. For example, after experiencing read alouds and LEA stories, students have a basic understanding of how sentences are made up, and they use those concepts. So they bring that knowledge of sentence patterns to the piece they are reading and take meaning from it. I was reading with a third grader, Ethan, one day and he was reading a story about a heron. (The man came upon a strange scene. The heron was struggling to move. He was covered with oil.) When Ethan came to the word *heron* in the second sentence, he stopped in his tracks and started to sound it out. He was using his orthographic cue first and said /her/ /on/, but he still struggled with the understanding of the word with these known chunks in it. He was still struggling with the word, so he moved to the semantic cue and looked for a picture cue to direct him to the meaning. The story didn't have pictures, so he reread the sentence before it. (The Man came upon a strange scene.) This didn't help him with clues from the story, so he looked up at me, using his syntactic cues, and said, "Hey this /Her/ /on/ is nothing I know about but it is important because it is covered with oil and can't move. It needs help!" He knew it was an IT, so he knew it was a noun. He had used his syntactic cue to figure out it was the noun in the sentence he was missing. I asked him to look at the cover of the book and tell me what he saw. Ethan closed the book with his finger on his spot and said, "There is a beach and in the ocean is a big big boat. There are black spots in the water and I see big birds." I assured him that I saw the black dots also and that we would find out in the story all about the boat and the black spots. I told him that the big bird was a heron. I turned back to his page and placed my finger under each letter as I read it. He said it after me and looked at me like he wasn't sure I was giving him correct information. "A heron is a big bird? It is flying right here [pointing to the cover picture]." I assured him that those black spots were really important to the story, so read on.

Research has added a fourth reading cue to our understanding of the sociolinguistic dynamics of reading. This one outlines how language is intentional and allows us to communicate. The more students perfect their communication in reading, speaking, listening, writing, and viewing, the more they bring those experiences to the piece they are reading or writing. So those rich phonological experiences in the classroom and the communication in the home and class scaffold the fourth cueing system: pragmatic (Hymes 1974; Halliday 1975; Tompkins 2013). If you remember, Ethan was trying to understand why the heron can't move, and as we read the next sentence, he found out that the big ship had spilled oil in the ocean. He looked up excitedly and told me that his daddy worked on a big ship in Galveston harbor and had told him that a big ship had put oil in the ocean somewhere. This illustrates that Ethan was bringing in his background knowledge from home, where they had spoken about how this might impact his dad's job. I watched Ethan turn back to the cover and look and look, then asked him what he was seeing. This time, he told me that the black spots were the oil and that they were going to get on the big birds when they came down to eat. When I asked him if he thought that was why the heron couldn't move, he raised his right index finger up to my face and said, "My dad said that the fish could die because they couldn't breathe. Is that why the heron can't move?"

Ethan was using all four of his informational cues to read this book. He was also very motivated to read this book now that he had a connection with what was happening. Many children would skip the word and then lose interest in the story, as it would not make sense to them. This is why we need to teach students to use all their cues to attack a story and to only go as far as one sentence past a word they don't know. If they continue on for paragraphs and pages, they will become more and more confused and distanced from the missed word, so they learn that reading is not for making meaning, it is for confusion. In the example above we also see all of Cambourne's conditions (Cambourne 1988, 1999; Rushton et al. 2003). Learning to read and write is a collaborative venture. We need to interact with experienced peers, parents, and teachers. This social and cultural exchange of knowledge becomes our cultural capital in literacy.

19

Sight Word Development

The more that you read, the more things you will know. The more you learn, the more places you'll go.

—Dr. Seuss

As readers make meaning from text, they use their budding phonemic awareness, but it is not always reliable in words that are multisyllabic or those words that defy the phonics rules. Our phonics rules are more generalizations than rules, as many of words are exceptions (Clymer 1996). This makes teaching young children difficult, as the rules tend to be a moving target. Research demonstrates that phonics generalizations are those phonics rules that have a high utility rate. Those children with strong phonological scaffolding and awareness are able to see these generalizations in the context of great children's literature. The list of phonics generalizations (Clymer 1996, 184–185) contains the basic forty-five, but beware of the utility rates when teaching emerging readers, as research tells us to teach those that have at least a 75 percent utility rate. This means that 75 percent of the words in our language follow the rule.

Sounding out words through phonics awareness helps emerging readers, but when only phonics is used as a method to figure out words, fluency is at risk. A reader's ability to recognize words quickly, on the spot, and with reliance requires help from sight word vocabulary. When readers access both sight word vocabulary and phonics support, their fluency can be greatly enhanced (Vacca et al. 2015). As we immerse our students in rich phonological awareness, we can bolster their fluency by supporting sight word recognition as well. This chapter covers three ways of celebrating sight words and creating an environment in which students can access again and again high-frequency and high-interest words as their classroom becomes a visual dictionary.

Instant Words

From the work of many researchers, teachers have come to recognize the value of high-frequency lists of words (Fry et al. 1993; Dolch 1948; Veatch 1979). These word lists are examples of high-frequency words that will help emergent literacy learners' fluency while reading as well as when writing. They will have these words at their disposal either on a word wall, in a keyword bank, or in a mini office. Schools all across our nation are creating mini offices for their students to have at their fingertips words they can find on the classroom word wall or word bank.

Many teachers have elected to teach instant words and Dolch sight word lists incrementally to their young readers, using rich children's literature to find the words embedded in context. There are many books that highlight high-frequency words in the context of rich language stories. For example, a teacher could read *Brown Bear, Brown Bear, What Do You See?* by Bill Martin Jr. and Eric Carle and highlight in different colors the words *what*, *do*, *you*, and *see* on each page. All four of these words are on the first 100 high-frequency list. Each time the word is read, the teacher can point to the highlighted word in different colors. After the students have read the predictable text a few times over a couple of days, the teacher can then give each of the students cards for each word to add to their sight word rings (figure 19.1).

The students see the words in context, and they become part of their sight word rings. The students may hang these on their desks or in a mini office. The mini office has gained favor over the last few years. It can contain any information that the class can add as it is encountered so the child has the material close at hand. The sample mini office in the pictures in figure 19.2 has a word wall that resembles the one in the classroom, theme words, map words, and so forth. The sight word ring could be attached on the side. The students love to put these rings up around them as they work, as in a small office, hence the name mini office.

The research is clear that teaching words is essential for young readers and writers (Graves 2006; Graves and Watts-Taffe 2008). As we teach students high-frequency and high-interest words, it is important to remember to provide the words in the context of language so the students can see and hear the word being used. Allow students enough time to internalize the word with multiple instances of word learning and meaning and to use the word in the context of the classroom inside books, conversations, and experiences (Graves 2006; Graves and Watts-Taffe 2008). Word play is also key to cementing the word in a child's lexicon so that the words are available for her to use in reading, writing, speaking, viewing, and listening in her world. The immersion of the words in the children's world creates repetition and familiarity with the word and its meaning. We know that the more we use the word, engage in word play, and find the word in the context of children's literature, the more the child will "own" the word.

High-Frequency Words Inside Word Walls

Another great way to teach high-frequency words is through a class word wall. A word wall is a systematically organized collection of words displayed in large letters on a wall or other large display surface in the classroom. It is a tool to use, not just display (Jasmine and Schiesl 2009; Graves 2006, 2008; Vacca et al. 2015) . Word walls are designed to promote group learning and be shared by a classroom of children. **Word walls contain high-frequency words.**

Word Wall

Goals

- Cull words from children's literature, LEA stories, and environmental print.
- Encourage students to find the words in context as they read.
- Encourage students to use the words on the Word Wall as they write.
- During Shared and Guided Reading and Writing, do a think aloud to teach the students how to access the Word Wall words.
- Help the student to know how to look for a word on the Word Wall by the shape of the word, parts of speech, or even by the first letter and alphabetic order.
- Play word games with the high frequency words found on the Word Wall to help them associate the words and their characteristics through play.
- Continue adding to the Word Wall all through the year so these high frequency words become part of the students' everyday writing and reading.

Guidelines

- Cull words form the context of rich language experiences.
- Highlight the words in context before you place them on the Word Wall.
- Take your time as you add the words so as not to overwhelm.
- Place the Word Wall at eye level for your students so they can access the words as they read and write.
- Write the words clearly and check their spelling to make sure the students access the word correctly.
- The teacher could color code the Word Wall for parts of speech, color words, questions words, etc.
- Use a high frequency word list to help you pick the most commonly used words for the Word Wall.
- Practice the high frequency words in play and in the context of the classroom and children's literature so the students have practice that will help the words become automatic.

The more the word wall is a part of your classroom and your day, the more the students will learn to access it when reading and writing. There are many games you can play with the word wall. For example, the teacher could call out clues to a word and see if the students can find it and call it out. "I see a word that begins with a w and has five letters. We see this word every day in our houses and our classroom. We use this word when we talk about getting a drink." Yes, it is water! The teacher could ask the students to find three words that have the same letter patterns on the word wall. The students could access their awareness of letter sounds (Cunningham 2013). A teacher could highlight suffixes or prefixes and graph them. I like to create literacy centers to help my students use and find high-frequency words in print and writing experiences. The rebus charts below are for a literacy center to support word wall words. These samples of literacy center rebus charts help students independently practice finding word wall words and make sentences with them.

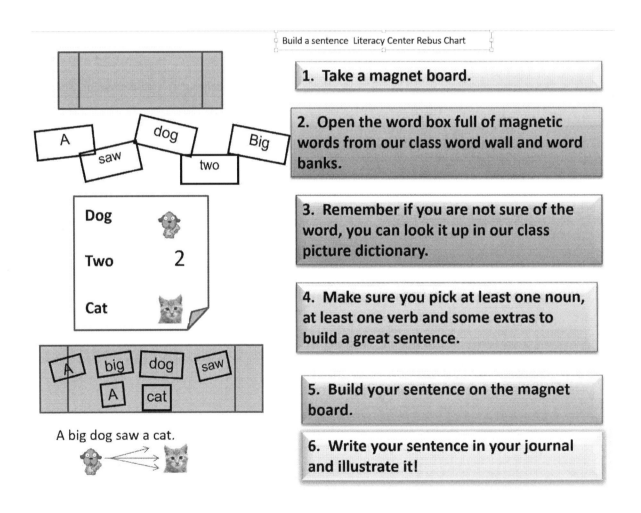

Build a sentence Literacy Center Rebus Chart

1. Take a magnet board.

2. Open the word box full of magnetic words from our class word wall and word banks.

3. Remember if you are not sure of the word, you can look it up in our class picture dictionary.

4. Make sure you pick at least one noun, at least one verb and some extras to build a great sentence.

5. Build your sentence on the magnet board.

6. Write your sentence in your journal and illustrate it!

A big dog saw a cat.

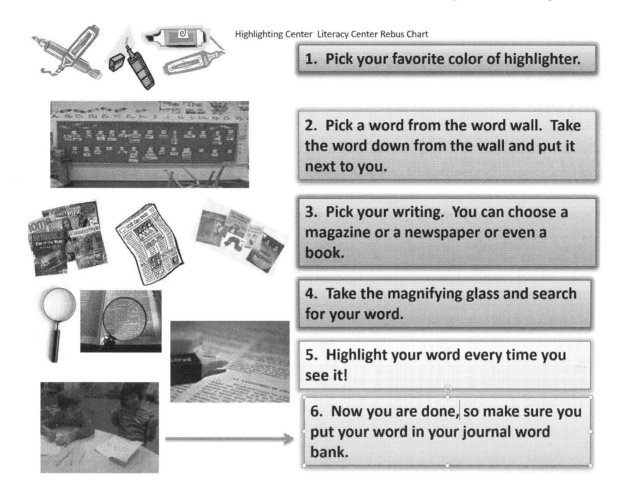

Highlighting Center Literacy Center Rebus Chart

1. **Pick your favorite color of highlighter.**

2. **Pick a word from the word wall. Take the word down from the wall and put it next to you.**

3. **Pick your writing. You can choose a magazine or a newspaper or even a book.**

4. **Take the magnifying glass and search for your word.**

5. **Highlight your word every time you see it!**

6. **Now you are done, so make sure you put your word in your journal word bank.**

High-Interest Words Inside Word Banks

Keywords are also a great way to find words, as the students are engaged in shared and guided reading. As I write an LEA story with my students, I pick out high-interest words we have accessed in our story, recipe, or map and highlight them with a key shape. In figure 16.5 (in chapter 16), you will notice small keys drawn on the bottom of stories listing the high-interest words students picked out of the stories. These are keywords (Veatch 1979). "Key vocabulary enhances and simplifies the language experience approach" (Veatch 1979, 18). In contemporary research, they are called high-interest words. These high-interest words are taken from the key and put on an anchor chart or large piece of chart paper and posted in the classroom. I like to draw the shape of the theme or topic of the word bank, as a visual, so it is easier for the students to find them when they need a word while writing. For example, Bill was writing a story about balloons at his birthday party after we read the story *The Blue Balloon* by Nick Inkpen. He went to where we keep the word bank anchor charts, found the one with the balloon shape, and borrowed *birthday* and *balloon* from the word bank for his story. These word banks become a visual dictionary for the students and create a shape, color, or key picture in the word banks, helping students access the memory of when we used the words.

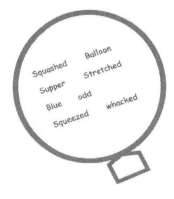

Word Banks

Description: A word bank is a collection of words. The collections could be from a common source or a theme. For example, the balloon word bank above words that were found in the book, THE BLUE BALLOON. The students shared the words that were new to them in the story. They also shared words they would like to use in future writing.

Word walls are made up of high interest words.

Procedures: Word banks can be created as a class, in a small group or individually. They can be put in a personal dictionary, a mini office or even individual word banks. Some teachers put pictures with the words if they are able to show a picture to represent the idea or word. The teacher could add words one at a time from frontloading the vocabulary or from picking the words as embedded vocabulary.

Frontloading: Teacher introduces words that she is sure her students might struggle with before they read a piece of writing.

Embedded Vocabulary: As the student, class, or teacher is reading a piece of writing, the child alerts the teacher to a word he doesn't understand or is new to him in that context. The teacher then defines the word quickly and then after the reading, or at a good stopping point, the student will look it up and clearly define it.

In my classroom I always utilized word walls, word banks, charts, individualized dictionaries, and quotes around the room as visuals. I told my kids to use the room when they constructed spellings in their writing. It was rewarding to watch them stretch to find a word or words on the word wall and dig in our word bank class charts hung around the room. There are many great books to help my students learn how to create and use word walls and word banks. *Rocket Learns to Read* and *Rocket Learns to Write* by Tad Hills are great for showing students how Rocket's teacher, the little yellow bird, shows him how to write down the words for the things he sees and wants to write about and then put them all together and create! Rocket's adventure of learning to write a story taught me to be explicit with word banks, word walls, dictionaries, and charts as resources and prewriting tools. Since these two books have come out, Tad Hills has written a board book, *Rocket's Mighty Words*, which is a great brief example of a word wall and word bank. One day before the students went to independent writing time, I took out a book, *Little Red Writing*, written by Joan Holub and illustrated by Melissa Sweet. The story follows the plot line of *Little Red Riding Hood*, but the main character is a red pencil who went on an adventure to write a story. On her way to a great story, she needed some exciting words. Her teacher, Mrs. No. 2, gave her a basket of fifteen red words to help her on her journey. The book is a beautiful story with loads of opportunities for lessons on descriptive writing. The story is an illustration of how to find the perfect word to construct a story. I read the book and challenged my students to use great descriptive words to show what was happening instead of just telling the reader. Children need to be surrounded by both print and language. They need both phonics and sight words taught in the context of rich children's literature that models how authors read and write fluently.

20

Literacy Lesson Development

You may have tangible wealth untold. Caskets of jewels and coffers of gold. Richer than I you can never be—I had a mother who read to me.

—Strickland Gillilan

At my grandmother's house there was a tree in the front yard that exploded with color in summer. Each year, I would wait for those purple, pink, and white blossoms to peek out. I knew that in a short time the yard would be filled with crepe myrtle blooms covering the tree. There were actually two trees planted in that spot in front of the house. My grandfather had planted them hoping to have a line of them by the sidewalk. Only two survived, and as they grew they held onto each other so tightly for survival that eventually the bright purple tree and the white tree became one. Each year the trees celebrated with variegated blooms, entwined so fully they shared both colors and even created a new one: pink, purple, and white blooms on each and every branch. The trees, by leaning on each other, had become one. Literacy works this way in a classroom that nurtures stories read and written, viewed, and heard. As we watch our young learners growing through the process, we see that their play represents the roots in their tree of learning. If we plant the roots deep enough and give them all the care we can, they will spread and branch out to form a strong base for the tree. From their play, children form a hearty trunk as they organize and internalize what they are immersed in. All around them they find print, quality children's literature, songs, rhymes, and chants. Their play has sprouted into an ability to internalize what they are engaged in and to organize the letters, words, and experiences to form stories. These stories that celebrate their experiences grow into branches that reach out to their families, friends, classmates, and members of the community in which they live. As they stretch their branches out into the literate world, they learn how their new literacy blooms. The more the process is nurtured, the stronger the tree. The stronger the tree, the more branches it will make and the brighter the blooms. Our job in the classroom is to immerse our emerging readers and writers in opportunities to explore literacy. All trees need sun, air, and room to grow. All learners need books, paper and pen, language, and a supportive, listening ear that celebrates approximation to grow.

Scaffolding Literacy Experiences with Children's Literature

So how do we organize our classroom and content to be that supportive ear for our students? How do we celebrate approximation while keeping an eye on where we want our students to go? How do we guide them by meaning? We start with strong child-centered lessons designed to engage the students in what they know and stretch them to expand their understanding of how language works. The students flourish when they are interested and motivated to learn. The first step to planning a great lesson is to tap into your students' interests. Remember that group of kindergartners I taught who were obsessed by penguins? The penguin and puffin house had just been opened at the Houston Zoo, and they wanted to learn everything about penguins. My first step, as always, was to find great children's literature to form a springboard for the lessons. Great literature tells a story the students can connect with (Haven 2007) and opens the door for those skills we teach via interactive strategies aimed at their developmentally appropriate level. In the figure below is an outline of scaffolding using children's literature to lead a lesson. Inside the lesson cycle, you will see the emphasis on priming the student and text. It is paramount to the success of the lesson for each child that he or she is motivated to learn. Rich story is a great way to bring students into a lesson.

Experiencing Children's Literature in All Facets of Literacy: Priming the Students and the Text

When introducing a text to a class or a student, it is important to take the time to prime the students for the book/story that is coming. I like to take a picture walk through the illustrations, predicting and inferring as we navigate through the story. Sometimes the book itself is the way I prime the students for a lesson. For example, as my class was exploring the alphabet and how each letter is formed, I read them *Alphabet Adventure*, written by Audrey Wood and illustrated by her son, Bruce Wood (2001). The story is about the order of the alphabet and how it goes a through z, but one day little **i** lost his dot, and the alphabet had a mystery. When I entered the classroom that day, I came and sat in my rocking chair and told my students that I had noticed a sad thing when I walked in that morning. When they saw my expression, they all sat up and asked what had happened. I pointed to the Word Wall that had the alphabet with lowercase and uppercase letters along the top. I asked them if they noticed anything about the alphabet letters on the top. As they were searching each letter for anything strange, I guided them to look in the area of the letter *I* by pointing to an area where I noticed something. We talked about how the capital I has only a line, but the lowercase I has a small line and a dot on top. I faltered as I spoke about little I and looked down. There are always one or two students who pick up on the missing dot. Yes, that is it, I told them, "Little I has lost his dot and without his dot, little I is only half of capital I and not his own letter."

"Where did it go?" shouted the class.

I looked down and sniffed, "I just don't know where it could be or what we will do!"

Outline of Scaffolding Reading

- **Prime the Students**
    - Check and assess prior knowledge.
    - Build excitement for the lesson.
    - Bring the lesson to their level.
    - Launch a purpose for the lesson.
- **Prime the Text**
    - Frontload new vocabulary
    - Preview or picture walk the book.
    - Connect prior experiences with the text.
    - Discuss the lesson and predict.
    - Discuss the cover and infer.
- **Move Students into Text**
    - Chorally read the text or share the reading.
    - Independently read the text with a partner.
    - Read aloud to students.
    - Individually read silently or whisper read.
- **Revisit the Text for Deeper Meaning**
    - Go back into the text and pull out and discuss characters, story parts, plot, main idea, etc.
    - Make connections with the text.
    - Discuss their predictions in light of the story.
    - Discuss their inferences in light of textual support.
    - Extend the lesson with a strategy or follow up the reading with a reader response.
- **Debrief the Lesson**
    - Observe the students throughout the reading and discussion to find out what the students learned.
    - Share the connections.
    - Talk with partners about the lesson.
    - Revisit the skills and strategies they learned in the lesson.

"We can go find it!"

So as a class we went on a scavenger hunt to find little I's dot. Of course I had hidden that dot already and guided us to find it, but not until we had searched and interviewed people along the way. When we found the dot, one of my friends carried it very carefully back to the Word Wall, and I placed it on top of the little I. After we were all back together, I brought them to the circle rug, where we saw a new book in my rocking chair. The title was *Alphabet Adventure*. I exclaimed, "Isn't that strange, as we just had an alphabet adventure!" This scavenger hunt primed the students for the book I would read to introduce the lesson of alphabet shapes. Each student had leaned in toward the book as I read about an adventure similar to our own. I had their attention and had set a purpose for the reading. Now when I prime a text, I simply show the students a few of the pictures in the storybook, and they are hooked. The book forms the basis for the lesson. The student now has a story and a memory of the storyline and pictures to hook the learning.

Extending the Story Experiences

For years and years we have read about the importance of reading aloud to our children, but just in the last ten years we have heard more and more about intergenerational literacy and the shifting landscape of our society. One thing remains constant: the importance of reading aloud to children (Trelease 1989). The changes are in the how, what, and who in the read aloud (Larson 2015; Muhtaris and Ziemke 2015; Bowcutt 2015; Morgan 2014; Trelease 1989). Children's literature is not just for children . . . it can motivate you to read in any genre and at any age! In recent years, with the onslaught of e-texts and tablets, read alouds have again evolved in both the medium and the impact on the reader and the listener. They are still powerful for both sides of the story. One day when I was walking in my neighborhood I saw my neighbor out in the yard on a blanket with her two-year-old, Jenny. They were lying on their stomachs reading. I walked over and was going to ask what they were reading but was surprised to see they were leaning over an iPad instead of a book. They had iBooks™ open and were reading *The Very Hungry Caterpillar* by Eric Carle Jr. (1994). Jenny was laughing and clapping just like my kindergarten students did while reading the book. She was counting the foods and calling out the days of the week just as my kindergartners did when I read aloud in the classroom; however, in this version she could touch each food and it would twirl and the numbers would be read aloud. I sat and interacted for a little while, and on my walk back home I thought about how books have adapted to the digital age. Their adaptations haven't killed the joy of sharing a great story together.

Children's books available on iTunes, Kindle, Nook, and other electronic formats (e-books) are very colorful and zoom in and out of the stories. There are also interactive books. One of my favorite books is *Scaredy Squirrel* by Melanie Watts (2008). I searched for versions of the book on the iPad and found an interactive version of the story. It was about $7, which was about the price of the paperback version of the book. I downloaded it and had hours of fun interacting with the story and illustrations. The electronic version really brought the story alive in a whole different way. I could click

Technology Tips

1. The use of technology is meant to supplement information and teacher instruction, not substitute for it.
2. There needs to be a balance between technology use and traditional methods.
3. Technology shouldn't be used as a digital paper and pencil worksheet; it should enhance the classroom learning.
4. Some modeling may be necessary, but students need to be allowed to explore.
5. Technology use in the classroom invites students to take more responsibility in their learning as they decide how to publish, present, research, and enrich their own learning.
6. When imagining technology use in the classroom, imagine engaged children exploring new ideas and thinking about ideas in different ways; imagine children working collaboratively to solve new problems.
7. Educators need to research the tools available in light of their classroom and student needs. There are many tools on the market, and it is okay to explore and experiment with technology, but remember the teacher still facilities, guides, and teaches the students.

Written by Rebecca Warren   Source: *Amplify: Digital Teaching and Learning in the K-6 Classroom*

on the microphone and let the program read the book as it highlighted the text, and I could move the characters and enlarge sections; bookmark pages; and even look up words, phrases, and clichés in a dictionary. I could also look up information about the author on Wikipedia™. I was hooked! I shared this with my neighbor, and now Jenny and Jenny's mom are hooked!

Oh, picture books have come a long way. They are terrific for activating prior knowledge with lessons for all ages. My favorite book for a history lesson is *So Far from the Sea* by Eve Bunting (Bunting and Soentpiet 2009). The book is a historical fiction picture book that deals with Japanese internment camps. By reading this book, kids can tap into story (Haven 2007) and picture how these camps affected Japanese families across America. When the content is read in the textbook, the students can look at the material with a new eye. This type of combination of textbook and trade book brings meaning in the form of the human impact to any event . . . to see it within a story.

One of my favorite books to read to young children is the story of a slug that learned to read. We were introducing word banks in a kindergarten class and I opened the book to the end paper, which was solid green, but I was completely stopped by the flap! On it (spoiler alert!) was a list of tips for teaching a slug to read a book:

1. Attach labels to Little Slug's favorite things.
2. Read out loud to him.
3. Point out words that repeat.
4. Sound out words.
5. Make a vocabulary list.
6. Be patient.
   AND, of course, it helps if Little Slug can see the book, so prop it up and set him on a rock!

Go ahead and read it again, and you will have the same feeling I did. This list is very close to what I share with my freshman children's literature students for when they read to young children in their first practicum. This list is also very close to Jim Trelease's *The Read Aloud Handbook* (2013) tips for parents reading to their children. Inside I found great strategies modeled by the slugs. Great book share and Word Bank label ideas are illustrated and modeled in big bold pictures. There is so much humor, and even Slug sounding out words in a think aloud. Mom slug highlights key vocabulary and shares nonfiction text features with Little Slug. Finally, toward the end Little Slug dreams of one day using reciprocal reading by turning the tables and reading a book to his mom. *How to Teach a Slug to Read* by Pearson (2011) is a great book to start Word Banks in your classroom.

Debriefing the Learning and Fostering Connections

As students connect with a book in the explorations above, they will make authentic connections with the book as it lingers in their minds. For example, a little later that day in the kindergarten classroom with the slug book, I overheard two little boys talking in library center.

"The book today had my favorite animal in it."

"Yuck, I hate slugs! You like them?"

"Yes, of course, a slug is like a worm and lives all over the place."

His little friend sat looking at the book and suddenly yelled enthusiastically, "Hey we read a book with a smug slug" (*Some Smug Slug* by Pamela Duncan Edwards, 1998).

As educators, we glory in moments when our students make those literary connections. We teach them, talk about them, and assign them, but a true connection like this one is authentic and powerful. How do we stimulate such connections? We read and read and read to our students every day from numerous genres. With a rich history of good books and conversations about character, setting, themes, and inferences, we can lay a foundation for such connections to germinate and grow. We can take the opportunity opened by the great stories and make those text-to-self, text-to-text, and text-to-world connections that little boy made (Keene and Zimmerman 2007). Taking the book into a lesson primes the student for the learning, primes the book for those connections, opens the story for extensions, ripens the environment for deeper meaning, and invites the reader and listeners to debrief the many connections they make in the lesson.

21

Reaching All Learners

Children are made readers on the laps of their parents.

—Emilie Buchald

In a classroom filled with young learners, there are as many learning styles as there are learners. It is our honor to reach them all. So far in this section of the book we have been learning about reaching emergent readers and writers guided by meaning. This information ties into the idea of implicit and explicit learning. Explicit learning is called "labeled learning" and is defined as traditional school learning in the areas of reading, writing, lectures, and talking. Teacher-led textbook learning and content area reading and writing are too often taught through these methods (Jensen 2001). The other type is implicit, which includes hands-on approaches, more trial and error, habits, role-plays, life experiences, drama, experiential learning, games, and active learning. Jensen calls this "unlabeled learning" (2001, 72). The more we facilitate connections with a child's interests in mind and create an environment in which hands-on learning can take place, the more we can offer a helping hand in the struggle some writers have finding concrete support in writing. In these two different teaching modes, the methodology of giving the opportunity to use implicit knowledge and integrating explicit teaching makes all the difference in students' affective and academic success.

Sarah was facing the possibility of failing second grade, and I knew her to be gifted in the elements of story and drama. She would make a dance or play from school events such as field day. She would hear the theme and create a performance or routine with her friends for the class or her family using music, creative dramatics, and even dance. Sarah went to drama and dance camps. She went to opera camp and can't carry a tune . . . why? She felt successful in the arts. Sarah created meaning in her life with HER intelligences to build her unique meaning for the information. How tragic it was to find that those creative ventures and interpretation of information were not upheld in the academic environment. She couldn't find such depth of creation and knowledge in her classroom. Story is a way of life, not a worksheet that she couldn't complete in the time allotted. Through Sarah's "village" support, she made it through second grade. In third grade she was assigned a teacher who saw all students' potential and unique gifts.

When given an assignment to do research, Sarah chose volleyball. She played volleyball for three years on a team. She began with attending a college volleyball game and also watching the US Olympic women's volleyball team. After noting the differences in the game and some techniques, she interviewed several of the players and coaches on tape and investigated the biographies of many US players. She added her kinesthetic intelligences and tried out some of the techniques they taught her. As she sat down to write, she had stimulated her brain with implicit learning about the topic and followed up with her explicit learning. Sarah wrote a "how-to" manual for new volleyball players. She also created a video for techniques and tips for new players. When we not only support but invite learning experiences that are built by the individual, as educators we use the arts as a way to stimulate, manipulate, support, and celebrate reading and writing authentically. Sarah produced and presented this to her class. Her friend Rachel presented her research by holding a yoga class, and Lizzie created a statue of Jack, her little brother, as she shared her research on sculpture. There were also "traditional" reports and research.

Levine (1991) sites an example of a student who was having trouble coordinating writing and thinking at the same time. The student was struggling with writing. "[The] child said, 'you know, I can think fast if I don't write, and I can write fast if I don't think. I just can't write fast and think fast at the same time'" (1991, 172). Had this writer been given the opportunity to utilize implicit skills, the experience could have supported his or her thinking, which would have led to the product. The process is enriched by the supportive tools in the arts. Each student in Sarah's third-grade classroom drew from his or her own experiences and curiosities to create meaning. The teacher saw each student as an artist (Jensen 2001; Cornett 2014). The tools for learning were not laid out by someone else. Each student drew from the arts because, as Jensen states, "The arts develop neural systems that often take months and years to fine-tune. The benefits, when they appear, will be sprinkled across the spectrum, from fine motor skills to creativity and improved emotional balance" (2001, 1). The key in this study was a teacher who did more than just carry out activities for multiple intelligences and then call that differentiated learning; she gave her students the room and acceptance of the creative process to guide their meaning through the arts and fine-tune new connections (Dorn and Soffos 2001). Students must be taught through, in, and about a variety of creative arts so they have usable tools to learn and think through situations in life as well as for a specific assignment (Jensen 2001; Cornett 2014). Using implicit learning to scaffold explicit understanding is how we learn for a lifetime. This idea is also pivotal to assessment to create germane individual instruction and assessment. We must assess as we instruct to have valid pictures of our students' true abilities. The arts each enhance natural abilities and interests and build thinking skills and support reading and writing:

> Music enhances the development and maintenance of our brain's memory systems in two ways. First, it activates our attentional systems. What we pay attention to increases our likelihood of remembering it. Second it activates and strengthens multiple memory systems for both explicit and implicit memory. By activating multiple memory pathways, we can dramatically improve our chances to retention and recall. (Jensen 2001, 40)

The same could be said of writing both reflexively and extensively about something we are passionate about. When Sarah was given the opportunity to use her implicit knowledge with her learning of her explicit understanding, she GOT IT!

Reading and Writing Benchmarks

In my kindergarten classroom, when I invite children to write a story, I observe a variety of things appearing on a piece of paper. I see large pieces of construction paper with fire and a house and animals running around on the page. I see letters and mock letters scattered all around the page and running right off the edge. I see small blue squares of paper with symbols and pictures mixed together. I also see many pages taped together to make a long sheet of paper, with pictures cut from magazines glued on the paper. I also look over a child's shoulder and see some words that I recognize written in a row down the side of a folded piece of paper with pictures next to them. No matter the writing I look at or listen to from the author's chair, I see pictures. Some may have been solely pictures, some may have been small pictures with some symbols and some letters and words, and some may have words on one page and pictures on the next, but ALL of the writing samples include pictures.

So when the students start to write, what comes first: the words, letters, symbols, or pictures? At least 90 percent of my students start by drawing to create meaning and in stages add the symbols, letters, and words. My emergent writers learn that creation of meaning is the goal. They are to get their ideas from their heads onto the paper in any way they can. On the first day of kindergarten, about thirty minutes before we gather our things to go home, I ask my kids to write about their first day of school. They usually look at me like I have a tiara on my head. One time a little girl who liked things to be perfect just burst into tears, and a little boy said, "My Mom said I can't write yet but you had to learn that from your teacher 'cause it ain't her job!" I asked the kids if they had ever drawn a picture, and they all said, "sure," "of course," uh huh," and "I do the best pictures!" I told them that in our heads, we think about stories or things that happen, like the first day of school, and then the ideas float down our heads and can come out of our mouths. I told them that as they told the story of their first day, I wanted them to hold the ideas in so they could float straight to their fingers. When they put a marker or pencil or crayon in their hands, their fingers just drain those ideas through the marker, pencil, or crayon right onto the paper. After they heard that they smiled and immediately put pencils to paper, creating all over the space.

In this instance they had to be given permission to "write" from their strengths. Drawing was their writing of ideas. Drawing cemented all their stories throughout kindergarten, from prewriting, writing, and revision to publication. **In a child's world, drawing is writing . . . REALLY!** I like to read *Dog Loves Drawing* by Louise Yates (2012). The book is the story of a dog who loves books. One day as he was reading, he received a package from his aunt. Inside the package was a journal with a note from his Aunt Dora, who had written inside it, "To my dearest dog, May the lines you draw open a door to some wonderful adventures. With love from your Aunt Dora X X X X." The new sketchbook/journal was exciting, and the dog first drew a person who could be his friend; they set off to draw other friends, a setting, and many great adventures. This fantastic book shows the pictures coming to life on the page just as the stories came to life in the dog's world. I share this book on the students' first day of kindergarten to demonstrate that pictures can tell a story now and later when they are writing words, then they can join in with the letters and help tell the story. This gives them permission to "write."

Teachers observe their students and learn from them when to nudge a skill or introduce a new book or strategy. This learning is ongoing throughout the year, guided by national and state standards and benchmarks for literacy development. However, most standards are borrowed from older grades and are simply adjusted to represent what the students learned before they advanced to the older grade. That is logical, but it is not all inclusive of what the child needs to scaffold later learning. There are so many precursors for reading and writing needed to build successful readers and writers. This need of the students to represent their day in drawing might not be found on a benchmark or scope and sequence of literacy skills, but it is important to scaffolding their writing. In early childhood, a teacher's role is to learn from the students' interactions what they need to meet those state and national standards. We also apply what we know about young learners' developmental needs. Standards, benchmarks, and literacy continuums are built of literacy skills to master and are designed to be spirally aligned as students develop, but they don't list the importance of **how** we teach those skills. A child might shine in phonics decoding but not comprehend the piece of text. As students learn, they can splinter in their skills, and if the teacher isn't leaning over their shoulders watching their interactions with others while they are playing in centers, reading with friends, and writing approximations, she might miss why a child is able to decode but not comprehend. Students could call out all the sight words on the word wall but not be able to understand a story written utilizing the same words. Why? They have missed a step, and if we keep our eyes and ears open, we can see what that step might be. The process and product are both important in a lesson. The product is only one piece of assessment. The process of their learning is where we delve into their learning and find the missing steps. Standards and benchmarks can tell us about what skill or product to look for to plot them on literacy continuums, but teachers in the classroom each day plan and implement how to get students to the next level.

As we are planning for our students, we must keep in mind the concepts and skills students need and then investigate how best to teach them those concepts and skills. Knowing each student's interests and processes, plus our knowledge of literacy processes, is a winning combination, and benchmarks, standards, and continuums help us. These great resources assist our planning in light of expectations for each year. Add to that knowledge our understanding of developmentally appropriate practices, and we know that young readers and writers must use the material in context and make concrete connections with the concepts to cement the learning into long-term memory. We have windows of opportunity for each child, and our authentic assessment informs our instructional decisions to take full advantage of those windows.

Developing Authentic Assessment

As we plan literacy lessons, we must know two things: (1) what our students know; and (2) the processes of literacy learning (Smith 2005). If we know our students and "kidwatch" as they play and learn about literacy, we can understand where they are on a continuum of literacy development. We can plot them on the continuum and follow them along their journey. For validity in our understanding of each learner, our lessons should mirror our assessment (Farr and Tone 1998; Afferbach 2010). For example, as Nancy came into class one day, she was upset and came right up to me and handed me an envelope with an American flag stamp and the full address of our school on it. I asked her if she wanted me to open it now or later. She put her hand on her hip and said I could open it right now. When I opened the letter, I realized she was not happy with her report card, which had been sent home the day before. I had had a hunch she would not be happy, as on our report cards that year, the students had to write their names on a line right on the report card. If she had written her name with a capital letter at the start and then lowercase letters, she would have received an S for Satisfactory. If she had written her name with all capitals or all lowercase letters, then she would have received an N for Needs Time. In her house, it was assumed that students brought home S report cards. They did not bring home report cards with Ns on them.

Nancy had written the note in a formal letter format with a salutation and signed it by writing her name with a capital letter and then lowercase letters. It was an S attempt! She hadn't known that on the report card writing a lowercase n would give her an N! I had to try to explain to a five-year-old that the report card didn't assess her ability to write her name in an acceptable S quality format. For when she wrote her name on all of her papers, she wrote it "Nancy," but not on report card assessment day. This assessment was not authentic. It is surprising what districts put on report cards. I understood that my district at the time had a report card committee, and they had made the call. The day I received Nancy's note, I decided to volunteer to serve on that committee to try and effect change. It seemed a small event, but not to Nancy or her family. They were immigrants from Colombia and had come in great distress to our country for a free quality education; they put strong emphasis in their household on school and education. I had brought the parents into the classroom, and Nancy and I had shared her portfolio with all the wonderful work she had done so far in kindergarten, but all they saw was that N on her report card, as in their eyes it was a formal assessment. This story makes me wonder how parents see high-stakes testing in our classrooms today. Do they see it as a one-shot picture of their child? No matter if the child started the day getting up late, eating breakfast in the car on the way to school, only to have the family frantic with worry the child would be late for TEST DAY! Then to the test, hurried and worried. This was one day like Nancy's report card. We call them high-stakes tests, as they carry so much weight in schools today and in the homes of our students.

Authentic assessment consists of real-life reading and writing during our instruction and in our assessment. As students have control over the topic and structure of their writing, we can observe their process and product, and as we watch we can see if they use the lessons they have learned in student conferences, small group guided reading and writing, and inter-active writing. For example, in Nancy's writing portfolio is a piece of writing she did about penguins (see below). She writes: *Penguins The seal is they enemy Penguins put they eggs undr they fets* She reads: "Penguins The seal is their enemy. Penguins put their eggs under their feets." She reads *they* as their. She looked on the Word Wall for the word and pulled down *they*, but called it *their*, which was right below it. She was so confident of the word that she used it over and over. She was approximating the plural of feet in this piece. When she read it, it still sounded okay to her. We placed it in her portfolio, and I made a note of the plural *feets*. This writing sample was done on

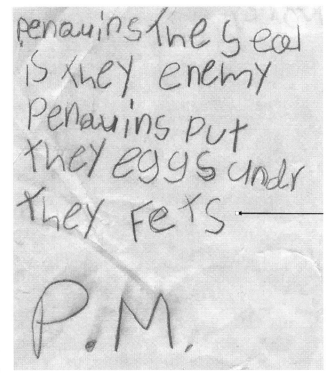

January 16. In the other sample, by March 30 she has worked out the plural of feet conventionally. She writes: *Insects his 6 legg sailors his 8 legg Butterflies, the lace wing sailors is not a insects Most of the time the puss hair streak the shiny pupa Butterflies tast with ther feet.* She reads: "Insects have 6 legs, spiders have 8 legs. Butterflies, the lace wing spider, is not an insect. Most of the time the puss hair streaks the shiny pupa. Butterflies taste with their feet." You can see she has worked out both the plural of feet and the correct word wall word for *their*. These portfolio entries illustrate authentic assessment for Nancy. I can see her writing and hear her reading, and she picks out what goes into the portfolio. She usually picks things she is proud of. I have her tell me why she is proud of each piece. For the penguin piece, she tells me that this is her first story about penguins. I also tell her I love how she has a title and a piece of nonfiction or a book that teaches. For her butterfly piece, she tells me that she wants to place it in her portfolio because she likes how she is teaching someone about how spiders and insects are different. I tell her that I love how she gives so much detail from her field notes next to the butterfly house. The conversations we have about her portfolio help this assessment be authentic as she shares her ownership and engagement in the pieces (Vacca et al. 2015; Afferbach 2007; Farr and Tone 1998; Afferbach, Hiebert, and Valencia 1994).

In November of that year I was given an assignment by my district to assess my students on their writing. The nonauthentic assessment consisted of four questions. The students weren't asked to write, so I couldn't note their writing, nor did it ask me to observe their writing in the classroom. The assessment was to ask the four questions. I asked Nancy the questions instead of putting a writing sample in her portfolio (Afferbach 2007), so what did I learn about Nancy's writing or Nancy's writing attitude? I learned that she will answer an abstract question with a concrete answer, but I didn't learn about her writing at all. From her answers (see below), I did learn about her tolerance for silly questions.

What do you like to write best? "*letters*"

What are you the best at in writing? "*pictures*"

What have you learned about writing? "*write*"

What do you want to learn about writing? "*ABC's*"

I use a multitude of assessments in my classroom to record how my students are doing in reading and writing. In the cluster of assessment for literacy below, you see the assessments I use to document a student's growth. Assessment should be authentic and from multiple sources. As the parents come in to talk about Nancy, I can show them her work, open my notebooks, and read snippets of her learning, and they can form a picture of her learning rather than leave just knowing their child is an "A student."

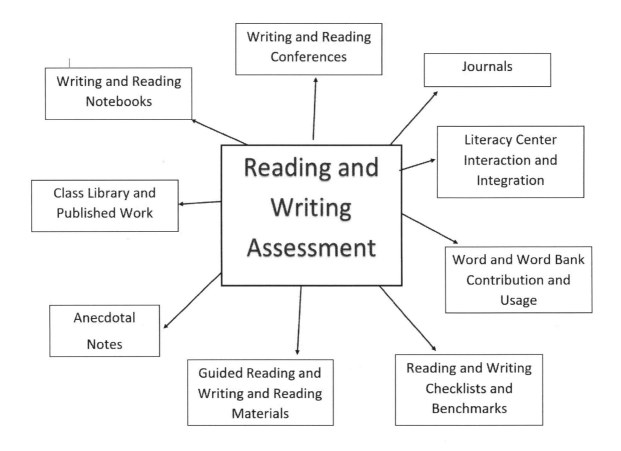

Lessons to Reach Out to ELL Students

In our classrooms we find all levels of learners, and all deserve to have equal opportunity to learn. When we plan our lessons, teachers have foremost in their minds their students' interests and cultural background, plus expectations of literacy development. We know that each child will come to learning in her own way, but the one thing all children share is the classroom environment they learn from. The classroom that contains culturally rich books and language stimulates the students to further their literacy journey. Students who are second language learners need to find meaning in the lessons they encounter in the classroom just as native English speakers do. They differ, however, in experiences with the language that is taught. Whereas our native speakers recognize the language we are speaking as one that is spoken in their homes and classroom, our ELL (English Language Learners) students may not. When I taught in Houston, our school had students who spoke over 100 different languages. Our school was in an area that was rich in immigrants to our country, and in my classroom, at any one time I might have students who speak Urdu, Spanish, Arabic, Mandarin, English, and Vietnamese, each of whom comes with rich language experiences that are different than my own. A classroom that puts meaning first is a classroom that includes all different languages and experiences (Boyd-Batstone 2015). Meaning-first classrooms focus on the child's needs first. For example, if I am teaching a lesson on possessive nouns in English, a child who has Spanish as his native language will not have the same prior knowledge as a native English speaker, because Spanish speakers don't use possessive nouns in their language. So as we plan our lessons, we must make sure to give the students as much context as possible and concrete examples of how the language is used in books to be shared and in conversations they might encounter. Reader's theater, puppet shows, creative dramatics, and singing are great ways to practice the language as well. Many classrooms design lesson complexity on text, and using leveled text for students is a common practice. The books used are at the instructional level or frustration level. The ELL students need concrete, contextualized lessons that support the text, teamed with texts aimed at their independent levels. This way they will have the safety of a text they understand to learn new skills from rather than using a text at an instructional or frustration level to learn those new skills. For example, native speakers have prior knowledge of the way the language sounds and the nuances in the way people speak and communicate, but ELL students come to the text without that knowledge (Shanahan 2013). They do possess that knowledge in their own language, but the text used in the class is not in their native language. So a safety net for them is essential. A teacher could take that independent level book and add meaningful tasks and materials to the lesson to build into what students find in the book. "Until we provide what is meaningful to ELLs, we cannot successfully move along a continuum of complexity. The Key is context, context and more context" (Boyd-Batstone 2015, 18). For example, a traditional lesson might consist of reading a passage in a book about penguins and completing a worksheet about sequence that includes putting the book events in order after they are cut out and mixed up. A contextually rich version of that lesson might include watching a short video about penguins in their habitat to build visual prior knowledge and then reading together a book about a little penguin that lost his tail. Then the students could create a puppet of the penguin and act out the character's events in the story, with the puppet speaking the repetitive words of the penguin from the story. In the second lesson the child would be engaged in all things penguin, viewing the penguins in their enviornment and then reading a story together in order to walk through the story, repeating the text with the teacher or another student. Finally, the child could use his creativity to make a puppet and practice the language with the character saying its lines. Additional lessons using this now-familiar book will form a safety net or scaffold for new language learners to further the sounds of the English language. The other children will flourish with these engaging, literature-based lessons as well.

Family Literacy: Inviting the Family into the Literacy Journey

Our schools are at risk! Alarming figures show that a significant number of American school-aged children lack positive peer socialization skills, respect for their teachers, appropriate classroom conduct, family communications, and positive self-esteem. These problems collectively are contributing to the increasing dropout rate in our schools and the high attrition rates among first-year teachers. To investigate these problems, we must look into the paradigm shift in the environments of our children. Each child comes to school with knowledge of her social world, which is built on two dynamic aspects: the home and the community. Within each individual world lies the potential for exchange. Households have a social interchange with each other, with a commonality of knowledge shared with other households. They read aloud great books, write letters, make phone calls, send notes, call from a kitchen window, and many other unique combinations. The community offers storytelling, group read alouds at the local bookstore, and even talking about books with others in the community (Smith 2005). Schools also rely on reciprocity in the exchange of knowledge. We read aloud, send notes, make phone calls, talk at bus stops, and so forth. A step toward making connections among home, school, and the community is also sharing books and information in a social context.

Literacy in the home scaffolds the school experience, and the same holds true in reverse. When we support and celebrate the exchange of experiences in every environment, we scaffold the child's emerging literacy. Each environment enriches the other. In activities in which the home is utilized in data-gathering expeditions online and with books, the school environment is enhanced and sophisticated. Literacy is mediated by the exchange. This integration of the funds of knowledge is enriched when all caregivers celebrate the potential of building up a student based on

- the home as an initiator,
- the school as a facilitator, and
- the community as both supporter and motivator.

Integrating a child's literacy awareness to encompass these three facets of his world builds a broader base of social context for literacy exploration and a greater potential for lifelong learning.

Examples of Family Literacy Activities

Scaredy Squirrel by Melanie Watts is a clever book that has a very "scaredy" main character. He worries about everything, from germs on the ground under his tree, to running out of nuts while perched on the branch, to not being able to exit in case of emergency! He has his plans and ideas all organized for every possible emergency. Think OCS, obsessive compulsive squirrel. I love the way the book is written to show the reader what his world is like and how he will overcome all obstacles.

> What to do in case of emergency according to *Scaredy Squirrel*:
> Step 1: Panic
> Step 2: Run
> Step 3: Get kit
> Step 4: Put on kit
> Step 5: Consult Exit Plan
> Step 6: Exit tree
> (if there is absolutely, definitely, truly no other option)

The book is a plethora of graphic organizers that we teach in our classrooms, shown in the real world of Scaredy in action. The interactive version of the book on iTunes™

for iBooks™ allows the reader to drag Scaredy along the book and listen to his panic and planning. The book reminds me of Eric Carle and Bill Martin Jr.'s style of teaching time, schedules, and counting with the story line. This book is written in diary style and follows the squirrel's day and how, when unexpected bees fly by, the plan must adjust!

I used the book with second graders and had them create an exit plan from their houses in case of fire. They had to gather information at home from their parents and do an investigation of the environment and bring all of that to school. We worked on the organization that Scaredy used as a model. The subsequent plans were hilarious. I asked the students to take them home and discuss them with their parents in case there was danger involved, such as jumping out a window! They had to have the plan approved by the teacher and then their parents.

Once the plans were revised to address safety concerns, they tried them out and brought back reader responses from their family and themselves. It was fun for the kids and also served as a family literacy reading-writing connection (Smith 1999). Not only was this intriguing for reading and language arts, it met the standards for health and safety and geography/social studies. Melanie Watts has written several books in this series. We know that every day our students are taking in the environment and learning, but we also want to empower them to learn *how* to learn as lifelong learners. We teach students to construct knowledge as they explore and discover the environment. We learn to watch their writing and observe their play to nudge their learning forward.

When we share our own cultural capital with each other, we broaden our understanding and tolerance of each other. In the following sample of Nancy's writing, you can see she has written about a brother and sister getting into an argument. I often tell my students stories about my brother and me as we were growing up. He and I would get into arguments, and then somehow the story always ended up with my brother getting into trouble and with me barely escaping punishment. I tell them these stories all year. The sample shows how much the students take in my stories about home as well as the stories of all their classmates, as Nancy wrote her own version of a brother-sister story that included my brother and me (Miss Smith). If you share your life with students, they will share their lives with you. Inviting the home life into the classroom increases the chances for us all of cultural capital growing.

Miss Smith push her bother in the water.
Tean her bother
push her in the water be got a
big tobgol
tean miss smith was so happy.

Part III References

Ada, A. 1995. *My Name Is Maria Isobel*. New York: Atheneum Books for Young Readers.

Afferbach, P. 2007. *Understanding and Using Reading Assessments K–12*. Newark, DE. International Reading Association.

Afferbach, P. (Ed.). 2010. *Essential Readings on Assessment*. Newark, DE: International Reading Association.

Afferbach, P., E. H. Hiebert, and S. Valencia. 1994. *Authentic Reading Assessment: Practices and Possibilities*. Newark, DE: International Reading Association.

Aliki. 1999. *A Visit to the Zoo*. New York: Trophy Picture Books.

Altman, G. T. 2002. "Learning and Development in Neural Networks—the Importance of Prior Experience." *Cognition* 85 (2): B43–B50.

Atwell, N. 2007. *The Reading Zone: How to Help Kids Become Skilled, Passionate, Habitual, Critical Readers*. New York: Scholastic Teaching Resources.

Atwell, N. 2014. *In the Middle, Third Edition: A Lifetime of Learning about Writing, Reading, and Adolescents*. Portsmouth, NH: Heinemann.

Avery, C. 1993. *And with a Light Touch: Learning about Reading, Writing, and Teaching with First Graders*. Portsmouth, NH: Heinemann.

Bergmann, O., J. Liebl, S. Bernard, K. Alkass, M. S. Y. Yeung, et al. 2012. "The Age of Olfactory Bulb Neurons in Humans." *Neuron* 74: 634–639 .

Bodrova, E., D. Leong, and D. Paynter. 1999. "Literacy Standards for Preschool Learners." *Redefining Literacy Educational Leadership* 57 (2): 42–46.

Bonini, L. 2016. "The Extended Mirror Neuron Network: Anatomy, Origin and Functions." *Neuroscientist* January 8. doi:10.1177/1073858415626400.

Bowcutt, A. A. 2015. "Discovering the E-relationship between Babies and Early E-literacy: A Case Study on the Responses of Babies Aged 0–12 Months to Traditional Texts and Electronic Readers." *Dissertation Abstracts International Section A*, 76. Ann Arbor, MI: University Microfilms International.

Boyd-Batstone, P. 2015. *Teaching ELLs to Read: Strategies to Meet the Common Core K–5*. New York: Routledge.

Brown, S. 2015. "Authentic Assessment: Using Assessment to Help Students Learn." *Electronic Journal of Educational Research, Assessment & Evaluation* 21 (2). http://dxdoi.org10.7203/relieve.21.2.7674.

Bunting E., and C. Soentpiet. 2009. *So Far from the Sea*. Boston: HMH Books for Young Readers.

Caine, G., and R. Caine. 1998. *Making Connections: Teaching and the Human Brain*. New York: Dale Seymour Publications.

Calkins, L. 1994. *The Art of Teaching Writing*. Portsmouth, NH: Heinemann.

Cambourne, B. 1988. *The Whole Story: Natural Learning and the Acquisition of Literacy in the Classroom*. New York: Ashton Scholastic.

Cambourne, B. 1999. "Conditions for Literacy Learning: Turning Learning Theory into Classroom Instruction; A Minicase Study." *The Reading Teacher* 54 (4): 414–429.

Carle, E. 1994. *The Hungry Caterpillar*. New York: Philomel Books.

Carroll, J. A. 1998. *Phonics Friendly Books*. Spring, TX: Absey & Co.

Carroll, J. A. 2002. *Dr. JAC's Reading/Writing Workshop Primer*. Spring, TX: Absey & Company.

Carroll, J. A. 2007. *Authentic Strategies for High Stakes Tests: A Practical Guide for English Language Arts*. Spring, TX: Absey & Co.

Carroll J. A., and E. Wilson. 2008. *Acts of Teaching: How to Teach Writing; A Text, a Reader, a Narrative*. 2nd ed. Santa Barbara, CA: Libraries Unlimited.

Castles, A., and M. Coltheart. 2004. "Is There a Causal Link from Phonological Awareness to Success in Learning to Read?" *Cognition* 91 (1): 77–111.

Charlesworth, R. 2014. *Understanding Child Development*. 9th ed. Belmont, CA: Wadsworth.

Choi, Y. 2003. *The Name Jar*. New York: Dragonfly Books.

Ciaramella, A., F. Salani, F. Bizzoni, M. Orfei, C. Caitagirone, F. Spalletta, and P. Bossu. 2016. "Myeloid Dendritic Cells Are Decreased in Peripheral Blood of Alzheimer's Disease Patients in Association with Disease Progression and Severity of Depressive Symptoms." *Journal of Neuroinflammation* 13: 18. doi:10.1186/s12974-016-0483-0.

Clay, M. 2000. *Concepts about Print: What Have Children Learned about the Way We Print Language*. New York: Heinemann.

Clymer, T. 1996. "The Utility of Phonics Generalizations in the Primary Grades." *The Reading Teacher* 16: 182–187.

Cornett, C. E. 2014. *Creating Meaning through Literature and the Arts: An Integration Resource for Classroom Teachers*. 5th ed. New York: Pearson.

Csikszentmihalyi, M. 2008. *Flow: The Psychology of Optimal Experience*. New York: Harper Perennial Modern Classics.

Cunningham, P. 1987. "Action Phonics." *The Reading Teacher* 41: 247–249.

Cunningham, P. 2013. *Phonics They Use: Words for Reading and Writing*. 6th ed. Making Words Series. New York: Pearson.

Cunningham, P., P. Cunningham, J. Hoffman, and H. Yopp. 1998. *Phonemic Awareness and the Teaching of Reading: A Position Statement from the Board of Directors of the International Reading Association*. Newark, DE: International Reading Association.

Dolch, E. W. 1948. *Problems in Reading*. Champaign, IL: Garrard Press.

Dole, J. A., G. G. Duffy, L. R. Roehler, and P. D. Pearson. 1991. "Moving from the Old to the New: Research on Reading Comprehension Instruction." *Review of Educational Research* 61: 239–264.

Donaldson, M. 1979. *Children's Minds*. New York: W. W. Norton.

Dorn, L. J., and C. Soffos. 2001. *Scaffolding Young Writers: A Writer's Workshop Approach*. Portland, ME: Stenhouse Publishers.

Edwards, P. 1998. *Some Smug Slug*. Repr. ed. New York: Katherine Tegen Books.

Estes, E. 2004. *The Hundred Dresses*. 1-Simul ed. New York: HMH Books for Young Readers.

Fanelli, S. 2001. *My Map Book*. New York: Harper Festival.

Farr, R., and B. Tone. 1998. *Assessment Portfolio and Performance*. 2nd ed. Orlando, FL: Harcourt Brace.

Fisher, B. 1997. *Joyful Learning*. Portsmouth, NH: Heinemann.

Flynn, R. 2004/2005. "Curriculum-Based Reader's Theater: Setting the Stage for Reading and Retention." *The Reading Teacher* 58: 360–365.

Fountas, I., and G. S. Pinnell. 1996. *Guided Reading: Good Teaching for All Children*. Portsmouth, NH: Heinemann.

Fox, M. 1990. *Teaching Drama to Young Children*. New York: Heinemann.

Fox, M. 2008. *Reading Magic: Why Reading Aloud to Our Children Will Change Lives Forever*. New York: Mariner Books.

Fry, E. B., J. E. Kress, and D. L. Fountoukidis. 1993. *The Reading Teacher's Book of Lists*. Englewood Cliffs, NJ: Prentice Hall.

Fuster, J. 1995. *Memory in the Cerebral Cortex*. Cambridge, MA: MIT Press.

Gallagher, K. 2015. *In the Best Interest of Students to What Works in the ELA Classroom*. Portland, ME: Stenhouse Publishers.

Goodman, K. 2014. *What's Whole in Whole Language in the 21st Century?* New York: Garn Press.

Goodman, Y., and G. Owochi. 2002. *Kidwatching: Documenting Children's Literacy Development.* Portsmouth, NH: Heinemann.

Goswani, U. 1986. "Children's Use of Analogy in Learning to Read: A Developmental Study." *Journal of Experimental Child Psychology* 42: 73–83.

Graves, D. 1994. *A Fresh Look at Writing.* Portsmouth, NH: Heinemann.

Graves, D., and P. Kittle. 2005. *Inside Writing: How to Teach the Details of Craft.* Portsmouth, NH: Heinemann.

Graves, M. F. 2006. *The Vocabulary Book: Learning and Instruction.* New York: Teachers College Press.

Graves, M. F., and S. Watts-Taffe. 2008. "For the Love of Words: Fostering Word Consciousness in Young Readers." *The Reading Teacher* 62 (3): 185–193.

Haken, H. (Ed.) 2016. *Self-organization in Complex Systems: The Past, Present, and Future of Synergetics.* Proceedings of the International Symposium, Hanse Institute of Advanced Studies, Delmenhorst, Germany, November 13–16, 2012. Springer Publishing AG Switzerland.

Halliday, M. 1975. *Learning How to Mean: Exploration in the Development of Language.* London: Arnold.

Hartman, G. 1993. *As the Crow Flies: A First Book of Maps.* New York: Harper.

Haven, K. 2007. *Story Smart: The Science Behind the Startling Power of Story.* Santa Barbara, CA: Libraries Unlimited.

Haven, K. 2014. *Story Smart: Using the Science of Story to Persuade, Influence, Inspire and Teach.* Santa Barbara, CA: Libraries Unlimited.

Henkes, K. 2008. *Chrysanthemum.* Buchanan, NY: Mulberry Books.

Higgins, B., B. Miller, and S. Wegman. 2006. "Teaching to the Test . . . Not! Balancing Best Practice and Testing Requirements in Writing." *International Reading Association Reading Teacher* 60 (December–January): 310–319.

Hindley, J. 1996. *In the Company of Children.* York, ME: Stenhouse.

Hoffman, J. 1985. *The Oral Recitation Lesson: A Teacher's Guide.* Austin, TX: Academic Resource Consultants.

Hoffman, J. 2011. "Constructing Meaning: Interactive Literary Discussion in Kindergarten Read-Alouds." *The Reading Teacher* 65 (3): 183–194.

Holdaway, D. 1984. *The Foundations of Literacy.* Portsmouth, NH: Heinemann.

Holdaway, D. 1992. *Models of Natural Learning in Literacy Development.* Portsmouth, NH: Heinemann.

Hoorn, V. J., P. M. Nourot, B. Scales, and K. R. Alward. 2014. *Play at the Center of the Curriculum.* 6th ed. New York: Pearson.

Hoyt, L. 2008. *Revisit, Reflect, Retell: Time-Tested Strategies for Teaching Reading Comprehension.* Portsmouth, NH: Heinemann.

Hubbard, R. S., and B. M. Power. 2003. *The Art of Classroom Inquiry: A Handbook for Teacher-Researchers.* Rev. ed. Portsmouth, NH: Heinemann.

Hutchins, P. 1990. *Goodnight Owl.* Repr. ed. New York: Aladdin.

Hyerle, D. 1996. *Visual Tools for Constructing Knowledge.* Alexandra, VA: ASCD.

Hymes, D. 1974. *Foundations of Sociolinguistics: An Ethnographic Approach.* Philadelphia: University of Pennsylvania Press.

Inkpen, M. 1990. *The Blue Balloon.* New York: Little, Brown Books.

Jasmine, J., and P. Schiesl. 2009. "The Effects of Word Walls and Word Wall Activities on the Reading Fluency of First Grade Students." *Reading Horizons* 49 (4): 301–312.

Jensen, E. 2001. *Arts with the Brain in Mind.* Alexandria, VA: ASCD.

Jensen, E. 2005. *Teaching with the Brain in Mind.* 2nd ed. Alexandria, VA: ASCD.

Jones, C. 1998. *Old MacDonald Had a Farm*. New York: HMH Books for Young Readers.

Keene, O,. and S. Zimmermann. 2007. *Mosaic of Thought: The Power of Comprehension Strategy Instruction*. 2nd ed. Portsmouth, NH: Heinemann.

Larson, L. C. 2015. "E-Books and Audiobooks." *Reading Teacher* 69 (2): 169–177.

Ledoux, J. 2013. *Synaptic Self: How Our Brains Become Who We Are*. New York: Penguin Books.

Lester, H. 1990. *Tacky the Penguin*. New York: HMH Books for Young Readers.

Levine, M. 1991. *Keeping Ahead in School: A Student's Book about Learning Abilities and Learning Disorders*. Toronto: Educators Publishing Service.

Levine, M. 2003. *A Mind at a Time*. New York: Simon and Schuster.

Martin, B., Jr. 1992. *Brown Bear, Brown Bear, What Do You See?* New Yor: Henry Holt.

McCarrier, A., G. S. Pinnell, and I. C. Fountas. 2000. *Interactive Writing: How Language and Literacy Come Together, K–2*. Portsmouth, NH: Heinemann.

Morgan, H. 2014. "Multimodal Children's E-Books Help Young Learners in Reading." *Early Childhood Education Journal* 41 (6): 477–483.

Morrow, L. 2012. *Literacy Development in the Early Years*. 7th ed. New York: Pearson.

Moscovitch, M. 1995. "Recovered Consciousness: A Hypothesis Concerning Modularity and Episodic Memory." *Journal of Clinical and Experimental Neuropsychology* 17: 276–290.

Most, B. 1990. *Dinosaur Cousins*. New York: Voyager Books.

Moustafa, M. 1997. *Beyond Traditional Phonics: Research Discoveries and Reading Instruction*. Portsmouth, NH: Heinemann.

Muhtaris, K., and K. Ziemke. 2015. *Amplify Digital Teaching and Learning in the K–6 Classroom*. New York: Heinemann.

National Institute of Child Health and Human Development. 2000. *Report of the National Reading Panel: Teaching Children to Read, an Evidence-based Assessment of the Scientific Research Literature on Reading and Its Implications for Reading Instruction*. NIH Publication No. 00-4769. Washington, DC: US Government Printing Office. http://www.nichd.nib.gov/publications/nrp/upload.smallbook_pdf.pdf.

Nell, V. 1988. *Lost in a Book: The Psychology of Reading for Pleasure*. New Haven, CT: Yale University Press.

Nyman, M. 2014. "A Quantitative, Comparison Study: Oral Language Development and High Stakes Testing." *Dissertation Abstracts International Section A*, 74. Ann Arbor, MI: University Microfilms International.

O'Keefe, T. 1996. *Taking Note: Improving Your Observational Notetaking*. Portland, ME: Stenhouse Publishers.

Pannell, M. 2013. "Relationships between Reading Ability in Third Grade and Phonological Awareness in Kindergarten." *Dissertation Abstracts International Section A*, 73. Ann Arbor, MI: University Microfilms International.

Pearson, P., and D. Jonson. 1978. *Teaching Reading Comprehension*. Austin, TX: Holt, Rinehart and Winston.

Pearson, P. D. 1999. "A Historically Based Review of 'Preventing Reading Difficulties in Young Children'." (Essay Book Review). *Reading Research Quarterly* 2: 231.

Pearson, S. 2011. *How to Teach a Slug to Read*. New York: Two Lions.

Piaget, J. 2001. *The Psychology of Intelligence*. 2nd ed. London: Routledge.

Ramachandran, V. S. 2012. *The Tell-Tale Brain: A Neuroscientist's Quest for What Makes Us Human*. New York: W. W. Norton.

Reber, A. S. 2003. *Implicit Learning and Tacit Knowledge: An Essay on the Cognitive Unconscious*. Oxford Psychology, no. 19. New York: Simon and Schuster.

Recourvits, H. 2014. *My Name Is Yoon*. New York: Square Fish.

Routman, R. 2002. *Reading Essentials: The Specifics you Need to Teach Well.* New York: Heinemann.

Rushton, S., J. Eitelgeorge, and R. Zickafoose. 2003. "Connecting Brian Cambourne's Conditions of Learning Theory to Brain/Mind Principles: Implications for Early Childhood Educators." *Early Childhood Education Journal* (31) 1: 11–17.

Savage, J. 2007. *Sounding It Out!* 3rd ed. New York: McGraw-Hill Higher Education.

Shanahan, R. 2013. "On Implementing the Common Core Standards Successfully, Grades K–2." In *Teaching with the English Language Arts, K–2,* edited by Leslie Mandell Morrow, Timothy Shanahan, and Karen Wixson, 184–200. New York: Guilford Press.

Shaywitz, S. 2003. *Overcoming Dyslexia.* New York: Knopf.

Smith, F. 2005. *Reading without Nonsense.* 4th ed. New York: Teachers College Press.

Smith-Barger, K. 1999. *Phonics Friendly Families.* Spring, TX: Absey & Co.

Spraque, C. 2015. "Phonics." *Research Starters: Education* (Online Edition).

Stillman, P. 1991. *Families Writing.* Portsmouth, NH: Heinemann.

Taylor, D. 1997. *Many Families, Many Literacies: An International Declaration of Principles.* Portsmouth, NH: Heinemann.

Teicher, Martin H., and Jacqueline A. Samson. 2016. "Annual Research Review: Endurin Gneurobiological Effects of Childhood Abuse and Neglect." *Journal of Child Psychology and Psychiatry* 57 (3): 241–266.

Tompkins, G. 2003. *Sharing the Pen: Interactive Writing with Children.* New York: Pearson.

Tompkins, G. 2013. *Literacy for the 21st Century: A Balanced Literacy Approach.* 6th ed. New York: Pearson.

Topping, D., and R. McManus. 2002. *Real Reading, Real Writing: Content-Area Strategies.* Portsmouth, NH: Heinemann.

Trelease, J. 1989. "Jim Trelease Speaks on Reading Aloud to Children." *The Reading Teacher* (3): 200.

Trelease, J. 2013. *The Read Aloud Handbook.* 7th ed. New York: Penguin Books.

Turner, P. 1999. *The War Between the Vowels and Consonants.* New York: Square Fish.

Vacca J., R. Vacca, M. Gove, L. Burkey, L. Lenhart, and C. McKeon. 2015. *Reading and Learning to Read.* 9th ed. New York: Pearson.

VanDycke, D. C., and A. A. Fox. 1990. "Fetal Drug Exposure and Its Possible Implications for Learning in the Pre-school and School-Age Population." *Journal of Learning Disabilities* 23 (3): 160–163.

Veatch, J. 1979. *Key Words to Reading: The Language Experience Approach Begins.* 2nd ed. New York: Merrill.

Vygotsky, L. 1978. *Mind in Society: The Developmental Higher Psychological Processes.* Boston: Harvard University Press.

Vygotsky, L. 2012. *Thought and Language.* Cambridge, MA: MIT Press.

Wackerle-Hollman, A., B. Schmitt, R. Bradfield, M. Rodriquez, and S. McConnell. 2015. "Redefining Individual Growth and Development Indicators: Phonological Awareness." *Journal of Learning Disabilities* 48 (5): 495–510.

Wasik, B. A., and M. A. Bond. 2001. "Beyond the Pages of a Book: Interactive Book Reading and Language Development in Preschool Classrooms." *Journal of Educational Psychology* 93 (2): 243–250.

Watts, M. 2008. *Scaredy Squirrel.* Repr. ed. New York: Kids Can Press.

Wells, G. 2009. *The Meaning Makers: Learning to Talk and Talking to Learn.* 2nd ed. Tonawanda, NY: Multilingual Matters.

Wilde, S. 1991. *You Kan Red This! Spelling and Punctuation for Whole Language Classrooms, K–6.* Portsmouth, NH: Heinemann.

Wood, A. 1993. *The Little Penguin's Tale*. New York: HMH Books for Young Readers.

Wood, A., and B. Wood. 2001. *Alphabet Adventure*. New York: Blue Sky Press.

Wood, D., and A. Wood. 1998. *The Little Mouse, the Red Ripe Strawberry, and the Big Hungry Bear*. Board Book ed. New York: Child's Play International Ltd.

Yates, L. 2012. *Dog Loves to Draw*. New York: Knopf Books for Young Readers.

Yim-Bridges, S. 2015. *Ruby's Wish*. New York: Chronicle Books.

Zinsser, W. 2013. *On Writing Well*. 5th ed. New York: HarperCollins.

Part IV

Guided by Meaning in Teaching Lessons

Karla James

22

The Arenas of Writing and Spelling: A Gradual Progression of Writing and Spelling Development

Writing should be meaningful for children, that an intrinsic need should be aroused in them, and that writing should be incorporated into a task that is necessary and relevant for life.

—Lev Vygotsky

A child's writing and spelling development is an incredible journey. So often we perceive this journey as taking place in stages, much like the stages of physical development. However, the writing and spelling development of a child is much more sophisticated than progressing through a universal timeline or moving up a growth chart. This process is so unique that Carroll and Wilson describe this progression as a "sphere of activity" known as arenas. They maintain:

> The word stage doesn't work because it suggests development that is linear or lock-step. The word characteristic doesn't work because while it denotes a distinguishing quality, it connotes that which is typical. Young children's writing is atypical since their language arenas are more closely tied to all of their other learning. (2008, 268)

Writing and spelling fit perfectly within the context of arenas because of the manner in which children move in and out of the processes throughout their development. Just as the writing process is recursive, so is the path by which students develop as writers and spellers.

An Overview of the Arenas of Writing and Spelling

Rhythms

There is nothing that can get us moving like rhythm. Whether it is the sound of water flowing down a stream, the ringing of a church bell at high noon, the cadence of a drum line, or the beat of a poem, rhythm moves our minds and bodies. Beginning in utero, humans develop a sense of and need for rhythm. This deep connection explains why more children memorize the alphabet, days of the week, and months of the year, among other concepts, to the tune of a song. Rhythms help children make meaning.

Strategies to Foster Development

- Read classic literature such as nursery rhymes: "One, Two, Buckle My Shoe"; "Hickory Dickory Dock"; "Jack and Jill"; "Hey Diddle Diddle"; and "The Itsy, Bitsy Spider."
- Read poems or books with a repetitive pattern: *Good Night Moon* by Margaret Wise Brown, *Brown Bear, Brown Bear, What Do You See?* and *Chicka Chicka Boom Boom* by Bill Martin Jr., or *One Fish, Two Fish, Red Fish, Blue Fish* by Dr. Seuss.
- Incorporate music into daily routines, such as singing the "Good Morning" song to welcome students each day or the "Clean Up" song to clean work areas, and transition songs when lining up to move from one location to the next.

Gestures

Children have the ability to make meaning at a young age through the use of gestures. In fact, there are a number of programs on the market that aim to teach infants a variety of signs for communication. Classroom teachers implement signs for students to communicate when they need to take a restroom break as an alternative to interrupting instructional time. No matter what message is being communicated, all gestures contain meaning and are believed to be the ultimate foundation for writing.

Strategies to Foster Development

- Create an environment that supports active listening, speaking, reading, and writing.
- Implement activities such as student of the day, show and tell, good news, turn and talk, and share time.

Good news is a great way to start each day in a positive way. Invite a few students each day to share something good that happened recently or something they are eagerly anticipating. Students build confidence through speaking to their peers while increasing their development as listeners, readers, and writers. Each of these learning activities invites students to become active participants in the learning process, which results in increased oral language development.

Initial Visual Signs

Think back to a piece of writing that consisted of random lines and scribbles. The writing that you are visualizing is an example of initial visual signs. These lines and scribbles are a by-product of gestures. As we continue to explore the seven arenas, notice how each arena is an extension of the previous one.

Strategies to Foster Development

- Model ways to write in a specific location on the paper. For example, write in a line from left to right or in the center of the paper.
- Encourage the child to tell you what the writing is about.
- Provide positive praise for the child's efforts.

Symbolic Play

Children emulate the behaviors and speech of those they are surrounded by most often. I recall my days as a young, school-aged girl watching my teacher's every move. I returned home after school and asked my mother to purchase things to set up my pseudo-classroom. I insisted on having books, stickers, stamps, and art supplies identical to those my teacher had. As I played with my brother and cousins, I would take on the persona of my teacher—even to the point of changing my name to hers, Mrs. Golden. Little did I know that by engaging myself in symbolic play, I was understanding and making meaning of the world around me while helping my brother and cousins do the same. This arena is critical in the development of writing and spelling, for it is the time when young children begin to gain control over what were once random marks on a page. Young children in this arena will demonstrate controlled scribbles, named scribbles, approximations and pre-phonemic spelling, and alphabetical writing and spelling.

Strategies to Foster Development

- Encourage children to talk about what they have written.
- Invite children to replicate the writing using different paper and crayons.
- Make use of environmental print such as logos, signs, and labels that are seen every day.
- Model thinking, that is, *think alouds*. Thinking aloud is a modeling approach that demonstrates how the teacher processes or comes to a conclusion. This thinking is verbally articulated, which allows students to see and hear the complexities of processing reading and writing for meaning.
- Incorporate opportunities for shared writing. Shared writing is a collective approach to writing. It offers a high level of support for emergent writers. The teacher is responsible for holding the pen while he or she works with the students to compose the text.

Symbolic Drawing

This arena is closely connected with symbolic play. The writing now begins to take on a new dimension. Writers demonstrate more control and show more attention to realistic details and meaning. The shapes and lines are more meaningful than the initial visual signs. Carroll and Wilson (2008) place drawings into two categories: *pictographs and ideographs.*

Strategies to Foster Development

- Model thinking and writing through shared writing and interactive writing.
- Provide opportunities for turn and talk, small group share, and whole group share.
- Utilize focal books as a model—a focal book is a purposefully selected piece of rich literature that serves as a model for a variety of techniques and strategies.

Transitional Writing and Spelling

Transitional writing and spelling is a critical turning point in the progression of an emergent writer's journey. No longer do these developing writers rely on pictures alone to make meaning; now they demonstrate the ability to use what they have learned about phonemes to write and spell simple words and sentences. Children in this arena may use initial consonants, final consonants, or a combination of the two to represent words.

Strategies to Foster Development

- Provide many opportunities for students to work with words using tactile materials such as building words with magnetic letters, Play-Doh™, beans, beads, or other objects.
- Incorporate word banks.
- Model thinking and writing through shared writing and interactive writing; shared writing involves the teacher and students working together to compose the text, as the teacher controls the pen. With interactive writing the teacher *shares* the pen while working with the students to compose a narrative or informational text.
- Utilize focal books as a model.

Standard Writing and Spelling

Students in this arena continue to make great strides in writing and spelling as they apply the conventional principles of phonics. Their writing shows intentional planning, details, and word choice. A student may use the standard conventions of writing and spelling; however, this does not necessarily mean he or she will write with

100 percent accuracy 100 percent of the time. What it does show is a student who has age appropriate literacy behaviors under control as well as the ability to absorb the teaching and make the learning generative, thus creating meaning.

Strategies to Foster Development

- Implement writing conferences and guided writing.
- Incorporate word banks.
- Model thinking and writing through shared writing and interactive writing.
- Utilize focal books as a model.

Application

Having an understanding of the arenas of writing and spelling development increases the literacy teacher's awareness of the development of his or her writers. This knowledge provides valuable insight into the child, the moves he or she makes as a writer, and why he or she makes them. This provides the teacher an outlet through which to instruct and foster continued progression in writing and spelling.

Samples of student writing should be analyzed to determine their status in the process of writing and spelling. In addition, examining a child's writing and observing what he or she knows about the writing process is an integral part of understanding a child's development over time. Implement strategies that will propel students forward through the seven arenas while teaching them to write with meaning along the way.

The Progression

Initial Visual Signs

Mark, an emergent kindergarten writer, demonstrates his awareness of print and that labels can be used to identify illustrations (see figure 22.1).

Next steps for Mark:

- ✓ Call attention to the location of print in mentor texts.
- ✓ Model standard letter formation using specific vocabulary.

Figure 22.1. Mark's Christmas tree.

✓ Encourage participation in interactive writing.
✓ Teach the strategy of stretching out unknown words, while listening to and recording the sounds that are heard.

Symbolic Play

Brent, a kindergarten student, labeled his self-portrait with his name scribbled to the left. Although Brent scribbled his name, he demonstrates the ability to control the writing. Not only does he recognize the purpose of a label, but he also knows his name has meaning relative to his identity (see figure 22.2).

Next steps for Brent:

✓ Invite Brent to share his story orally in a writing conference or with his peers.
✓ Point out Brent's name on the name chart or word wall.
✓ Model how writers use words to communicate a message.
✓ Direct Brent's attention to environmental print that includes the same letters as those found in his name.

Figure 22.2. Brent's self-portrait.

Addison, a kindergarten student, wrote about her dreams of growing up to become a singer. Addison's writing demonstrates her ability to make approximations. She obviously recognizes that symbols are used to make meaning. Here, she zeros in on one symbol and repeats that symbol in a variety of ways (see figure 22.3).

Next steps for Addison:

✓ Invite Addison to take part in the interactive writing experience by *sharing the pen*. Encourage her to highlight words she recognizes. Guide her to notice that words are used to express thoughts. Show examples of writing such as environmental print, magazines, advertisements, and postcards.
✓ Model your thought process for forming letters and words during shared writing.
✓ Teach Addison to access resources such as the word wall or word banks for needed information.

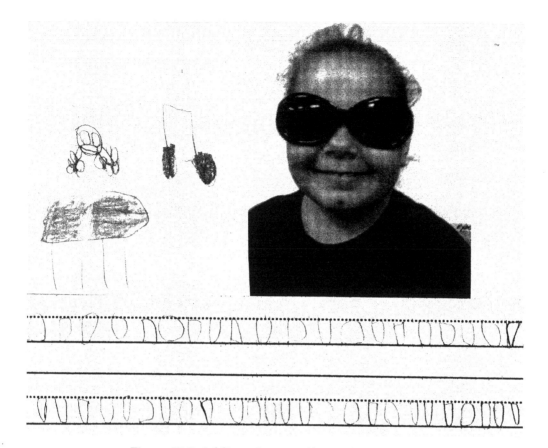

Figure 22.3. Addison dreams of becoming a singer.

Symbolic Drawing

Bryce, a first grader, wrote about his family vacation to Cancun. While on vacation he saw a monster truck show. In the original piece of writing, Bryce colored the tree in the corner a pale gray, and the center—which he stated was the ground—was bright blue. When asked to speak about his writing, Bryce explained that the ground was spray painted blue and the palm trees were gray. What Bryce was describing was the trunk's transition from green to gray. It is evident that Bryce's writing represents his fun-filled family vacation (see figure 22.4).

Next steps for Bryce:

- ✓ Share picture books, drawing Bryce's attention to the details of the illustrations and showing the relationship between the text and the illustrations.
- ✓ Invite Bryce to view the work of other student authors and show how they master finding the relationship between the illustrations and text.
- ✓ Provide a variety of opportunities for writing.

Figure 22.4. Bryce writes about his vacation to Cancun.

Transitional Writing and Spelling

Liz, a first grader, wrote a story about the day she played with Leland because he did not have anyone to play with. Liz shows knowledge of how some words work, and it appears as though she has a core of high-frequency words she is familiar with and can spell accurately (see figure 22.5).

Figure 22.5. Liz's story about being a friend.

Next steps for Liz:

- ✓ Encourage Liz to utilize resources such as the word wall, word banks, and human resources (peers).
- ✓ Revisit phonics lessons of specific spelling rules that prove to be a challenge.
- ✓ Continue to model through think alouds, shared writing, and interactive writing.

Standard Writing and Spelling

Brooklyn, a first grader, used standard conventions to write about her friend Christian and the things they do together at school. Brooklyn recognizes that print carries meaning and that it can be used to communicate ideas that are important to the writer (see figure 22.6).

Next steps for Brooklyn:

- ✓ Model strategies that focus on adding details.
- ✓ Encourage the use of word banks in order to raise the level of word choice.
- ✓ Model the use of grade-appropriate conventions.

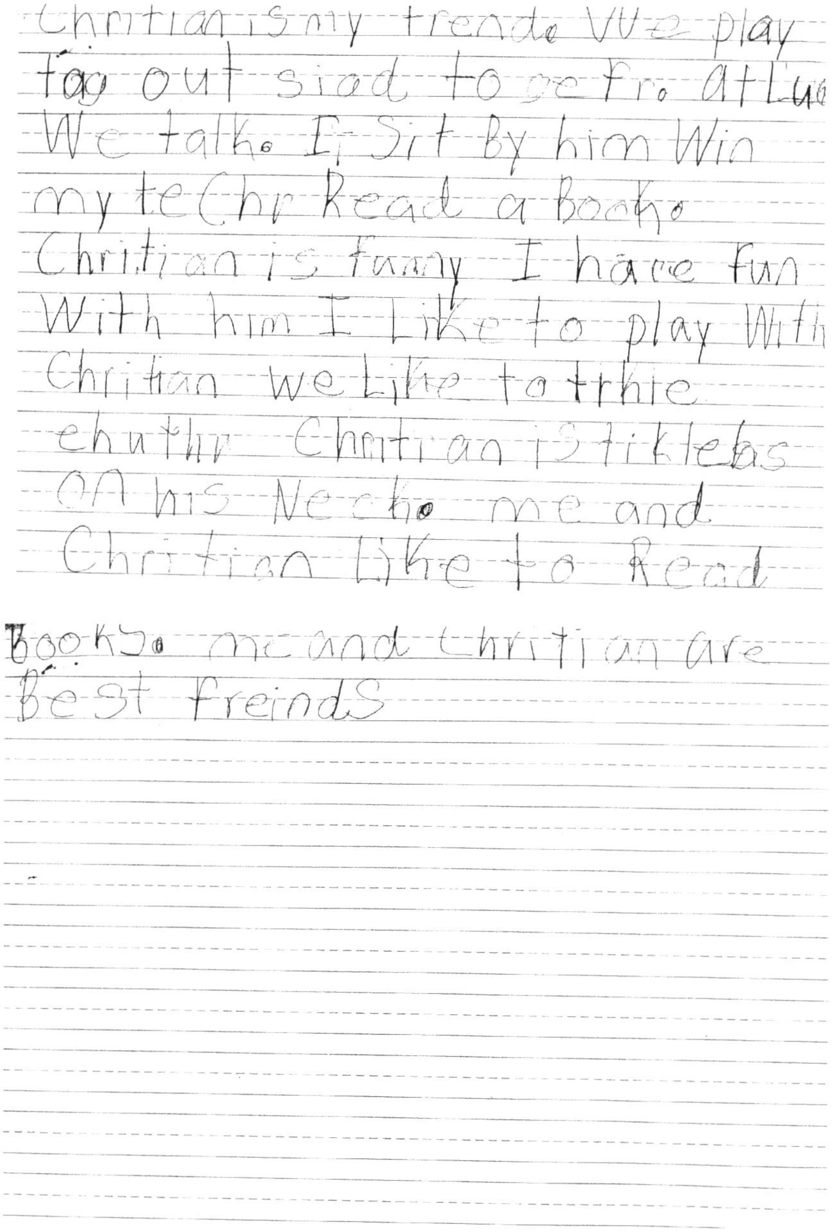

Figure 22.6. Brooklyn's essay about her friend Christian.

Consider This

The arenas of writing and spelling development form a model that guides teachers to an understanding of the progression of writing and spelling. Teachers who have a deep understanding of their students' beginnings will inevitably be better equipped to differentiate instruction based on the needs of every writer. Consider getting to know your students by creating a writing portfolio for each student, and spend time getting to know the students up close and personal through their writing.

23

Ready, Set, Go! Practical Lessons to Engage, Explore, and Execute the Writing Process

It is significant to realize that the most creative environments in our society are not the ever-changing ones. The artist's studio, the researcher's laboratory, the scholar's library are each deliberately kept simple so as to support the complexities of the work-in-progress. They are deliberately kept predictable so the unpredictable can happen.

—Lucy Calkins

Children enter schools each year with varied experiences with language. Some engage in articulate storytelling about past personal experiences, family traditions, and interests such as favorite books and movies. Conversely, there are children who enter the same doors who are in the developing or early stages of language acquisition.

A number of children come to school with a sense of eagerness to read and write, while others sit in silence from fear of taking risks to share what they know and therefore demonstrating reluctance. Because of the vast differences that are evident in our classrooms, the need for preparedness to meet our youngest writers where they are developmentally is integral to the progress and to the success of our writers. Preparation begins with knowing all students' academic behaviors and motives, specifically their early literacy behaviors. You should ask yourself, "What skills do my writers demonstrate consistently, and what skills require my attention?" And yes, you should take note of their motives. Consider the motives of the students who sit in your classroom each day. Using their motives as leverage is the secret to reaching all writers, including the reluctant ones. It's plain and simple: give them what they want.

Two years ago I worked with a class of kindergarten students who exuded great passion for writing. It was an exciting time to witness their progress as writers. I recall one particular student, whom I will call *Jack*. Jack preferred other activities to writing unless he engaged in writing stories about his favorite character, Super Mario. I'm sure you've taught this student. He owned the Super Mario shoes, the shirt, the backpack, and every other piece of merchandise imaginable. The only topic Jack wanted to write about was Super Mario. There was no way I was going to convince him to select other topics. I finally came to the conclusion that if Jack could find meaning in a fictional character, then I had to take advantage of this opportunity to teach Jack as much as possible about the writing process using the one thing that held meaning for him, Super Mario. Super Mario eventually became my golden ticket to many conversations with Jack about other topics. These conversations revealed other topics that proved to be just as meaningful to Jack. Once those connections surfaced, more writing followed. Writers need and want choice, and the freedom to choose fosters learning that is relevant and meaningful. Caine and Caine assert, "If we want students to use their brains more fully, we have to teach for meaningfulness" (1991, 99). Topics I considered important were secondary to Jack. Finding meaning in his world proved to be time well spent, as it yielded a plentiful harvest of topics he could potentially tap into as well as stretching his mental capacity to think deeper than ever before.

To engage students in the writing process, their interests should be placed first and foremost prior to delving into planning those *go to* lessons. When lesson design and the writing process are approached with the interests of the students in mind, we are inevitably forced to step outside of our comfort zone to deliver lessons that are guided by meaning, because our design becomes more about the students and their process and less about the teacher.

The following pages will guide teachers of writing through a series of practical lessons that include research-based strategies proven to engage all writers in exploring and executing the writing process.

Getting Started with Writing Workshop

The Structure

Each element of the primary writing workshop is essential to the efficiency and effectiveness of every lesson. Although there is flexibility within the framework of the writing workshop, the structure should be predictable (see figure 23.1). Ensuring a predictable structure alleviates any unnecessary anxiety. It assures young writers that this treasured time is valued and that there will be supports in

---

Structure of the Primary Writing Workshop

The Minilesson: 5–10 minutes
- Includes the objective and rationale for the lesson.

The Model: 5–10 minutes
- The teacher provides a model to demonstrate how writers will apply the strategy (focal book, shared writing, interactive writing, teacher model, anchor charts, and student writing).

You Try It: 5–10 minutes (optional)
- Writers visualize, turn and talk, practice on dry erase boards.

Independent Writing: 15–30 minutes
- Writers apply the minilesson independently; teacher confers and/or pulls small groups to provide additional support.

Share: 1–10 minutes
- Writers have the opportunity to share with others in a variety of ways.

Figure 23.1. Structure of the primary writing workshop.

place to guide their learning. This assurance builds the confidence they need to feel safe and to be free to take risks in the writing classroom.

Necessities

Teachers prepare for writing workshop not only by knowing the strengths and needs of their students, but also by preparing the physical classroom environment. Having the necessary supplies and resources will aid in a smooth launch (see figure 23.2). This serves as evidence that the writing workshop is an important part of the day. When you are ready, so too will your little writers be ready.

The Launch

Launching the writing workshop is always an exciting time for me. It is the time to lure students into what I think of as the highlight of the day. The launch is a grand affair and should be treated as such. I don't know if there is any other time in which students will have as much freedom as they

Supplies
• Easel
• Chart paper
• Sentence strips
• Markers
• Highlighter tape
• Post-it® Cover Up Tape
• Dry erase boards
• Plastic or magnetic letters
• Focal books
• Student folders or spirals
• Variety of paper
• Flesh tone pencils
• Student dictionaries
• ABC Chart
• Consonant Clusters Chart

Figure 23.2. Supplies.

do during writing workshop. Because students love to exercise choice, I emphasize that when introducing what writing workshop is all about. Let's think about the mile-long buffet of choices writing workshop offers. Writers have the option to choose (1) topic, (2) genre, (3) purpose, (4) audience, (5) focal books to study, (6) words, (7) craft, (8) syntax, (9) text layout, (10) illustrations, (11) strategies for revising and editing, (12) paper for publishing, and more.

This is a critical time because it is when you establish the writing community, as well as expectations. You will want to invest a great deal in focusing on creating a writing environment in which students feel safe to take risks and where their ideas will be valued. Writing workshop without a community of writers is like a refrigerator without food—empty. As you begin to launch the writing workshop, not only will you teach lessons specifically about the writing process, but you will also teach many lessons on management. A well-managed writing workshop provides structure, consistency, predictability, and an understanding of the expectations. A well-managed writing workshop empowers writers to carry on each and every day no matter the circumstances. Management lessons teach students how the class functions during the writing workshop. These lessons include where ideas for writing can be found; how to use resources such as the word bank, the word wall, and personal dictionaries; where to locate and how to use supplies; what level of voice to use while engaged in writing conferences; whom to go to for help; what can be done when a student is finished; and where writing is to be turned in (see figure 23.3).

Minilessons for Launching the Writing Workshop

- What is writing workshop?
- What writing workshop looks like, sounds like, and feels like.
- Structure of the writing workshop.
- How to hold a pencil.
- How to turn and talk.
- How to find and care for supplies.
- How to care for the writer's notebook/folder.
- Ways writers choose topics.
- Pictures can convey meaning.
- What to do when writing is completed.

Figure 23.3. Minilessons for launching the writing workshop.

What Is Writing Workshop?

At the beginning of the year, one of the first lessons I teach to get students acquainted with the writing workshop is "What is writing workshop?" I share the minilesson orally so the students are aware of the *what* and *why* of the work in which they will be engaged. It seems as though humans are born to question the world around them, and there is no doubt that children are the masters of asking *why*? Their curiosity is always piqued. Giving students the *what* is only one piece of the puzzle. If we want students to fully understand the relevance of the work we design, we should offer the *why*. Eventually, students will begin to establish the *why* for themselves.

The Minilesson: Writers write every day during writing workshop, so they become strong authors.

I begin by inviting all of the students to the whole group meeting area. This is a designated place in the classroom where all students can sit together for instruction. Once everyone is seated, I open a discussion about something special *we* will do each day. I stress *we* because I am of the belief that young writers fall in love with reading and writing when they see their teacher's love for reading and writing. This love can only be demonstrated by doing, that is, thinking aloud and visibly exposing yourself as a writer. I continue explaining that the special activity I am referring to is writing workshop. *Writing workshop is a time when we will come together to learn about writing. We will learn how to be strong writers. We will share oral stories, draw illustrations, create lists, invitations, and letters. We will write stories and make books. Every day at the beginning of writing workshop, we will meet in our special area. We will learn about authors and read the books they have written. We will also think about all the choices that writers can make in order to make our writing strong.*

The Model: After a brief minilesson, I read aloud *Pete the Cat: Rocking in My New School Shoes* (Litwin 2011). During the read aloud, students have the opportunity to listen to the text and view the detailed illustrations while thinking about the story the author is telling. After the read aloud, I inform the students that each of us has a story to tell. *The author of* Pete the Cat: Rocking in My New School Shoes, *Eric Litwin, had a story to tell about a cat who discovers all of the places in his new school shoes, so he wrote a book about that story.* I go on to explain that *each of us has a story to tell. In fact, we have many stories to tell, and that is what we will do during writing workshop.* I proceed to ponder a story I want to tell. I sit in the author's chair facing the students and commence sharing my story. I conclude with helping students to understand that it is important to share stories about what we know.

Independent Writing: (Typically, independent writing is the time when students are engaged in the writing process themselves. However, during the writing workshop "launch" phase, independent writing is in the form of oral storytelling.) At this point, I invite a student who is ready to come up before the class and sit in the author's chair to share his or her story.

Share: (I value share time just as much as any other component in the writing workshop, for this is when writers receive the feedback necessary to take their work to a deeper level. It is also a great time to initiate those confidence boosters.) At the conclusion of the storytelling experience, we celebrate the monumental accomplishment of the writer by cheering a special cheer for the author. The students get creative when thinking of special cheers: the cowboy/cowgirl, firecracker, roller coaster, and the list goes on and on. The type of cheer is not the *key*. The key is the validation that comes with the cheer, the validation that their story is something worth celebrating.

Interactive Writing

Interactive writing, also known as *share the pen*, is a powerful instructional tool that not only demonstrates how words work phonologically speaking, but also invites students into the world of written text—how text is composed in order to convey meaning (McCarrier, Fountas, and Pinnell 2000). Interactive writing offers the highest level of writing support, which explains why it is an integral component of the literacy framework at the primary level. Many concepts can be taught within one lesson, from letter formation to the writing process, from one-to-one correspondence to reading and summarizing. The possibilities are endless.

Tips for an Effective Interactive Writing Lesson

Interactive writing lessons have the potential to be highly effective. To be successful, interactive writing must (1) have purpose, (2) be written for an authentic audience, and (3) include all writers.

There is purpose in all messages that are composed. Whether it is a grocery list or a letter to a loved one, all writing should have meaning. Interactive writing is no different. Young writers are more likely to be engaged in interactive writing if they have a hand in establishing a purpose for the writing they will be composing and constructing.

Emergent writers are never too young to think about their audience. When writers think about their readers, they automatically begin to craft their voice and choice of words. The meaning they convey will dictate the form, or the way they deliver that message: list, letter, invitation, diagram with labels, and more (see figure 23.4).

All writers are included in the process of interactive writing. The community of writers works together, along with the teacher, to brainstorm ideas for the message. The writers work to write the message, and they think of ways to revise and edit. They also work together to summarize the relevance of each piece of writing to confirm its meaning. Anytime learners are able to find a link between what they have learned and future situations, they are making meaning. This is the image of long-term memory.

Ways to Incorporate Interactive Writing

- Summarizing text by creating a mural
- Steps for a process
- Lists
- Thank-you notes
- Holiday cards
- Letters
- Reader's response
- Invitations
- Research project
- Rewriting a new version of a familiar book
- Book recommendations
- "I Can" workstation labels
- Math problem solving
- Timelines for social studies

Figure 23.4. Ways to incorporate interactive writing.

The Minilesson: Writers can write classroom or workstation rules in order to remember what to do (see figure 23.5).

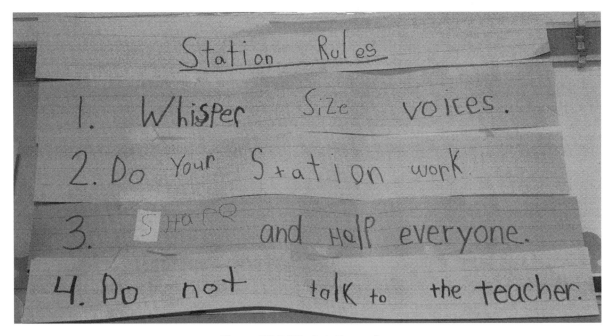

Figure 23.5. Workstation rules.

The Model: Using a previously read focal book, highlight examples of classroom rules. Invite writers to turn and talk about possible rules for their classroom. It is important to monitor the discussions of the groups. As a class, decide on a few rules that are necessary for the class to function as a safe learning environment.

You Try It: Continue this process once or twice depending on the level of engagement.

Share: Invite one or two students to share one thing they like about interactive writing. (See figure 23.6.)

A Structure for Teaching Interactive Writing

1. The writers come to a consensus about the first idea or sentence.
2. Repeat the sentence in unison.
3. Count the number of words in the sentence. Students should hold up one finger for each word counted.
4. Share the pen by calling on individual writers to help write the sentences. Writers are invited to write the words or word parts that are familiar. Teachers are encouraged to support the writing at this time by writing unknown words or word parts. The other writers can participate from their seats by practicing writing in the air, on the floor, or on the palm of their hands. Writers can utilize their very own "palm pilot."
5. Reread the sentence in unison. Be sure to use a pointer while pointing to each word.
6. Revise and edit as needed.
7. Summarize the learning.
8. Reflect.

(McCarrier, Fountas, and Pinnell 2000)

Figure 23.6. A structure for teaching interactive writing.

Suggested Focal Books

Lilly's Purple Plastic Purse by Kevin Henkes
The Art Lesson by Tomie dePaola
Countdown to Kindergarten by Allison McGhee

Oral Storytelling

Oral storytelling is the gateway to independent writing. Most primary students I know love to engage in conversation. From telling stories about a new baby sibling to unbelievable pet adventures, all children have a story to tell. Because written language requires a high level of abstract thinking, young children must first be immersed in literacy opportunities that are rich and meaningful before expecting them to reach that point of higher-level learning; therefore, if the expectation is for writers to develop and progress to higher levels of writing proficiency, then it only seems natural to invite oral storytelling as a means to teach the writing process. Providing a structure for oral storytelling has a variety of benefits that will serve each student well.

1. It affords every child the opportunity to extend and elaborate on his or her time of play by sharing his or her unique voice, which eventually transfers to the written work. In *the boy who would be a helicopter*, Vivian Gussin Paley writes of her experience as a kindergarten teacher and how she used storytelling as an innovative tool for teaching writing. She says this about play and writing:

   > Amazingly, children are born knowing how to put every thought and feeling into story form. If they worry about being lost, they become the parents who search; if angry, they find a hot hippopotamus to impose his will upon the world. Even happiness has its plot and characters: "Pretend I'm the baby and you only love me and you don't talk on the telephone." It is play, of course, but it is also story in action, just as storytelling is play put into narrative form. (Paley 1990, 4)

2. It is a means for students to establish their place within their learning environment. Children feel the need to belong, to take ownership. Oral storytelling is a nonthreatening atmosphere in which children can become their own community of learners while making it known to their teacher and peers that this place is *theirs*.

3. In addition to interactive writing, students begin to instinctively discover the writing process. If the teacher optimizes this structured time, this is the perfect opportunity to expose students to all steps of the writing process. This can be achieved through careful observation, assessment, and questioning: (1) observing and taking note of what the student has shared, (2) assessing important next steps, and (3) forming questions that will lead the student to elaborate and clarify any misconceptions.

4. Placing oral storytelling in its rightful place within the literacy framework builds confidence. Young writers thrive on positive learning experiences. Oral storytelling is just that. When students are encouraged to share stories about experiences that are important to them and interesting to others, this creates a stage for them to perform on and to be affirmed for their performance. When a child's work is validated, he or she is instantly boosted. This boost pushes the child to share more and more until it becomes an addiction—an addiction that takes students to places of great depth.

The Minilesson: Writers tell interesting stories about what they know.

Prior to the lesson, students experience a focal text. I begin by inviting all of the students to the whole group meeting area. I display a variety of previously read focal books and quickly discuss the authors' purpose for writing the books. I follow up with:

Today we read The Art Lesson *by Tomie dePaola [1989]. It is about a young boy, Tommy, who wants to become an artist. He can't wait to go to art class at school. Once there, his dreams are crushed because of all the rules set by his teacher. His art teacher later comes up with an idea that is sure to please Tommy. The author wrote* The Art Lesson *to tell us a story. Each of us has a story to tell. In fact, we have many stories to tell and that is what we will do during writing workshop. We will tell and draw and write our stories. As we were reading* The Art Lesson, *I started thinking about my two children. My story will not be about school or art class. It will be about the day I became a super hero.*

The Model: *One late, summer afternoon my sons P. J. and Christian asked if they could go outside and play. It was a beautiful evening, so of course I agreed. "Yes," I replied cheerfully. They bolted out of the door as if the house were on fire. Boy, do they love playing outdoors! As they played, I washed dishes (a never-ending chore). Every once and a while, I looked out the back window just to make sure they were okay. They played sword fighting, they played with our dog Ace, they swung like trapeze artists at the circus on the monkey bars, and they dug up the ground looking for toads to play with. It was while they were digging, they noticed something dark gray coiled up stiff as a board on the ground. Christian shouted, "Mom. Mom. Come out here. It's a snake!" I ran out frantically. What am I going to do? I thought. My husband was usually the one to take care of this sort of crisis, but he was away. It was up to me to save the day, and I was determined to do just that. I thought about trying to capture the snake, but that was not a smart plan. I even considered just throwing a box over it, but it just would have slithered away. The only thing to do was to calmly escort my boys back inside, and let nature take care of itself. And that's what I did! Remaining calm in that situation automatically made me a super hero!*

You Try It: Using the app Random Name Selector, I call upon a few students to share stories about an experience they think is interesting. This is a great time to teach students to tell personal stories using the pronoun "I." Invite authors to sit in the author's chair when sharing their stories.

Share: After each author shares, invite one student to tell the author one thing he or she liked about the story. After the positive feedback has been offered, invite the author to choose the type of celebratory cheer he or she prefers for that day. Remember, keep the feedback positive!

Consider This

Students buy into the idea of writing when they know, without a shadow of a doubt, that their teacher is sold on the process. A teacher's passion for writing is demonstrated when he or she thinks with the students, writes with the students, and celebrates with the students. Consider how you will establish a community of young writers who are comfortable taking risks while fostering a culture of independence, problem solving, and creative thinking.

24

The Writing Process

Everyone has a process, but each writer's process is idiosyncratic. Recognizing that process not only frees the writer but frees the teacher to facilitate not commandeer writing.

—Joyce Armstrong Carroll and Edward Wilson

As we embark upon this journey known as the writing process, it is important to note that you will have many opportunities to teach a variety of skills, from choosing a topic, to craft elements, to choosing ways to share writing with others. Teaching the process is critical to the development of a proficient writer (see figure 24.1). Because of the complexity of the writing process, intentional scaffolding and modeling is required in order for emergent writers to understand the expectations as well as to achieve success. I am reminded of the quote, "If you don't model what you teach, then you're teaching something else." Young children learn best by imitating the language and actions of those around them. Vygotsky's study of learning and development proves this:

In the child's development imitation and instruction play a major role. They bring out the specifically human qualities of the mind and lead the child to new developmental levels. In learning to speak, as in learning school subjects, imitation is indispensable. What the child can do in cooperation today she can do alone tomorrow. Therefore the only good kind of instruction is that which marches ahead of development and leads it; it must be aimed not so much at the ripe as at the ripening functions. (1962, 104)

While numerous strategies have been developed to teach the writing

Figure 24.1. The Writing Process

235

process, the strategies that I share here are the ones that I have found to support emergent writers: those who find it difficult to establish an idea, to move from one thought or idea to another, to move from one process to the next. These strategies will create a fertile ground in which seeds can be planted and later cultivated into well-crafted pieces of writing to be enjoyed by all.

The Writing Process

Prewriting
- Brainstorming ideas
- Selecting a topic

Drafting
- Forming complete thoughts using prewriting
- Tinkering with craft

Revising
- Adding or removing words
- Adding details to composition and illustrations

Editing
- Working with a teacher or peer to proofread for proper conventions: spacing, capitalization, punctuation, spelling

Publishing
- Sharing with others

Prewriting

Prewriting is where all great writing begins. It is the place where seeds are planted. Prewriting can be as unique to each writer as fingerprints are to each human being. Writers may stare, sketch, doodle, list, make connections, map, or confer. Prewriting is the means by which a writer finds purpose or ideas for writing. Carroll and Wilson state that prewriting strategies "are meant to be experienced not ordered" (2008, 5). In order for prewriting to be effective, students must be taught in a way that allows for connections to be made. Teaching prewriting strategies in isolation contradicts the process paradigm. According to Vygotsky, "When taken out of context, it may only foster 'pseudo concepts' that seem to be grasped abstractly but are not" (1962, 66).

The consistent teaching, modeling, and practicing of prewriting strategies support students in a number of ways. They are able to stockpile a variety of strategies to be used at their discretion. Giving students choice fosters creativity and critical thinking.

Carroll and Wilson (2008) describe how oversimplifying prewriting, jumping from prewriting to publishing, staying on prewriting, and internalizing prewriting can cause potential problems for students. In "Write Before Writing," Donald M. Murray contends that the reason students struggle with transferring their thoughts to paper is that they are not given the opportunity to prewrite. Murray states that all too often textbooks, as well as teachers, "pass over it rather quickly" (1978, 375).

Not only is prewriting recursive, but so are the processes within the process. A teacher who has a deep understanding of the writing process acknowledges that it is necessary to allow ample time for students to revisit their prewriting before requiring them to complete a task. "To sum up prewriting, it could be said that prewriting is looking at ones thinking and seeing another" (Carroll and Wilson 2008, 30). The prewriting strategies discussed below are those that I find not only grade level appropriate, but also effective in helping young writers generate ideas and select topics for writing in a variety of genres. These strategies can be introduced and integrated into the prewriting process at any time during the year.

Listing

The Minilesson: Writers create lists in order to brainstorm ideas for a story or book.

The Model: Initiate a discussion about reasons for keeping a list. *We keep lists to help us remember important information. For example, if I am planning a party, I want to remember the people I would like to invite; therefore, I write a guest list. I go shopping weekly for groceries. When I go to the store without a list, I usually forget an important ingredient or a snack my son wants for his lunch. Authors create lists when they wish to remember topics or details for writing projects.* Select a previously read focal book and call attention to the ways the characters used lists.

You Try It: Encourage students to turn and talk about topics they can write about. Invite them to help create a list using the ideas they shared in their turn and talk. Record the responses on an anchor chart titled "Brainstorming."

Independent Writing: Distribute one 9-by-6-inch sheet of colored construction paper and four 3-by-2½-inch index cards to each student. Have students fold one-fourth of the paper upward. Glue the outer edges to create a flap, and glue the center in place to allow the cards to be separated (see

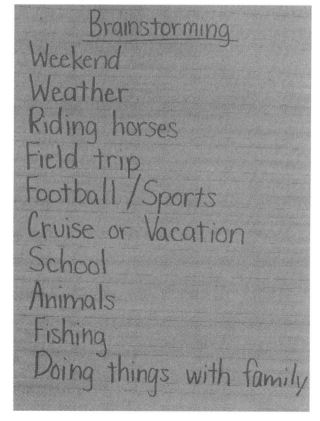

Figure 24.2. Brainstorming Anchor Chart.

figure 24.3a–d). Encourage the students to brainstorm and write a variety of lists, such as family, hobbies, favorite foods, and favorite music. Have additional index cards available for those students who want to add more ideas. Once the students have completed their lists, they may place them in the pockets of the book. Allow time for students to decorate the cover of the book.

Figure 24.3a.

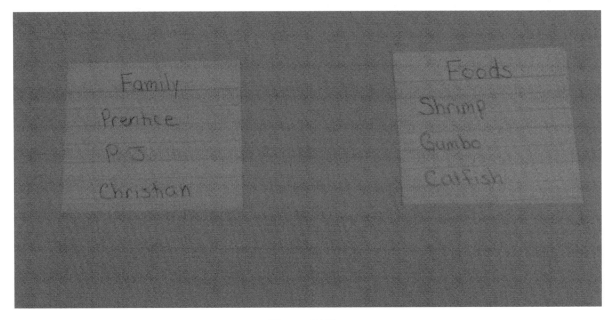

Figure 24.3b.

Family	Hobbies	Foods
Prentice	Cooking	Shrimp
P. J.	Canning	Gumbo
Christian	Traveling	Catfish
Dad	Writing	Green Beans
Mom		Chips & Salsa

Figure 24.3c.

Figure 24.3d.

Share Time: Invite one or two students to share one idea from the list that they would like to write about in the future.

> ### Suggested Focal Books
>
> *Wallace's Lists* by Barbara Bottner
> *Put It on the List* by Kristen Darbyshire
> *Eddie Gets Ready for School* by David Milgrim
> *Shopping with Dad* by Matt Harvey
> *Oliver's Must-Do List* by Susan Taylor Brown
> *Scaredy Squirrel* by Melanie Watt

Sketching

The Minilesson: Writers sketch pictures in order to gather ideas for writing.

The Model: The teacher should model this strategy using a personal story. Share your thinking aloud; this is also known as a *think aloud*. Provide students with as many details as possible. Sketch the supporting details on chart paper. Do support students who do not see themselves as artists. Writers need not be artists in order to generate ideas for writing.

You Try It: Invite students to turn and talk to their knee-to-knee partner about a picture they have created in their minds about a topic they want to write about.

Independent Writing: Encourage students to sketch a picture of the details that were shared with their partners.

Share Time: Place students in quads, or other variations, and invite students to share their sketches.

The Pentad

The Minilesson: Writers use a five-point star called a pentad to zoom in on one moment.

The Model: Using a focal book, or a common experience, complete each point of the pentad, answering who, what, when, where, and why. The center of the pentad is reserved for the title. Model whole group as needed before requiring students to complete the pentad independently (see figure 24.4).

You Try It: Invite students to close their eyes and imagine a story they would like to write. Encourage them to make a picture of the who, what, when, where, and why. Instruct the students to turn and talk to their knee-to-knee partners about their *mental* pentads.

Independent Writing: Encourage students to return to their tables to plan their stories, transferring the ideas from their mental pentads to their official pentads (see figure 24.5).

Share Time: Select one or two students to share the details of their pentads.

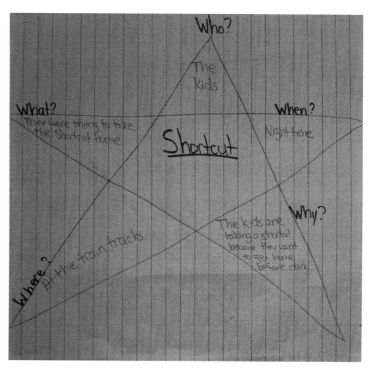

Figure 24.4. Model pentad with the focal book *Shortcut*.

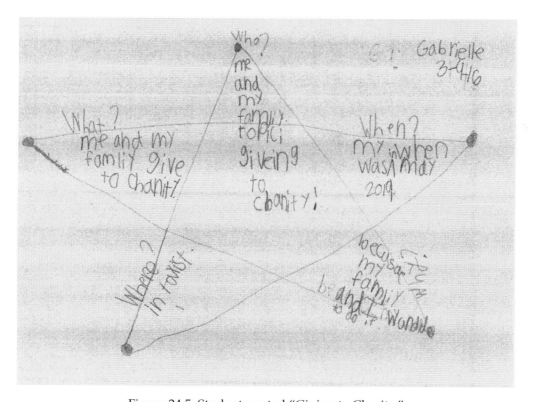

Figure 24.5. Student pentad "Giving to Charity."

Blueprinting

The Minilesson: Writers can map important places in order to brainstorm ideas for writing.

The Model: Bring in blueprints for students to view. Point out the details of the blueprint. Inform students that many of us live in different types of homes: apartments, mobile homes, homes with one level, and homes with multiple levels. Using a focal book, guide students in identifying rooms or places that are labeled. Invite students to think of possible topics that would be a good match for the label. Create a blueprint of your home. This can be done on manila construction paper or parchment paper for novelty (Carroll and Wilson 2008). As you create and label your blueprint, share with students the rooms you are sketching as well as any special memories that were made in those rooms.

You Try It: Place students in dyads and encourage them to share details about their homes with their partners. Challenge students to share any memories they can recall.

Independent Writing: Writers will map a room or several rooms and label spaces that hold special memories.

Share Time: Gallery walk—students can walk around the room and view the blueprints of other students.

Suggested Focal Books

Me on the Map by Joan Sweeny
Mapping Penny's World by Loreen Leedy
My Map Book by Sara Fanelli

Free Association

The Minilesson: Writers brainstorm ideas for writing by making connections.

The Model: Engage the students by explaining that they will take ordinary objects and magically transform those objects into new things. For example, I bring in a mini, galvanized planter to model the strategy. This particular container does not have a handle. You may choose any object that can be modified. Hold the planter for all students to observe. Explain that one can take something so simple, add a few details, and turn it into something completely different. Proceed to unfold a jumbo paper clip and attach it to the container, and with a wave of your "magic" wand it becomes a bucket for storing small items. Continue the lesson using pictures. Invite students to select a picture from a variety of living or nonliving things: baseball bat, ball, snake, flower, stick, or something of relevance. You may have them vote on a favorite picture. Connect that picture with the subsequent idea based on some attribute. Take a picture of a sunflower, for example; perhaps the students will associate the sunflower seeds with a corn maze. A picture of a corn maze is placed adjacent to the sunflower, with an arrow connecting the two ideas. The students then brainstorm an object that is associated with a corn maze. This process continues using a determined number of pictures, with the final picture connecting back to the first in some way. Once you and the students have illustrated all ideas, text can be added. In one activity, I posted a floatie on butcher paper, then during interactive writing, the students and I brainstormed, composed, and constructed the following poem:

The floatie turns into a soccer ball
The soccer ball turns into a flower
The stem is long like a bat
The bat splits into a stick
The stick snaps into a snake
The snake slithers into a floatie
The floatie saves lives

You Try It: The students try the process as stated above, with high levels of teacher support and scaffolding. Upon completion, students can share their brainstorming orally by using a voice-recording app or computer program. Writers love to hear their ideas over and over! This is also a great way to build fluency. The oral storytelling will also support writers when they are ready to add written text.

Independent Writing: Invite students to independently create associations using ideas from a choice of pictures, or give them the option to brainstorm their own ideas. Challenge students to write a story or poem using one or more of their associations.

Share: Invite students to sit in the author's chair to share their ideas.

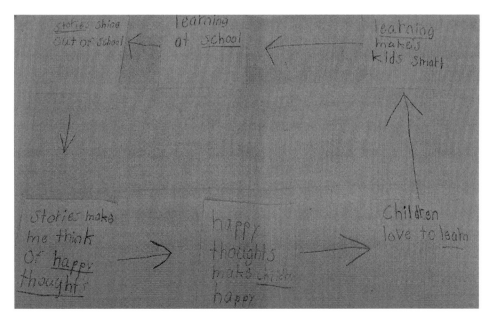

Figure 24.6. First grader Mariam makes associations with the topic: "Stories."

Suggested Focal Books

"Good Water" by Diane Wiskowski
The House in the Night by Susan Marie Swanson
Meggie Moon by Elizabeth Baguley
Emeraldalicious by Victoria Kann

Drafting

Drafting is the activity in which the seeds of writing begin to germinate and take root. Lucy Calkins states, "[A]s a writer I have come to know that significance cannot be found, it must be grown" (1986, 7).

During this step in the writing process, students revisit their lists, sketches, pentads, blueprints, and associations to select a topic, an audience, and a purpose for writing. Often the teacher must nudge the student to find value in his or her life. Writers must also understand there is a purpose for writing. This understanding comes partially through teachers sharing their personal experiences as a writer. Even if teachers do not see themselves as writers, they must model how writers draw from positive, personal experiences when finding purpose. The difference between mediocre teaching and great teaching is helping students realize their lives are important enough to write about. Young writers also begin to experiment with the author's craft and borrow ideas from mentors they have grown to love and adore. In *Acts of Teaching*, Carroll and Wilson state, "In prewriting students find meaning; in writing they find form. To do it the other way around is artificial" (2008, 31). Writing should be of utmost significance to the writer. "Teaching writing is a matter of faith. We demonstrate that faith when we listen well, when we refer to our students as writers, when we expect them to love writing and to pour heart and soul into it" (Calkins 1986, 17).

Labeling

The Minilesson: Authors label their illustrations to help the reader understand their message.

The Model: Facilitate a discussion about labels. Ask students to share the meaning of the word *label*. Invite students to share examples of labels they have seen or have made. Show the students food labels and discuss the reasons that producers use labels. Next, show examples of how authors use labels as a text feature in books or magazines. Take students on a scavenger hunt around the school. Distribute a scavenger hunt record form to each student and challenge them all to sketch or write examples of the labels they find (see chapter appendix 1). The classroom is a great place to begin. Visit places such as the library, nurse's clinic, and cafeteria. Stop in the hallway and, if weather permits, take the students outdoors. As you travel throughout the building, invite staff members from each area to speak to the students or demonstrate how they use labels to help themselves and others understand. Once students have completed the scavenger hunt and have returned to the classroom, open a discussion about the various places they visited and the ways labels were used in those places. The students can use the scavenger hunt guide to spark ideas.

You Try It: Explain to the students that you will sketch a picture of one place they visited. Invite the students to choose. Tell the students there is a chance others will see their writing, but they might not understand the message that is written. Ask students to name something they can add that would help the reader to understand their message. Invite students to "share the pen" as you write the labels for the illustration.

Independent Writing: Explain to the students that they will revisit their list of potential topics. Challenge the students to select a topic, draw pictures, and label the pictures so their readers will understand their story.

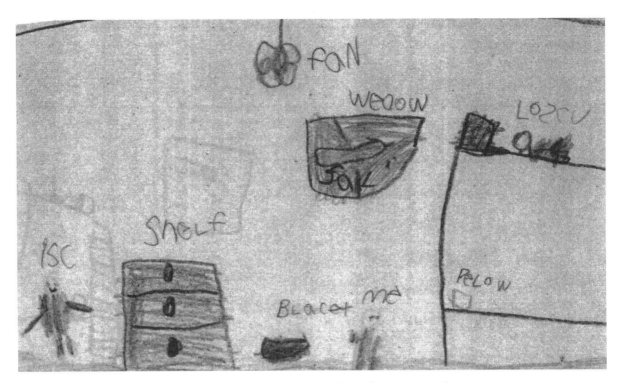

Figure 24.7. Grace labels her story about her sister and room.

Share: Select students to sit in the author's chair to share their topic and two of their best labels.

> ### Suggested Focal Books
>
> *The Bird, the Monkey, and the Snake in the Jungle* by Kate Banks
> *Growing Vegetable Soup* by Lois Ehlert
> *A Ball for Daisy* by Chris Raschka
> *It's a Butterfly's Life* by Irene Kelly
> *Diary of a Worm* by Doreen Cronin

Writing Small Moments

The Minilesson: Writers zoom in on the important details in order to write about a small moment.

The Model: The teacher should model this strategy using a personal story. Share your thinking aloud. This is a great time to model the difference between a *watermelon* story and a *seed* story. A watermelon story is synonymous to a broad topic that tells many stories within it, whereas a seed story focuses on one small moment. An example of a watermelon story is one about a trip to New York City. A seed story would be about taking the ferry to Staten Island.

Model for students that when photographers take pictures, they use their lenses to zoom in on the object in order to get a close-up shot. Writers should do the same when zooming in on a small moment to write about. Demonstrate this analogy with some photographs that depict a broad range and one that shows a more focused shot.

You Try It: Invite students to turn and talk to their knee-to-knee partners about a picture they have made in their minds about a "seed" story, or small moment.

Independent Writing: Distribute an image of a camera photocopied on cardstock to each student. Encourage students to sketch a picture of the details that were shared in their dyads on their cameras.

Share: Place students in quads, adjust groups as needed, and have students share their sketches. The students will continue by taking the writing through the writing process.

Leads

The Minilesson: Writers begin their stories in interesting ways to lead the reader to a strong story.

The Model: Teaching young writers to craft strong leads during the drafting stage of the writing process may seem like a daunting task; however, students will prove time and time again that they are ready for the challenge. Begin by prepping the lesson in advance. Select focal books that students are familiar with, as students love to revisit their favorites even when studying specific pages or sections. Be sure to choose books that demonstrate the types of leads you would like to introduce: action, setting, dialogue, or exciting thought. For this lesson, I begin sharing *Shortcut* by Donald Crews (1992a). I prefer using this focal book because of the length. Although it is short, it packs a powerful punch. The immediate action builds the reader's suspense. I find that students enjoy experimenting with this type of lead because they feel confident that they can try it in their own writing.

Explain to the students that they will practice reading like a writer, which means that as they read, they will be thinking of ways they can imitate or borrow the ideas of the writer. Inform students that you are only focusing on the lead or the beginning of the story.

This is the lead Donald Crews wrote for *Shortcut*:

> We looked . . .
> We listened . . .
> We decided to take
> the shortcut home.

This is a short lead, but there is so much action. It makes me excited to read more. A lead that shows action is one in which the characters are doing something. What did the characters do at the beginning of the story?

Create a three-column anchor chart titled "Leading the Way to a Strong Story." Write the term that identifies the lead "action," sketch a picture that represents action, and conclude by writing the lead. Repeat the previous steps using a second focal book. This time invite the students to share their thinking along with you and assist them with identifying the lead. Continue this process until you have introduced the leads you desire your students to explore. This can take several days depending on the grade level. Thinking aloud, model your thought process on selecting a just-right lead for your story. Model writing the lead.

You Try It: Have students turn and talk to their knee-to-knee partners about a lead they would like to try in their stories. Invite a few students to share the leads they will attempt in their writing.

Independent Writing: Challenge the students to try the selected leads in their stories.

Share: Invite a few students to share only the leads.

Endings

The Minilesson: Writers write endings that will leave the readers satisfied.

The Model: This model mirrors the lesson on leads. Spend time exploring familiar focal texts that have strong endings. Explain to students that they are going to explore more focal texts; this time they are looking for strong endings. Help students understand that the ending should be just as strong as the beginning. Create an anchor chart titled, "Strong Endings Leave Lasting Memories." Invite students to add their favorite endings to the anchor chart. Model writing a strong ending for your story.

You Try It: Invite students to turn and talk to their knee-to-knee partners about an ending they would like to try in their stories. Have a few students share.

Independent Writing: Encourage students to think about and write strong endings for their stories.

Share: Select students to share their endings.

Revising

Revision is a process that most novice writers react to adversely. "I'm done." "I don't have anything else to add." It's already perfect." In their eyes, the writing process ends with the draft. However, as teachers of writing, we understand that the revision process is the step in which those budding plants grow strong, take on shape and color, and infuse the environment with its sweet aroma. Writers begin to grapple with the idea of making decisions about words, meaning, voice, and punctuation, and how they affect the overall message. It is here that writers add, delete, and move words around on the page. We clarify meaning and make images crystal clear for the audience. We're preparing for the harvest. Calkins sees revision as a way to use her draft to "see more, feel more, think more, and learn more" (1986, 39). In *Craft Lessons: Teaching Writing K–8*, Fletcher and Portalupi (1998) contend that most young writers overlook craft and revision, moving from drafting to publishing.

The terms *modeling* and *scaffolding* have been repeated throughout *Guided by Meaning* because they are fundamental to the success of every writer. As with anything we expect our students to accomplish and accomplish well, we must provide them with multiple opportunities to see, hear, and experience, and revising is no different. In "What Writing Is and Isn't," Jeff Anderson states, "Writing instruction has little to do with kits and worksheets. It's messier—and more joyous—than that" (Anderson 2014, 10).

Figure 24.8. Sydni revises personal narrative book.

Prove-Its

Prove-its, a strategy that is outlined in *Dr. JAC's Guide to Writing with Depth* (Carroll 2002), is a foolproof way to teach emergent writers the skill of adding depth to their writing. When challenging students to revise their writing, this is one of my "go to" strategies, because it is easy for young writers to access and apply.

The Minilesson: Writers add more details to their writing in order to help the reader make a picture in his or her mind.

The Model: Using the focal book *When Sophie Gets Angry . . . Really, Really Angry* by Molly Bang (2004), read a telling sentence. Students chant: "Maybe yes, maybe no. Prove it!" Share with students how the author adds more details to the simple telling sentence.

You Try It: Choose an additional sentence from the focal book. Encourage students to chant "Maybe yes, maybe no. Prove it!" Select one student to share his or her thinking about ways in which the author added more details using the Prove-It strategy. Continue by selecting a telling sentence from the teacher's model and elicit the help of your students to brainstorm ways to "prove it."

Independent Writing: Invite students to reenter their writing and find a place where they can add more details. Instruct the students to highlight or circle the telling statement that requires more information. Encourage the students to elaborate by adding the missing details to their stories, therefore proving the telling statement.

Share: Call upon a few volunteers to share how they added more details using Prove-Its.

Suggested Focal Books

Say Hello to Zorro by Carter Goodrich
Wilfrid Gordon McDonald Partridge by Mem Fox
Charlie Goes to School by Ree Drummond
Yard Sale! by Mitra Modarressi

Statement, Extend, Elaborate (SEE)

The Minilesson: Writers help the reader to "SEE" the meaning of their writing by adding more details.

The Model: Read aloud the focal book *Ten Black Dots* by Donald Crews (1992b). The teacher creates an object using black die-cut dots or stickers. For example, place the dots in a circular formation to create a wreath. The creation of an object is a visual representation of how writers extend and elaborate meaning. The teacher orally shares his or her creation by simply providing one telling sentence. *Wreaths are popular items used for decorating.* Do not show the students the creation. By concealing the creation, you are encouraging students to visualize the object in order to make meaning.

You Try It: Challenge students to make their own creations. Divide the students into pairs or triads. Invite them to share their creations. Again, students should not reveal the object. Reconvene the whole group and inquire if the meaning was clear. Allow students time to share their thoughts. The teacher should then model again orally, this time giving a topic sentence, followed by extending and elaborating. For example: *Wreaths are popular items used for decorating. Most people buy or make wreaths to hang on their front doors or on the walls of their home. The ribbons and bows can be customized for any occasion—holidays, school, or even seasons of the year.* The students should be able to identify how extending and elaborating provided clarity and meaning to the object. Invite the students to join the same group and apply the strategy above. This should be practiced orally. Challenge the students to write the name of the new creation and an informational paragraph that supports their idea. If the students require more scaffolding, provide a handout with pictures of things such as a cylinder, circle, star, raindrop, cloud, or others. Students choose one figure, then add lines and other details to extend and elaborate. Allow time to write about the new figure.

Share: Invite a brief discussion about why authors should extend and elaborate upon their writing.

The Minilesson: Writers explore nonfiction books in order to notice how authors use the SEE strategy in their writing.

The Model: Create an anchor chart that explains what it means to *SEE*. As a whole group, explore other focal books that illustrate the use of SEE. Write examples on sentence strips and have students circle words to show the connection from one sentence to the next. The teacher should model the application of SEE with his or her writing (Carroll, 2002).

You Try It: Revisit the focal book *Ten Black Dots* by Donald Crews. You may provide students with the following prompt or one of your choosing: *Writers often think outside of the box in order to generate ideas for writing. If you were given 10 black dots, explain what you would create.* Invite students to turn and talk to their knee-to-knee partners about their ideas. Students may opt to use the object that was created during the first lesson.

Independent Writing: Students will begin writing about their ideas. Challenge students to use *SEE*.

Share: Invite those students who are willing to share to do so.

Editing

I love to observe students in this phase of the writing process. Young writers are just as passionate about their writing as adult writers. Critical thinking takes on a whole new meaning, because the work they have done is now being critiqued by an "outsider." Writers quickly climb up the rungs of Bloom's taxonomy during the editing process—justifying their writing moves is the main objective of this game. Although most developing writers are convinced their work is perfect and is exempt from correction, eventually they invite the help of their peers and consider their suggestions.

The Minilesson: Writers work with a friend to help them *spice up* their writing before publishing.

The Model: Use the teacher-created rubric and invite a student to help you *spice up* your writing (see chapter appendix 2). Encourage the rest of the class to watch and listen while you and your student editor model. If this is your first time introducing editing, perhaps focus on beginning capitals and end punctuation. As conventions are taught, gradually increase the number of items to be checked. Model how to use the rubric. When errors are found, tag them with a small Post-it® flag. This will help writers find their errors easily when they go back to fix them up. Modify or extend based on the needs of your students. Call upon a few students to share what they noticed the teacher and student doing during the model.

You Try It: Invite two students to demonstrate how they can help each other *spice up* their writing by using the teacher-created rubric. Guide the discussion and practice as needed.

Independent Writing: Place students in pairs. Provide each student with a copy of the rubric. Have the writer point to each word and read his or her story while the reader looks on. The reader should be looking for beginning capitals and ending punctuation. The writer then asks the question: "Do my sentences make sense?" The reader will circle the face that answers the question. The pair will proceed to the next question on the rubric: "Did I start my sentences with a capital letter?" The reader will circle the face that answers the question. The pair will complete the last question: "Did I use punctuation at the end of all of my sentences?" The reader will circle the face that answers the question. The reader will then complete the rubric by totaling the number of happy faces and sad faces. Have partners switch roles and repeat the process. Once each partner has helped the other edit, students can go back to their table to correct any errors that were discovered.

Share: Have students share how they helped each other edit.

Publishing

What greater joy is there for a child than knowing he or she has become a published author? Young writers want and deserve to be affirmed for reaching this point in the writing process. The level of engagement it takes to endure the writing process is no small feat for a beginning writer; therefore, his or her accomplishment is definitely worth celebrating. Writing celebrations can be as small scale or as grand as you would like them to be. Either way, variety is always great because it keeps them wanting more.

Author's Chair

Select a special chair that will be designated as the author's chair. This chair can be decorated by the students using a sheet of poster board or recycled fabric like a pillow case. Allow students to personalize the author's chair so that it becomes theirs. Each student who volunteers to share or is selected to share his or her writing has reserved seating in the author's chair.

Students at all levels feel comfortable and are proud to sit in this special seat before their audience.

Circle of Authors

Circle of authors is a small group, typically four to five students, who come together to share their writing. Circle of authors is an effective method to implement when several students are sharing lengthy pieces of writing. Each student is encouraged to share his or her writing with those in the circle. The audience is allowed to share positive feedback at the conclusion of each share.

Museum Walk

This method allows students to walk around to each piece of writing within a small group or an entire classroom. The students stop at each sample to read, enjoy, and admire the work of their peers before the teacher signals the students to move to the next writing sample. If students are trained, they can leave positive, handwritten notes.

The Minilesson: Writers share their stories with others so they can enjoy them.

The Model: The teacher shares his or her story with the class. Invite one student to point out one idea he or she liked.

You Try It: Encourage the students to turn and talk to their knee-to-knee partners and share their favorite part of their stories. The partners should then point out one idea they liked and share it with the authors. The partners then switch roles and repeat the process.

Application: Divide students into groups and invite each student to share his or her favorite part of the story. The audience should practice being good listeners. Once the author has shared his or her writing, each member of the audience can point out one positive word, sentence, or detail that was noticed in the writing and/or illustration (Carroll and Wilson 2008).

Figure 24.9. Circle of authors share their writing.

Self-Reflection

As teachers we constantly reflect about our relationships with our students. We evaluate our teaching moves and our motives for what we do. However, what would happen if we asked our young students to reflect upon what they have learned about becoming a writer? I recall completing a three-week project on personal narratives with a group of first graders. I was thrilled that we had come to the point of celebrating their accomplishments, but a part of me was not ready for the project to end. It was as if something was tugging at me, beckoning me to extend the project. There was really nothing else to be done, because the celebration had taken place. Then I had a eureka moment! I posed the idea of a reflection to my coteacher, and we went for it. Not only did we have our students pause to take time to intentionally think about the work they had completed, but we also challenged them to record their reflections (see chapter appendix 3). What a profound way to end such a project: to have first-grade students take a moment to think about all they had learned over the three weeks of study and provide honest feedback. Yes, we encouraged them; in fact, we demanded their honesty. We truly wanted to know how they felt about spending, what probably seemed like an eternity, three weeks on one project. Not only did students have to choose the way they felt, but they had to explain why. Their responses were enlightening. One way to know if students are internalizing the lessons we are teaching is by asking them to articulate what they have learned. If we want students to adapt their thinking in an interdisciplinary way, we must offer opportunities for them to engage in the act of thinking about their thinking.

Figure 24.10. Ariana reflects on a three-week writing project.

Figure 24.11a. Gabbi's self-sponsored reflection.

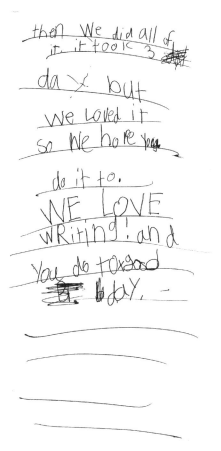

Figure 24.11b. Gabbi's self-sponsored reflection.

Consider This

This entire chapter focuses on strategies and best teaching practices that can be implemented to guide and support authentic writing. As you begin planning the course your students will take along this journey called the writing process, consider how you will scaffold, model, and allow opportunities for peer collaboration and self-reflection.

Name:_____

Writing Scavenger Hunt

Hunting for Labels

Library	Nurse's Clinic	Classroom

Hallway	Cafeteria	Outdoors

Author:_____

Editing Partner:_____

My Editing Rubric

My sentences make sense.	☺	☹
I started my sentences with a capital letter.	☺	☹
I used punctuation at the end of all my sentences. . ? !	☺	☹
Total	____ / ☺	____ / ☹

Author:_____

Editing Partner:_____

My Editing Rubric

My sentences make sense.	☺	☹
I started my sentences with a capital letter.	☺	☹
I used punctuation at the end of all my sentences. . ? !	☺	☹
Total	____ / ☺	____ / ☹

Name:_____

My Writing Reflection

How Do I Feel About My Writing Project?

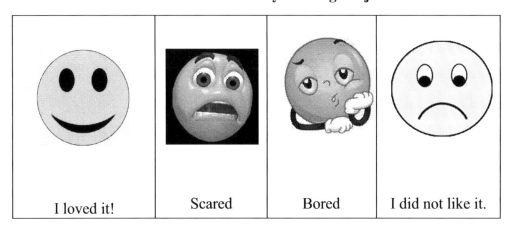

| I loved it! | Scared | Bored | I did not like it. |

_____

_____

_____

_____

Author:_____

Editing Partner:_____

My Editing Checklist

Does my writing make sense?	Yes	No
Did I start my sentences with a capital letter?	Yes	No
Did I use punctuation at the end of all my sentences? . ? !	Yes	No
Do my words look right?	Yes	No

Author:_____

Editing Partner:_____

My Editing Checklist

Does my writing make sense?	Yes	No
Did I start my sentences with a capital letter?	Yes	No
Did I use punctuation at the end of all my sentences? . ? !	Yes	No
Do my words look right?	Yes	No

25

Units of Study

The fact that a writer pauses to establish the genre in which he is writing may seem obvious to you, but it is not obvious to children.

—Lucy Calkins

Exposing students to a variety of genres during their primary years establishes a strong foundation for reading and writing. Many district curricula introduce genres such as personal narrative, procedural or expository writing, and poetry. Through this introduction, students may be assigned or choose a topic within the genre. Subsequently they will work toward taking the piece through the writing process. Once that project is complete, then it is on to the next genre. This sampling of genres does not support young writers in establishing a genuine understanding of various forms of writing. The goal, then, is to go deep (Ray and Cleaveland 2004). Designing units of study is a meaningful context for teaching primary writers the specific characteristics of any given genre. When students are engaged in a unit of study through an inquiry approach, they study rich literature up close, gleaning as much information as possible regarding craft and features of the genre. Studying genres in this way aids young writers by strengthening observation skills, fostering higher-level thinking, and increasing awareness and knowledge of the features and characteristics of a variety of genres.

When students become knowledgeable about the inner workings of the genre they are writing in, they rely on their understanding to make important decisions about purpose, audience, organization, and craft. These important decisions lead to growth, which ultimately points to a stronger writer.

The structure for implementing a unit of study is outlined in the lessons that follow. Prior to beginning any unit of study, carefully select the texts you will study alongside your students. Collect several mentor texts that include clear examples of the features and characteristics of the genre you are studying.

Text Discovery
- The teacher and students work together to read, tag, notice, name, and chart the characteristics and/or features of the genre.

Text Discovery: Cooperative Inquiry Approach (CIA)
- Students work together to read, tag, notice, name, and chart the characteristics and/or features of the genre.

Prewriting
- Students brainstorm ideas and plan writing in the genre.

Drafting
- Students settle on a topic and begin organizing writing in the genre. Students experiment with craft elements that were noticed and named during text discovery.

Revising
- Students consider ways to add or remove details to strengthen the meaning of the draft.

Editing
- Students work with the teacher or peers to correct spacing, capitalization, punctuation, spelling, and sentences.

Publishing
- Students make writing public by sharing it with others.

Personal Narrative Unit of Study

Text Discovery

The Minilesson: Writers learn how to write personal narrative books by studying other authors.

The Model: The teacher reads a preselected narrative and has students share what they noticed about the writing (the book is written in story form, includes story elements, speech bubbles, etc.).

You Try It: Create an anchor chart titled "What We Know About Personal Narratives." Invite students to share ideas for the chart.

Independent Writing: Distribute discovery text sets of narratives for students to explore. Encourage the students to tag features that interest them.

Share: Encourage students to share something new they learned or something they want to try when writing their personal narrative books.

Text Discovery : Cooperative Inquiry Approach (CIA)

The Minilesson: Writers work in groups to investigate personal narrative books by studying other authors.

The Model: Review the anchor chart from the previous day.

You Try It: Select a new focal book to read and analyze. Explain to the students that they will be assisting you with tagging ways the author used special strategies to make the writing more interesting. As you read, stop and tag craft techniques such as internal dialogue, speech bubbles, word choice, text layout, use of punctuation, and bold or italic print. Challenge students to identify strategies.

Independent Writing: Encourage the students to explore various narrative mentor texts. Have students tag the pages that show various craft techniques with Post-it® notes. Remind them to search for ways authors have written words, how and where authors have placed words on the pages, and so forth. As students tag the pages, have them name what they notice on their Post-it notes.

Share: Have students share the craft techniques they have discovered. Ideas can be recorded on the "What We Know About Personal Narrative" chart.

Prewriting

The Minilesson: Writers can use a flow map to plan their personal narrative books.

The Model: The teacher creates a flow map using a focal book. The teacher models the parts of the flow map using ideas from the focal book.

You Try It: Invite students to turn and talk about the topic they want to write about. Challenge the students to share some of the craft elements they will try in their writing.

Independent Writing: Using their chosen topic, students will begin planning their personal narrative books using the flow map. Walk students through each step if necessary.

Share: Have students share something they learned while using the flow map.

Drafting

The Minilesson: Writers write personal narrative books with a beginning, middle, and end.

The Model: Introduce or revisit beginning, middle, and end using short texts such as nursery rhymes. Choose one that students are familiar with, like "Hickory Dickory Dock."

Write the nursery rhyme "Hickory Dickory Dock" on sentence strips prior to the lesson:

Sentence strip 1: Hickory, dickory, dock.
Sentence strip 2: The mouse ran up the clock.
Sentence strip 3: The clock struck one,
Sentence strip 4: the mouse ran down.
Sentence strip 5: Hickory, dickory, dock.

Every strong story has a beginning, middle, and end. The beginning introduces the reader to the characters and setting of the story. The middle reveals the problem or the most important part of the story, along with the events and other details. The end includes how the problem is solved or how the story ends.

Display the sentence strips in random order. Invite students to put the lines of the nursery rhyme in sequential order. Challenge the students to assist you with identifying the beginning, middle, and end.

You Try It: Provide each table with a nursery rhyme cut into strips. Students are to work in groups to arrange and identify the nursery rhymes' beginning, middle, and end. Extend the lesson by having the students justify their decisions.

Display the model flow map and call attention to the beginning, middle, and end. Explain that you will add more details when writing your book.

Independent Writing: Students will write the beginning, middle, and end using the teacher model as a guide.

Share: Select a student to share beginning, middle, and end.

Revising

The Minilesson: Writers choose exact words to add details to their writing.

The Model: Read the focal book *Diary of a Worm* by Doreen Cronin (2003). Call attention to pages three and four. Read the telling sentence on page three. Lead the chant, "Maybe yes, maybe no. Prove it!" Invite students to choral read page four. Challenge students to evaluate the author's ability to prove her declarative statement.

You Try It: Turn to page eight. Write a declarative statement on chart paper. Lead the chant, "Maybe yes, maybe no. Prove it!" Place students in pairs, and challenge them to revise the telling statement. Remind them to choose specific words to add details. Call upon a few groups to share their revisions.

Independent Writing: Encourage students to reenter their drafts to find a declarative statement. Encourage students to choose exact words to "prove" what they are attempting to communicate.

Editing

The Minilesson: Writers work together to help one another make their stories stronger.

The Model: Display a piece of writing that someone helped you edit. Share examples of how your editor helped you strengthen your writing.

You Try It: Select two volunteers to model peer editing using the teacher-created rubric or editing checklist (see appendix 4 in chapter 24).

Independent Writing: Assign peer editing partners and have the students work together to peer edit one another's personal narrative using the teacher-created rubric or editing checklist.

Publishing

The Minilesson: Writers share their stories so others can celebrate their work.

The Model: Select a student to share his or her story. Remind students of the qualities of a good audience.

You Try It: Select two to three students to share what they noticed while the author shared his or her writing. Challenge the students to use that information to reach their goals for share time.

Share: Select students to sit in the author's chair to share their books.

Discovery Text Set for Personal Narrative

First Person
Grandpa's Awesome by Mary H. Wright
Something Beautiful by Sharon Wyeth
A Chair for Always by Vera Williams
A Chair for My Mother by Vera Williams
Kitchen Dance by Maurie Manning
I Love My Hair! by Natasha Tarpley
When I Was Young in the Mountains by
    Cynthia Rylant
Tulip Sees America by Cynthia Rylant

Other Narratives
Jennie's Hat by Ezra Keats
Peter's Chair by Ezra Keats
Roller Coaster by Marla Frazee
Rosie Sprout's Time to Shine by Allison
    Wortche
The Paperboy by Dav Pilkey
The Relatives Came by Cynthia Rylant
*When Sophie Gets Angry—Really, Really
    Angry . . .* by Molly Bang
Fred Stays with Me! by Nancy Coffelt
Max's Dragon by Kate Banks

Figure 25.1. Discovery text set for personal narrative.

How-To Unit of Study

Text Discovery

The Minilesson: Writers can learn how to write how-to books by studying other authors.

The Model: The teacher reads a how-to focal book and invites the students to share what they notice about the craft of the writing. (The book is written in narrative or expository form. It includes lists, steps, layout of text, etc.)

You Try It: Create an anchor chart titled "How-To Discovery Chart." Challenge the students to share ideas for the chart. Record the students' ideas on the anchor chart.

How-To Features in My Writing

Characteristics/Features of the How-To	Ways I Can Explore with My Writing

Independent Writing: Distribute discovery text sets of how-to books for students to explore. Encourage the students to tag features that interest them.

Share: Invite a few students to share something new they learned or something they want to try.

Text Discovery: Cooperative Inquiry Approach (CIA)

The Minilesson: Writers work in groups to investigate how to write how-to books by studying other authors.

The Model: Review the "How-To Features in My Writing" anchor chart. Select a new focal book and explain to the students that they will explore many how-to texts together. Remind students of how to tag the pages with Post-it® notes to identify various characteristics or features of the how-to you are exploring. Share with students ways the author has crafted the text and text layout, as well as how and where illustrators have placed illustrations on the pages. The teacher models by reading his or her writing and that of other students. The teacher should focus on the craft techniques that were applied.

You Try It: Project a focal book for the purpose of analysis. Guide students to share what they notice about the words or illustrations. Record the students' ideas on the anchor chart.

Independent Writing: Place discovery text sets of how-to books on each table. Allow time for students to explore the text sets and tag various techniques they notice with Post-its. Students can make notes and use the notes as a discussion starter for share time.

Share: Have students share the craft techniques they discovered. Ideas can be recorded on the anchor chart.

Prewriting

The Minilesson: Writers can plan out the details of what they want to teach others by counting their fingers.

The Model: Model counting your fingers to brainstorm directions for teaching others. Begin by holding up your index finger. State the first step of the directions for what you are teaching. Next, hold your middle finger and state the second step. Continue until all steps have been stated. Add details to Post-its. Post-it® notes work well because they can be manipulated and placed in sequential order as students plan the layout of their book.

You Try It: Students turn and talk about their ideas, using their fingers as they share.

Independent Writing: Have students choose paper for their how-to books and begin planning the layout of the book. The students can also begin sketching the layout of their books.

Share: Select a student to share the technique that will be applied to his or her how-to book.

Drafting

The Minilesson: Writers write directions that are clear and easy to understand.

The Model: The teacher chooses a student's prewriting to share with the rest of the class. The class helps the writer determine if the directions are clear and easy to understand.

You Try It: Select another prewriting sample. Share the steps and invite the students to vote on whether the directions make sense.

Independent Writing: Students will write their drafts.

Share: Select a few students to share. Encourage the audience to provide feedback.

Revising

The Minilesson: Writers can *spice up* or revise their own writing so that it makes sense.

The Model: Model revising with a student sample. Invite a student to read the steps he or she is attempting to teach others. The class should try to complete the task to determine if the steps are precise. Demonstrate for the students how to revise by adding or removing words using Post-its. Students may also add a picture to explain directions.

Independent Writing: Students will reread their how-to books and look for ways to revise them. Have students mark their confusing parts with Post-its and then revise them.

Share: Have students share ways they revised.

Editing

The Minilesson: Writers can learn how to use punctuation by studying other authors.

The Model: The teacher models how other authors use punctuation with how-to mentor texts.
Display a page or write an excerpt on chart paper and have students identify the types of punctuation they observe. Discuss the purpose for each type.

Independent Writing: The teacher confers with the students and encourages them to reenter their writing to look for places where punctuation needs to be added.

Share: Choose a few students to share ways they added punctuation.

Publishing

The Minilesson: Writers can publish their writing by sharing with others.

The Model: The teacher models sharing using the *fishbowl* method. Arrange five chairs in a circle. Choose four students to join the circle. The teacher shares his or her writing while the chosen participants model being a good audience.

Share: Divide students into small groups and have them share their how-to books.

Discovery Text Set for How-To

Henry Builds a Cabin by D. B. Johnson
How to Bicycle to the Moon to Plant Sunflowers: A Simple but Brilliant Plan in 24 Easy Steps by
  Mordicai Gerstein
How to Babysit a Grandpa by Jean Reagan
If I Built a Car by Chris Van Dusen
How to Read a Story by Kate Messner
Ralph Tells a Story by Abby Hanlon
How to Wash a Woolly Mammoth by Michelle Robinson
How to Teach a Slug to Read by Susan Pearson
Everyone Can Learn to Ride a Bicycle by Chris Raschka
The Pumpkin Book by Gail Gibbons

Figure 25.2. Discovery text set for how to.

Poetry Unit of Study

Text Discovery: Poetic Language

The Minilesson: Poets can listen to the words people say in order to find poetry.

The Model: Words that we speak can be *seeds* of poems. Begin a structured conversation by sharing something that is important to you.

You Try It: Ask the students to share good news or choose a focal book to prompt a discussion. Invite the students to engage in a conversation about the good news that was shared or the topic of the focal book. Listen for the words they speak and record poetic words on an anchor chart titled "Poetic Words."

Introduce poetry bags, which are brown or white lunch bags that can be used for collecting words.

Independent Writing: Distribute strips of paper and encourage students to write words they love on the slips of paper and drop them into their poetry bags. The collection of words can be used for future writing. Students can decorate their poetry bags.

Share: Have students place their decorated bags on the table, and invite students to go on a museum walk to view each bag.

Text Discovery: Cooperative Inquiry Approach (CIA)

The Minilesson: Writers can use their *magic* eye to look at ordinary objects in a new way.

The Model: Poets must learn to look at everyday objects in new ways to discover hidden poetry. In order to do this, poets must use their *magic* eye. In other words, poets must view ordinary objects in an extraordinary way. They observe the world around them from a different perspective. Model by taking an ordinary object in your classroom or bring in an object from your home and demonstrate how you would use your magic eye. When poets write about ordinary, everyday objects in creative and imaginative ways, they look at those objects through another eye—a *magic* eye. Share the poem "Picture Puzzle Piece" by Shel Silverstein. Share your thinking about how the poet used his "magic" eye

You Try It: Display the poem "A Stick Is an Excellent Thing" from the book *A Stick Is an Excellent Thing: Poems Celebrating Outdoor Play* by Marilyn Singer (Singer 2012). Invite students to choral read, then invite them to share what they noticed about how the poet used her "magic" eye.

Independent Writing: Set up a poetry center. Have items available on the table for students to explore their five senses. Invite students to write sensory words to describe the items explored. Independent writing can be differentiated by allowing the students to sketch. Challenge students to use their *magic* eyes to think of those objects in a different way.

Share: Have students share what they discovered.

Text Discovery Continued: Cooperative Inquiry Approach (C.I.A.)

The Minilesson: Writers collect amazing words from the books that they read.

The Model: The teacher will read aloud a selected poem and have students help highlight beautiful, vivid, unusual, or poetic words. Students can add words they like to their poetry bags.

You Try It: Distribute one short poem and one highlighter to each group of four. Assign each student a role: reader, highlighter, discussion director, and communications director. Have the reader read the poem while the others listen. The discussion director guides the discussion, which focuses on poetic words. The highlighter highlights the words chosen by the group. Once all groups have completed the task, the communication director of each group can share the learning with the whole class.

Independent Writing: Have discovery text set of poetry or individual poems available for students to read and explore. Encourage students to collect new words that are beautiful, vivid, unusual, or poetic.

Share: Invite students to share the words they collected during the CIA.

Text Discovery

The Minilesson: Writers share special experiences in order to find poetry.

The Model: Do a poetry walk. Take students on an expedition around the school grounds. If the weather is inclement, an indoor walk will provide a similar experience. Provide examples of adjectives they may write down before the walk to describe their observations of the senses.

You Try It: Shortly after you begin the poetry workshop, stop for a moment and challenge the students to share something they have noticed. Encourage the use of adjectives to describe the senses.

Independent Writing: Invite students to record the sounds they hear. They can also write words to describe what they see, feel, and smell.

Share: Have students share the new words they collected.

Extension

Popcorn Activity: Seat students in a common area and have them observe corn popping in a popcorn machine. Initially, they should be focused on three of the five senses: sight, sound, and smell. Once the popcorn has popped, the students may explore the sense of taste and touch. After sampling the popcorn, have students record words on gold paper to describe taste, touch, smell, sound, and sight.

Prewriting

The Minilesson: Poets think about what they know about poetry in order to write their own poems.

The Model: The teacher and students create an anchor chart titled "What Do We Know About Poetry?" Then they list everything the students know about poetry.

The teacher will read a newly selected poem. After reading the poem, invite the students to share what they know about poetry. Highlight the ideas in the poem that support what the students know.

You Try It: Invite students to think about a topic they know and love. For example, foods, cars, amusement park

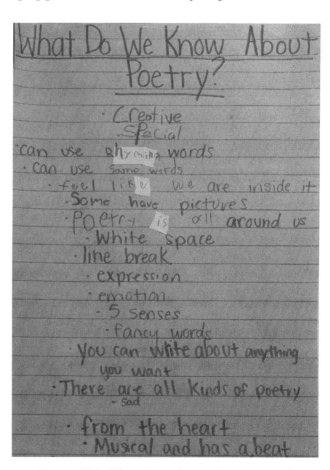

Figure 25.3. What do we know about poetry?

rides, books, flowers, or insects. Students can turn and talk to share their ideas. They should share one thing about the topic in a complete sentence. Choose one idea to write on the board. Model for students how a poet can choose important words to create a poem. Share the new poem using the model.

Model: *The buttery popcorn filled the room with a wonderful aroma. Aahh.*

Independent Writing: Have students give it a try with the ideas that they shared with their partners. Students should write the sentences they shared with their partners on a sentence strip or sheet of colored paper.

Share: Choose a few students to share their sentences with the class.

Drafting

Minilesson: Poets experiment with words in order to create interesting poems.

The Model: Display the model sentence from the previous day's lesson. Cut the words apart and model how you can use important words and arrange them in a specific way to create a poem.

Model:

> The buttery popcorn filled the room with a wonderful aroma. Aahh.
> ~~The~~ Buttery popcorn
> filled the room
> with a wonderful aroma—
> Aahh.

You Try It: Compose a sample sentence with the students and write the sentence on a sentence strip. Cut out each word. Keep the important words and manipulate them to create a poem. Encourage the class to read the poem in unison.

Independent Writing: Have students give it a try with the sentences they wrote on the previous day during independent writing.

Share: Choose a few students who experimented with line breaks and white space to share with the class.

Revising

The Minilesson: Poets can add descriptive details to their poems to make them interesting to the reader.

The Model: Display the model. Think aloud as you demonstrate ways to add specific words to create more interest.

You Try It: Display the class model and challenge the students to revise their sentences.

Independent Writing: Assign peer-conference groups. Students should take turns reading their poems. The peer should point out a place in the poem where descriptive details can be added to make the poem interesting. Students return to their table to revise. Encourage students to use words collected in their poetry bags.

Share: Invite a few students to share ways they revised.

Editing

The Minilesson: Poets work together to help each other check their writing.

The Model: Select a student to partner with you. Model how to help check the poem for his or her name, the title of the poem, spelling of known words, and spacing. An editing checklist can be used to check for these items.

You Try It: Invite the class to help you check your writing. Model how to correct your writing using their ideas.

Independent Writing: Have students work with their editing partners to edit their poems. Encourage students to complete the editing checklist and to use the checklist to make changes to their writing.

Share: Select a few students to share the edits that were made.

Publishing

The Minilesson: Poets can go on a museum walk to enjoy the work of other poets.

The Model: Have students clear their tables and place their published writing in their designated areas. Place your writing on one of the tables. Model walking around the table, stopping at each poem to read and enjoy.

You Try It: Select a few students to model the process.

Share: All students participate in the museum walk following the model that was demonstrated. At the conclusion of the museum walk, gather students at the whole group meeting area and discuss some of the poems and the positive things the students noticed.

Discovery Text Set for Poetry

Bug Off! Creepy, Crawly Poems by Jane Yolen
Button Up! Wrinkled Rhymes by Alice Schertle
Dizzy Dinosaurs by Lee Bennett Hopkins
Dreaming Up by Christy Hale
My Teacher Dances on the Desk by Eugene Gagliano
Pattern Bugs by Trudy Harris
Pick a Picture, Write a Poem! by Kristen McCurry
Poem Runs: Baseball Poems and Paintings by Douglas
    Florian
School Fever by Brod Bagert
Silver Seeds: A Book of Nature Poems by Paul Paolilli
Volcano Wakes Up! by Lisa Westberg Peters

Figure 25.4. Discovery text set for poetry.

Consider This

The inquiry approach to genre study leads directly to meaning. Relevance is found when meaningful interactions abound while students are engaged in the discovery and exploration of a variety of genres and craft techniques. This is just what young writers need in order to transfer new learning from short-term memory to long-term memory. Consider the implications for incorporating units of study into your existing writing curriculum.

Part IV References

Anderson, J. 2014. "What Writing Is and Isn't." *Educational Leadership* 71 (7): 10–14.

Bagert, B. 2008. *School Fever*. New York: Dial Books for Younger Readers.

Baguley, E. 2005. *Meggie Moon*. Intercourse, PA: Good Books.

Bang, M. 2004. *When Sophie Gets Angry—: Really, Really Angry . . .* New York: Scholastic.

Banks, K. 1999. *The Bird, the Monkey, and the Snake in the Jungle*. New York: Farrar, Straus, and Giroux.

Banks, K. 2008. *Max's Dragon*. New York: Farrar, Straus and Giroux.

Bottner, B., and G. Kruglik. 2004. *Wallace's Lists*. New York: Katherine Tegen Books.

Brown, M. W. 1947. *Goodnight Moon*. New York: HarperCollins.

Brown, S. T. 2005. *Oliver's Must-Do List*. Honesdale, PA: Boyds Mills Press.

Caine, R. N., and G. Caine. 1991. *Making Connections: Teaching and the Human*. Alexandria, VA: Association for Supervision and Curriculum Development.

Calkins, L. 1986. *The Art of Teaching Writing*. Portsmouth, NH: Heinemann.

Carroll, J. A. 2002. *Dr. JAC's Guide to Writing with Depth*. Spring, TX: Absey & Co.

Carroll, J. A., and E. Wilson. 2008. *Acts of Teaching: How to Teach Writing*. 2nd ed. Westport, CT: Teacher Ideas Press.

Coffelt, N. 2007. *Fred Stays with Me!* New York: Little, Brown.

Crews, D. 1992a. *Shortcut*. New York: Greenwillow Books.

Crews, D. 1992b. *Ten Black Dots*. New York: Greenwillow Books.

Cronin, D. 2003. *Diary of a Worm*. New York: Joanna Cotler Books.

Darbyshire, K. 2009. *Put It On the List!* New York: Dutton Children's Books.

DePaola, T. 1989. *The Art Lesson*. New York: Putman.

Drummond, R. 2013. *Charlie Goes to School*. New York: Harper.

Ehlert, L. 1987. *Growing Vegetable Soup*. San Diego: Harcourt Brace Jovanovich.

Fanelli, S. 1995. *My Map Book*. New York: HarperCollins.

Fletcher, R. J., and J. Portalupi. 1998. *Craft Lessons: Teaching Writing K–8*. York, ME: Stenhouse.

Florian, D. 2012. *Poem Runs: Baseball Poems and Paintings*. New York: Harcourt Children's Books.

Fox, M. 1985. *Wilfred Gordon McDonald Partridge*. La Jolla, CA: Kane/Miller.

Frazee, M. 2003. *Roller Coaster*. San Diego, CA: Harcourt.

Gagliano, E. 2009. *My Teacher Dances on the Desk*. Chelsea, MI: Sleeping Bear Press.

Gerstein, M. 2013. *How to Bicycle to the Moon to Plant Sunflowers: A Simple but Brilliant Plan in 24 Easy Steps*. New York: Roaring Brook Press.

Gibbons, G. 1999. *The Pumpkin Book*. New York: Holiday House.

Goodrich, C. 2011. *Say Hello to Zorro!* New York: Simon & Schuster Books for Young Readers.

Hale, C. 2012. *Dreaming Up: A Celebration of Building*. New York: Lee & Low Books

Hanlon, A. 2012. *Ralph Tells a Story*. Las Vegas, NV: Amazon Children's Publishing.

Harris, T. 2001. *Pattern Bugs*. Brookfield, CT: Millbrook Press.

Harvey, M. 2008. *Shopping with Dad*. Cambridge, MA: Barefoot Books.

Henkes, K. 1996. *Lilly's Purple Plastic Purse*. New York: Tupelo Books.

Hopkins, L. B. 2011. *Dizzy Dinosaurs: Silly Dino Poems*. New York: Harper.

Horn, M., and M. E. Giacobbe. 2007. *Talking, Drawing, Writing: Lessons for Our Youngest Writers*. Portland, ME: Stenhouse.

Johnson, D. B. 2002. *Henry Builds a Cabin*. Boston: Houghton Mifflin.

Kann, V. 2013. *Emeraldalicious*. New York: Harper.

Keats, E. J. 1966. *Jennie's Hat*. New York: Harper & Row.

Kelly, I. 2007. *It's a Butterfly's Life*. New York: Holiday House.

Leedy, L. 2000. *Mapping Penny's World.* New York: Henry Holt.

Litwin, E. 2011. *Pete the Cat: Rocking in My School Shoes.* New York: Harper.

Manning, M. 2008. *Kitchen Dance.* New York: Clarion Books.

Martin, B. 1970. *Brown Bear, Brown Bear, What Do You See?* New York: Holt, Rinehart and Winston.

Martin, B., and J. Archambault. 1989. *Chicka Chicka Boom Boom.* New York: Simon & Schuster Books for Young Readers.

McCarrier, A., I. C. Fountas, and G. S. Pinnell. 2000. *Interactive Writing: How Language and Literacy Come Together, K–2.* Portsmouth, NH: Heinemann.

McCurry, K. 2014. *Pick a Picture, Write a Poem!* North Mankato, MN: Capstone Press.

McGhee, A. 2002. *Countdown to Kindergarten.* San Diego, CA: Harcourt.

Messner, K. 2015. *How to Read a Story.* San Francisco, CA: Chronicle Books.

Milgrim, D. 2011. *Eddie Gets Ready for School.* New York: Cartwheel Books.

Modarressi, M. 2000. *Yard Sale!* New York: DK Publishing.

Murray, D. M. 1978. "Write Before Writing." *College Composition and Communication* 29 (4): 375–381.

Paley, V. G. 1990. *the boy who would be a helicopter.* Cambridge, MA: Harvard University Press.

Paolilli, P., and D. Brewer. 2001. *Silver Seeds: A Book of Nature Poems.* New York: Viking.

Peters, L. W. 2010. *Volcano Wakes Up!* New York: Henry Holt.

Pilkey, D. 1996. *The Paperboy.* New York: Orchard Books.

Raschka, C. 2011. *A Ball for Daisy.* New York: Schwartz & Wade Books.

Raschka, C. 2013. *Everyone Can Learn to Ride a Bicycle.* New York: Schwartz & Wade Books.

Ray, K. W., and L. B. Cleaveland. 2004. *About the Authors: Writing Workshop with Our Youngest Writers.* Portsmouth, NH: Heinemann.

Reagan, J. 2012. *How to Babysit a Grandpa.* New York: Alfred A. Knopf.

Robinson, M. 2014. *How to Wash a Woolly Mammoth.* New York : Henry Holt.

Rylant, C. 1982. *When I Was Young in the Mountains.* New York: E. P. Dutton.

Rylant, C. 1985. *The Relatives Came.* New York: Bradbury Press.

Rylant, C. 1998. *Tulip Sees America.* New York: Blue Sky Press.

Schertle, A. 2009. *Button Up! Wrinkled Rhymes.* New York: Harcourt Children's Books/Houghton Mifflin Harcourt.

Seuss, D. 1960. *One Fish Two Fish Red Fish Blue Fish.* New York: Random House.

Silverstein, S. 1981. *A Light in the Attic.* New York: Harper & Row.

Singer, M. 2012. *A Stick Is an Excellent Thing: Poems Celebrating Outdoor Play.* Boston: Clarion Books.

Swanson, S. M. 2008. *The House in the Night.* Boston: Houghton Mifflin.

Tarpley, N. 1997. *I Love My Hair!* Boston: Little, Brown.

Van Dusen, C. 2005. *If I Built a Car.* New York: Dutton Children's Books.

Vygotsky, L. 1962. *Thought and Language.* Cambridge, MA: MIT Press.

Watt, M. 2006. *Scaredy Squirrel.* Toronto: Kids Can Press.

Williams, V. B. 1982. *A Chair for My Mother.* New York: Greenwillow Books.

Williams, V. B. 2009. *A Chair for Always.* New York: Greenwillow Books.

Wortche, A. 2011. *Rosie Sprout's Time to Shine.* New York: Alfred A. Knopf.

Wyeth, S. D. 1998. *Something Beautiful.* New York: Doubleday Books for Young Readers.

Yolen, J. 2012. *Bug Off! Creepy, Crawly Poems.* Honesdale, PA: Wordsong.

Epilogue

Joyce Armstrong Carroll

Stories of all kinds are coming back into their own; adults as well as children thirst for them.

—John Thomson

I have always been fond of the alpha and the omega, the call back, the return to an earlier allusion, so I find myself drawn to Joyce Elizabeth's writing once again to make my final point as well as the final points made by Kelley, Karla, and Kristy. It's quite simple, really: We learn to talk by talking. We learn to walk by walking. We learn to write by writing. We learn to read by reading. Literate people engage in literate events. Rich environments—even for experimental rats—produce rich results. Limiting human creativity, curiosity, and learning produces limited results. PERIOD! We hope we have proved that simple yet profound truth in this book.

Here comes the support. When Joyce Elizabeth was five and one-half years old, after only about six months under the aegis of a superior kinder teacher, Stephanie Phipps, and immersed in the rich literate environment of the Center for Teaching and Learning at the Woodlands, a progressively positive private school, she began real and independent writing—not the laborious fashioning of letters, but writing what was in her head. As Emma Martinez, a fourth grader in E.C. Mason Elementary School in Alvin ISD, Texas, said on a video about AbydosPRO, our integrated writing/grammar curriculum, "Writing reads my mind." Joyce Elizabeth began realizing that writing was thinking on paper.

First came short notes to classmates and family. Then she wrote a book—independently—and placed it in her portfolio. She had been reading books on flowers and had figured out how flowers grow. She was eager to place her newfound knowledge in the permanency of writing an informational book. What makes her book so astonishing is how she went about writing it. First, for the cover, she drew a flower, complete with a title, her name, and a butterfly, all in soft pastel colors.

Imagine what she already knows at five and a half years of age—what belongs on the cover of a book: title, author, illustration. But what is so telling is that she drew the flower first and then went on to analyze *how* she drew it and in what order. That she

follows her own cognitive process shows how she is guided by meaning—her meaning—in the way she drew her flower. The implication is clear: if this process works for me and if you follow it, you, too, will produce a flower.

On page two she begins her instruction with: *First you draw the middle.* And in the center of the page, a bright yellow oval illustrates her words. That is the last spot of color until the final page—the flower in full bloom.

Moving to page three, Joyce Elizabeth introduces the petals. *Then you draw the petals.* Using her consonant spelling and her knowledge of phonics in context, this page is easy to read.

Pages four, *Then you draw the stem*, and five, *Then you draw the leaves*, direct the reader to add the stem and leaves.

What is interesting about these pages is the width of the stem—she obviously wanted the reader to be sure about its sturdiness—and the fact that Joyce Elizabeth's flowers do

not have leaves. Clearly, she is able to produce an ideograph of not only what she sees, but what she knows—flowers have leaves! She doesn't forget the grass—after all, she had to place the flower in a setting. *Then you draw the grass.*

Pages two through five are written totally in pencil—no colors.

Finally, her last page has the return of a colorful flower and green grass but is without words. "Why didn't you write any words on this page?" I asked.

"Because then I made the whole flower," she responded, pointing to it and making me feel just a little bit silly about my question and the obviousness of the answer. Notice, too, how she framed her expository text by beginning and ending with the flower. Her conclusion relates back to her cover, her promise to show the reader how to make a flower. She uses the call back technique effortlessly and efficiently. Who ever said little children cannot write exposition? They can and do—when they are guided by meaning—their meaning.

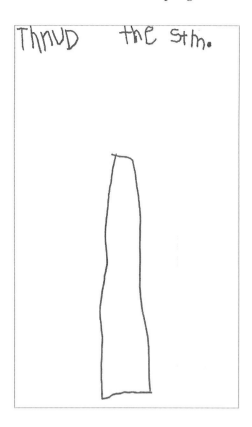

To Recap

Contrary to many myths about children, they rarely act in random, chaotic ways even though it often looks that way. In their minds there is a reason, a rationale behind their actions, their pretend play, their actual play, and their writing. To watch them is to learn. To read what they write is to be humbled. To teach them is the highest calling, as their brains are so malleable and so open.

And so our book comes to a close. We have tried to be cumulative; we have tried to be succinct; and we have tried to convey our messages. So, we shall tie all our words off not with "the end" or "they lived happily ever after," but with the couplet so satisfying at the end of the folktale 'The Three Billy Goats Gruff":

Snip, snap, snout,
This tale's told out.

Appendix A: Mentor Texts for Library Lessons

Mentor Texts for Nonfiction

Actual Size by Steve Jenkins
Sharks by Seymour Simon
Coral Reefs by Seymour Simon
Lightning by Seymour Simon
Locomotive by Brian Floca
Mesmerized by Mara Rockliff
The Right Word: Roget and His Thesaurus by Jen Bryant
Balloons Over Broadway by Melissa Sweet
The Scraps Book: Notes from a Colorful Life by Lois Ehlert
I Could Do That! by Linda Arms White
Martin's Big Words by Doreen Rappaport
Subway by Larry Dane Brimner
Stargazer's Alphabet by John Farrell
A Second Is a Hiccup by Hazel Hutchins
Gravity by Jason Chin
A Seed Is Sleepy by Dianna Hutts Aston and Sylvia Long
Beachcombing: Exploring the Seashore by Jim Arnosky
Owls by Gail Gibbons
Marsupials by Nic Bishop
The Art Box by Gail Gibbons
Ice Cream: The Full Scoop by Gail Gibbons
Saving Audie: A Pit Bull Puppy Gets a Second Chance by Dorothy Hinshaw Patent
If You Decide to Go to the Moon by Faith McNulty
Moonshot: The Flight of Apollo 11 by Brian Floca
How to Build a Fizzy Rocket by Lori Shores
My Light by Molly Bang

Workshop by Andrew Clements
The Edible Pyramid: Good Eating Every Day by Loreen Leedy
The Fantastic Ferris Wheel: The Story of the Inventor George Ferris by Betsy Harvey Kraft
Spidermania: Friends on the Web by Alexandra Siy and Dennis Kunkel

Mentor Texts for Hexagonal Writing

The Fantastic Flying Books of Mr. Morris Lessmore by William Joyce
The Christmas Tapestry by Patricia Polacco
The Keeping Quilt by Patricia Polacco
The Flower Man: A Wordless Picture Book by Mark Ludy
Seven Blind Mice by Ed Young
The Sweetest Fig by Chris Van Allsburg
Brave Irene by William Steig
The Chicken Chasing Queen of Lamar County by Janice N. Harrington
Harriet, You'll Drive Me Wild by Mem Fox
The Matchbox Diary by Paul Fleischman
Louise, the Adventures of a Chicken by Kate DiCamillo and Harry Bliss
Stellaluna by Janell Cannon
Song and Dance Man by Karen Ackerman

Mentor Texts for Grammar

The Web Files by Margie Palatini
Click, Clack, Moo by Doreen Cronin
Knuffle Bunny by Mo Willems
Punctuation Takes a Vacation by Robin Pulver
Chicka Chicka Boom Boom by Bill Martin Jr.
Eats, Shoots, and Leaves by Lynne Truss
Exclamation Mark by Amy Krause Rosenthal
The Girls Like Spaghetti: Why You Can't Manage Without Apostrophes by Lynne Truss
Creepy Carrots by Aaron Reynolds
I'm Dirty by Kate and Jim McMullan
Mustache by Mac Barnett

Mentor Texts for Poetry

Mirror, Mirror by Marilyn Singer
Poems in the Attic by Nikki Grimes
Follow, Follow: A Book of Reverso Poems by Marilyn Singer
Rutherford B. Who Was He? Poems About Our Presidents by Marilyn Singer
I Hear a Pickle by Rachel Isadora
This Is Just to Say by Joyce Sidman

Earthshake: Poems from the Ground Up by Lisa Westberg Peters
The Kitchen Talks by Shirley Mozelle
Animal Snackers by Betsy Lewin
Dirty Laundry Pile: Poems in Different Voices by Paul B. Janeczko
Color Me a Rhyme by Jane Yolen
Grumbles from the Forest: Fairy Tale Voices with a Twist by Jane Yolen and Rebecca Kai Dotlich
Loose Leashes by Amy Schmidt
Come to My Party and Other Shape Poems by Heidi B. Roemer
I Am the Book by Lee Bennett Hopkins
Got Geography by Lee Bennet Hopkins
Dogku by Andrew Clements
Amazing Faces by Lee Bennett Hopkins
Face Bug by J. Patrick Lewis

Mentor Texts for General Reading and Writing Strategies

Zoom by Istvan Banyai
Unspoken by Henry Cole
What Do You Do with an Idea by Kobi Yamada
The Best Story by Eileen Spinelli
Ninja Red Riding Hood by Corey Rosen Schwartz
Emily's Blue Period by Cathleen Daly
A Fine Dessert: Four Centuries, Four Families, One Delicious Treat by Emily Jenkins
The Day the Crayons Quit by Drew Daywalt
Dot by Randi Zuckerberg
Chester by Melanie Watt
Bugs in My Hair by David Shannon
Memoirs of a Goldfish by Devin Scillian
Battle Bunny by Jon Scieszka
Otis and the Tornado by Loren Long
Crazy Like a Fox: A Simile Story by Loreen Leedy
Lacey Walker Nonstop Talker by Christianne Jones
Snow Sounds: An Onomatopoeic Story by David A. Johnson
Pancakes for Supper by Anne Isaacs
Rocket Writes a Story by Tad Hills
No Pirates Allowed Said Library Lou by Rhonda Gowler Greene
Emily's Blue Period by Cathleen Daly
The Memory String by Eve Bunting
The Lonely Book by Kate Bernheimer
The Plot Chickens by Mary Jane and Herm Auch
Story County by Derek Anderson
Crankee Doodle by Tom Angleberger
Nothing by Jon Agee

Mentor Texts for Sight Words

Spoon by Amy Krause Rosenthal
Elephant and Piggie Series by Mo Willems
How to Teach a Slug to Read by Susan Pearson
Five for a Little One by Chis Raschka
Grumpy Cat by Britta Teckentrup
Green by Laura Vaccaro Seeger
Chewy Louie by Howie Schneider
Nugget and Fang by Tammi Sauer
The Bookshop Dog by Cynthia Rylant
Huff and Puff by Claudia Rueda
Stand Tall, Molly Lou Melon by Patty Lovell
Mountain Dance by Thomas Locker
Water Dance by Thomas Locker
Punk Farm by Jarrett J. Krosoczka
Flight School by Lita Judge
Perfect Square by Michael Hall
The Looking Book by P. K. Hallinan
Clark the Shark by Bruce Hale
Is Your Mama a Llama? by Deborah Guarino and Steven Kellogg
The Hermit Crab by Carter Goodrich
Noises at Night by Beth Raisner Glass and Susan Lubner
Hattie and the Fox by Mem Fox
Where the Giant Sleeps by Mem Fox
In the Tall, Tall Grass by Denise Fleming
A Neat Line by Pamela Duncan Edwards
Chicken Cheeks by Michael Ian Black

Appendix B:
Abydos Customized Book Bundle List of Titles for Grades PreK–2

PreK

Hardcover editions are indicated by (hc).

Scaredy Squirrel by Melanie Watt
My Map Book (hc) by Sara Fanelli
Rufus the Writer (hc) by Elizabeth Bram
Rocket Writes a Story (hc) by Tad Hills
Sleepy Little Alphabet (hc) by Judy Sierra
Chrysanthemum by Kevin Henkes
Tacky the Penguin by Helen Lester
Little Penguin's Tale by Audrey Wood
The War Between the Vowels and the Consonants by Priscilla Turner
Harry and the Terrible Whatzit by Dick Gackenbach
Little Red Writing by Joan Holub
Red Knit Cap Girl and the Reading Tree (hc) by Naoko Stoop

Grade K

Oddrey (hc) by Dave Whamond
Kindergarten Luck (hc) by Louise Borden
Lemonade in Winter: A Book about Two Kids Counting Money (hc) by Emily Jenkins
Good News, Bad News (hc) by Jeff Mack
Me and My Place in Space by Joan Sweeney
Farmer Duck by Martin Waddell

Police: Hurrying! Helping! Saving! by Patricia Hubbell
Too Many Tamales by Gary Soto
No Dragons for Tea: Fire Safety for Kids (and Dragons) by Jean E. Pendziwol
Dogs on the Bed by Elizabeth Bluemle
A Kiss Means I Love You (hc) by Kathryn Madeline Allen
My New School by Kirsten Hall
Pete the Cat: Rocking in My New School Shoes (hc) by Eric Litwin
Good Luck Bear (hc) by Greg Foley
Officer Buckle and Gloria (hc) by Peggy Rathmann
Albert the Fix-It Man by Janet Lord
Leo the Late Bloomer by Robert Kraus
Miss Bindergarten Celebrates the 100th Day of Kindergarten by Joseph Slate
You Can't Buy a Dinosaur with a Dime by Harriet Ziefert
Mousetronaut: Based on a (Partially) True Story (hc) by Mark Kelly
I Love Saturdays y Domingos by Alma Flor Ada
Woof: A Love Story (hc) by Sarah Weeks
That Is Not a Good Idea! (hc) by Mo Willems

Grade 1

Soon by Timothy Knapman
Ralph Tells a Story (hc) by Abby Hanlon
Shortcut by Donald Crews
One Bean by Anne Rockwell
Mr. Tiger Goes Wild (hc) by Peter Brown
The Kissing Hand (hc) by Audrey Penn
Courage (hc) by Bernard Waber
What a Wonderful World (hc) by Bob Thiele
How to Babysit a Grandpa by Jean Reagan
If You Plant a Seed (hc) by Kadir Nelson
Horsefly and Honeybee (hc) by Randy Cecil
The Best Story (hc) by Eileen Spinelli
Me on the Map by Joan Sweeney
Bigmama's by Donald Crews
Do unto Otters: A Book about Manners by Laurie Keller
Friends: True Stories of Extraordinary Animal Friendships (hc) by Catherine Thimmesh
Wemberly Worried by Kevin Henkes
Lola Plants a Garden by Anna McQuinn
Lucky Duckling by Eva Moore
Pick a Picture, Write a Poem! by Kristen McCurry
Bug Off! Creepy, Crawly Poems by Jane Yolen
Drawing from Memory by Allen Say
Everyone Can Learn to Ride a Bicycle by Chris Raschka
Library Mouse: A World to Explore (hc) by Daniel Kirk

Grade 2

First Day Jitters by Julie Danneberg
You Have to Write by Janet Wong
Stand Tall, Molly Lou Melon by Patty Lovell
When Sophie Gets Angry, Really, Really Angry by Molly Bang
Platypus Lost by Janet Steven
Aunt Isabel Tells A Good One by Kate Duke
How I Became a Pirate by Melinda Long
The Chicken Sisters by Laura Numeroff
A Sick Day for Amos McGee by Phillip Stead
I Wanna Iguana by Karen Orloff
Roller Coaster by Marla Frazee
The Important Book by Margaret Wise Brown
Silent Letters Loud and Clear by Robin Pulver
The Perfect Pet by Margie Palatini

Index

About the Authors

JOYCE ARMSTRONG CARROLL, EDD, HLD, is codirector of Abydos Literacy Learning. She is the author of more than twenty professional books and more than fifty professional articles. She has taught every grade from kindergarten to graduate school in her 57 years in the profession. Carroll holds an honorary degree from Georgian Court University for her "mark on the world of education and in so doing influenced the future for good" and was awarded the Edmund J. Farrell Lifetime Achievement Award from the Texas Council of Teachers of English Language Arts.

KELLEY BARGER, EDD, is professor and director of reading programs at Fontbonne University, St. Louis, MO. She is the author of *Phonics Friendly Families* and part of an author collegium for AbydosPro, a dynamic writing and grammar curriculum for grades pre-K through twelfth. Barger has taught reading and writing methodology, emergent literacy, educational research, family literacy, early childhood curriculum, and children's literature in both undergraduate and graduate programs at Texas A&M University–Commerce, University of Houston, Stephens College, and Fontbonne University. She taught kindergarten in Houston, TX; served as a team leader; and created and coordinated a vibrant family literacy program, KID Connection, in Spring ISD. She is cohost of a children's literature blog, www.whisperingspines.com, and is a diamond level trainer with Abydos Learning International.

KARLA JAMES is an educator with fifteen years of experience with the Alvin Independent School District in Texas. As literacy coordinator and writing trainer, James has developed expertise in the area of early literacy while working with primary teachers and students to support the implementation of best literacy practices. She has written curriculum for kindergarten and first grade audiences, presented numerous professional development sessions and conferences across the state, and is the recipient of the Abydos Sue German Award and the Abydos Jan DeBlance Memorial Award for Instructional Excellence.

KRISTY HILL, MLS, is a library media technology specialist for Keller Independent School District, Keller, TX. She has worked in education for fifteen years. She is an ABYDOS writing trainer and has brought that knowledge to the library, where she teaches literacy as part of her library lessons. Hill is also a member of the Texas Library Association.

Made in the USA
Lexington, KY
22 August 2019